ACTORS' VOICES

ACTORS' VOICES

THE PEOPLE BEHIND THE PERFORMANCES

Edited by Patrick O'Kane

OBERON BOOKS

LONDON

WWW.OBERONBOOKS.COM

First published in 2012 by Oberon Books Ltd
521 Caledonian Road, London N7 9RH
Tel: +44 (0) 20 7607 3637 / Fax: +44 (0) 20 7607 3629
e-mail: info@oberonbooks.com
www.oberonbooks.com

A catalogue record for this book is available from the British Library.

ISBN: 978-1-84002-956-7

Cover design by James Illman

Printed and bound by CPI Group (UK) Ltd, Croydon, CR0 4YY.

CONTENTS

INTRODUCTION

I HAVE BEEN an actor since leaving Central School of Speech and Drama in 1990. In the subsequent years it has been my good fortune, great privilege and occasional frustration to have worked, across the media of film, television and theatre, on a regular basis. In 2005, to my great surprise, I was invited to apply for a NESTA Fellowship. To my even greater surprise, my application was successful. At the heart of my fellowship was an interest in how I and other actors might usefully articulate our personal processes and consider the actor's position within the process of making theatre.

I had not always been so interested in analyzing the hows and whys of what actors do; I remember, as a young actor, telling my agent, when she asked me what it was I wanted to do, that I wanted to play the big parts in the big plays in the big theatres. In a sense, little has changed, for I still hunger to be involved in the telling of the great stories that define and engage us as a society and I am still excited by the genuinely, viscerally transformative powers of theatre. In 1998, the birth of my first child prompted me to scrutinize just what it was I was doing, for I would no longer be doing it simply for my own creative expression but also to provide for my children. At that time I had also experienced the archetypal volte-faces that actors are prey to. Twelve months previously, I had enjoyed the life of a West End actor in an acclaimed and popular production, followed by a film and TV production, before the longest fallow period of my career. At the time of my son's birth I was playing a great part in a great play – in a room above a pub in West London, for no money. During the West End production, I had also been dropped by my agent when I had the temerity to express a desire to participate in my own career. This was a shocking experience for me. I had long appreciated that, as an actor, I had little or no control over a career, as such, because I would never know what was coming next, but I was surprised that a genuine curiosity about how I might best advance my career was received as an attack on the integrity of my agent. I began to

7

take artistic and professional stock. So I took down my old university books that had been gathering dust on my shelves and began to re-read them with no particular expectation, only to be amazed at how eloquently they now spoke to me, how profoundly they affected me, giving an articulacy to those things that I'd been unconsciously grappling with and stumbling towards in my everyday work as an actor. I also began to consider the broader hierarchies, which go beyond the particular circumstances of personality clashes and which affect the business of being an actor.

In 2000 I was invited to be one of a team of artistic associates at Nottingham Playhouse. I used this opportunity to work as a director on unperformed play texts with young actors and professional actors, based in Nottingham. This experience prompted me to apply for a three-week intensive directors course at the National Theatre Studio, for emerging directors. By having substantial access to a broad range of visiting tutors, we were able to experience many different directors' processes both practically and conceptually. Two events occurred on that course, which set me on the path to constructing this book of discourses:

When I revealed that the bulk of my experience had been as an actor, my status, within the group of students, fell through the floor and it took considerable effort to regain the lost ground over the rest of the course.

Nearly every visiting tutor/director talked about what actors want and how you need to deal with them in rehearsals.

I was disappointed that my fellow student directors showed little interest in hearing what an actor's experience of rehearsals and performance might have been and I was curious about what it was that I, as an actor, wanted of a director in a rehearsal process. I began to realize that much of what is written about acting and actors has been written by academics and directors, but, celebrity biographies apart, little was known about the thoughts and creative processes of working – and, indeed, non-working actors.

What follows is not an actor's manual, but a range of very personal reflections – part biographical, part process analysis and part contemplation of art, theatre and our role, as actors, within the artistic landscape – based on the evidence of each individual's articulated experience. I have tried to get to the essence of what the reality of being an actor in the theatre is, as opposed to the notion that the public might have of fame and fakery and to unravel what it means to each of us to be an actor. The conversations which follow are focused primarily on mainstream literary theatre-making practice. The actors you will meet have all worked and continue to work within the framework of our mainstream, literary theatre. In addition to their work on stage, sometimes out of neccessity, curiosity or, occasionally, frustration, some of them also teach in drama schools, some have become writers and some have become directors and one, at the time of our conversation, had fallen out of love with the theatre. By dint of these alternative contributions to the theatre landscape, they have all been forced to examine their own theatrical values as well as to confront the limits of their ambitions. I think these various divergences serve to enrich the experience and perspectives of each actor in turn. I cannot claim, nor did I attempt, to create a representative picture of what it is to be an actor, but through the broad range of experiences and disparate points of interest detailed here, some common themes, shared values and points of contention emerge with regard to actor training, rehearsal periods and director/actor dynamics. Furthermore, all the actors who have contributed to this book share a passion for their art and a concern for how we might make it better, which goes way beyond the limited horizons of self-interest. Each actor has seen this as an opportunity to contribute to a conversation about how we make the making of theatre better for everyone – actors, directors, writers and, of course, audiences.

I would like to thank each of the actors for the generous way in which they have given their time and energy to share their reflections on the how, what and why of what they do. I also applaud their courage in this because, for many actors, to give articulation to their methodology is to bestow the kiss of death upon their art. I appreciate such an apprehension, for while words can provide a ready portal for a fertile imagination, they can also entrap a creative process in a mesh of cerebral definition, limiting other possible expressions of creativity. Furthermore, while an academic or cerebral intelligence is undoubtedly very useful, it is not necessarily the primary intelligence for the actor in the moment of rehearsing and creating a performance.

I am also grateful for the candid nature of the actors' observations on the nature of the hierarchies within theatre. Some actors were simply too nervous to make a contribution to this book, for fear of finding themselves

on some sort of creative blacklist. Even among some of those who participated, there was an anxiety about potential career suicide. This is both
interesting and ironic: interesting because it suggests that actors reside in
an environment of perpetual uncertainty and even fear, with regard to their
relationships with directors, theatre managers and even their agents; ironic
in that, at the heart of our art lies a fundamental compulsion to communicate, generously, openly and truthfully, through the enactment of character-based stories. It cannot be useful if one set of artists – actors – do not
feel enabled to participate fully in the creative discussions, which underpin
how and why we are making theatre. All theatre-makers – writers, directors, designers and actors – in the act of making theatre are engaging in an
act of generosity. When we act, we make a huge personal investment in the
work; when we act in good faith, the capital is our soul. There can be a price
to pay for such investment, but the dividend, when it is good, provides the
life-blood for one's creative spirit.

To students and those who are considering entering the profession; to
actors, directors and theatre managers, who are already engaged in the
making of theatre, I hope you find in these actors' voices, which reveal
the people behind the performance, information and inspiration, food for
thought and food for the soul.

*I would like to thank NESTA, whose fellowship afforded me
the encouragement to imagine this book and the space to complete it.
I would also like to thank Helen Prosser, Niamh Dowling, Lynn Haill and
Jodi Myers for their generous assistance; Alex Giannini, Colin Mace and
Indira Varma whose invaluable contributions, unfortunately, do not appear
on these pages. Finally, a very big thank you to all of the actors featured here,
without whose generosity this book would not have been possible.*

The interviews that follow were conducted in 2008

CLAIRE PRICE

Claire Price, the daughter of actor parents, was only ever interested in working as an actor. In 2002 she won The Ian Charleson Award for the role of Berinthia in *The Relapse* at the National Theatre and has subsequently performed many leading classical roles in the plays of Shakespeare, Schiller, Webster and Ibsen. In 2009 she won a TMA award for her performance as Elizabeth I in *Mary Stuart* at Theatr Clywd and in 2011 she won a second TMA award for her performance in *The Pride* at The Crucible Theatre, Sheffield.

POK   *What was your first encounter with theatre?*

CP   My dad, the actor John Price, took me to see Karl Johnson's *Hamlet* and I was bewitched. I was about four but I can remember all sorts of details: Karl wore a jacket with corduroy elbow patches. I remember being transfixed when someone came on carrying a head in a bag, when Rosencrantz and Guildenstern were killed. That's my first proper memory of the theatre – coming home after *Hamlet* and sitting up all that night in my bed playing all the parts.

Can you identify what it was that so thrilled you?

When it's what your parents do, what they talk about over breakfast there's an apprenticeship aspect to it. For example, we really did have conversations over the breakfast table about how to make Shakespeare accessible and what it means when Macbeth says this or that. Every part my father played was brought home, talked about and worked out and I was taken into rehearsal, so there was no getting away from it.

Did you ever consider an alternative career?

No, it was always going to be this. I did the National Youth Theatre when I was 16 and had a miserable experience. I was shy, I couldn't speak up, so I got quite small things to do. In the first year, we spent three weeks playing drama games and at the end we devised a show. The thing I didn't have was confidence. I've got courage but I didn't have much confidence: courage is what you need to stand on stage and play a part and confidence is what you need to be yourself in games. I remember thinking 'Oh, maybe this is not going to be my life', and that was devastating. Then I thought, 'No, no, I just don't like doing it here.'

Then you went to university to study English, in London.

Yes, the University of London, Queen Mary College, where I joined the Queen Mary Players. I remember the first audition, the terror of walking up to that door, thinking this is the most scared I've ever been; but I was given stuff to read and immediately I thought, 'Now, I can do this, everything will be fine!' In the final year I played Lady Macbeth and a very good friend of my family, the actor Jimmy Hazeldene, who died a few years ago, came to see it and wrote me a card saying, 'You are an actor'. My father died when I was quite young, so to hear that from Jimmy – a great friend of my dad's – felt like permission to give it a go. Later he was to give me my first proper job when he directed me in an episode of *London's Burning*.

Did a mentoring relationship develop?

I didn't think of him as a mentor, but I suppose he was in a way. He said, 'You're unusual for your generation because you have a poetic sensibility; you've approached it from a poetic angle and that's not common now.' That was fantastic to hear. He also helped me through that first television experience with advice that still bears fruit now. For example, he explained the difference between stage and camera work – on the screen you mustn't tell the story at all, and I still find that really hard. He said it's about thinking it rather than showing you're thinking it. To this day I'm still not entirely sure how to bridge the gap between screen and stage. I'm a stage actor by nature and on stage you tell the story with every single part of you, with your back, the tips of your fingers, everything.

You then went to Guildford for one year?

I didn't want to go into the business without an agent and I thought the showing at the end of a drama school course would be the way to get one.

Was your reason for going to drama school entirely strategic?

I did think I could do with some voice work. Yes, it probably was mostly strategic when I look back.

Were your expectations of your training satisfied?

I enjoyed it very much but there were elements that I hated and there were a lot of things that I came away thinking were failings in me. For example, in a private tutorial session a voice teacher really laid into me about my voice. It was absolutely devastating: she said your voice is very breathy and at some point in your life you've chosen to do that in order to manipulate men and you'll never be able to change it, you're going to be one type of actor. Even though I was devastated by that session I didn't consider stopping, but I left not really knowing how to use my voice. Most of what I know about how to use my voice, I learned from my mother; she went to RADA in the 1950s, learnt rib reserve and she taught me that. If you have three years to teach something you can really start from basic principles and build it; when you've got three terms, you have to teach it very quickly and if people were not getting it the teachers were quite personal, because they didn't have the time to be properly personal.

Was the nature of the course at fault?

Yes. We spent the first term with the first-year students, second term with the second-year students and the third term with the third-year students. That's not good enough: you need to think, right, this is a one-year course so we're going to do something completely different from the three-year course. I think it's very different now, I think they changed the whole system.

When you left, would it be fair to say your head was slightly a jumble?

Because my mother was incredibly supportive and we'd talk about acting a lot, I had a framework. A lot of people on that course were in their 30s, 40s and 50s, had paid off the mortgage and thought, 'Right that's it, I'm not going to be a financial advisor any more, I'm going to be an actor', and I felt for them because they had nothing to go back to, except suddenly having no income. I think I'm the only one who is still an actor.

One out of how many?

Out of about eighteen.

Would it be fair to describe your relationship with acting as an obsession?

Once I started to get great parts, I realized I was expressing myself through those parts, so, in that way, it is an obsession. I am obsessed by the craft of it as well. I'd love to learn Russian fluently enough to go and work with the Mali for ten years, to just get really good at it. I'm obsessed by the way other people do it and doing it well myself.

What was your first job? What were your hopes and expectations of it?

It was a fringe production of *A Midsummer Night's Dream*, by the London Classic Theatre Company, at the New End, Hampstead. I played Helena. My agent at the time was cross with me for doing it; he thought it was almost a betrayal. I'd joined him, fresh out of drama school and I'd been out of work for about three months. I'd been writing letters to PCR, got this job and told him I was going to do it. He wanted me to stay free so he could send me up for television work and get my career going in a different way. He said, 'Three months out of work is nothing, I want to build a career for you. Doing this is going to get in the way of other work I could send you up for.' At the time I thought that was madness and just to be doing something was what was important. I appreciate his point now, as I've just had six months off during which I've been turning stuff down and my current agent has been completely behind me because it's about waiting for the right thing.

Presumably you're in a more secure financial position, having had a couple of series of Rebus, *to take that voluntary unemployment?*

Exactly. Although back then I lived with my mother, because I wanted to be free to take the right kind of jobs to build my career in the first ten years. I knew that was going to be theatre and that theatre didn't pay very well, so I thought if I commit to a big outgoing, I would have to make certain compromises and I refused to make them. My mother used to say to me 'what kind of an actress do you want to be?' and I said Juliet Stevenson; I wanted a career in great classical theatre parts. My first agent wanted me to be a Bond girl really, to be very, very thin.

Did he tell you to lose weight?

Yes, when I first joined him he made me take my cardigan off and he said, 'you're lovely but you won't get television work that size, you need to lose weight. Leave the work issues to me and I'll sort it out. Ring me every now and again and tell me how much weight you're losing.' I'd just come from a drama school which was predominantly musical theatre, so I was spending a lot of time with people who were hearing that a lot, because they wanted to be dancers. I'd thought that didn't apply to me because I'm an actress. However, his assertion that success was contingent on a certain level of weight loss was a seed that bore very ugly fruit over the years. I left him in the end because he didn't tell me about a job that I'd been offered and when I rang him to confront him he said, 'the real problem we have here is that you're so overweight. I want you to go on the jockey diet over Christmas and really drastically waste, as jockeys do, and then we can really get your career going'. I wrote him a letter that day to terminate the representation. I thought I'll represent myself if that's what I have to do; but it's out there all the time that weight-loss thing.

What were the key events or people, in the early years that shaped your career?

The job that began the arc of my career so far was Howard Barker's *Ursula*, with his company The Wrestling School. I played Ursula, the virgin martyr. I met John Cannon, who was casting at the RSC at the time, when he came to see it and a few months later I was brought in by the RSC for two fantastic jobs and everything has led on from that.

Was it a good experience working with The Wrestling School?

Fantastic, I loved that job. Howard writes proper, muscular tragedies and you can't do them half-heartedly, or ironically. *Ursula* ends with all the virgins getting their heads cut off – fantastic. That's the kind of theatre I want to be in and see. It explored issues of womanhood, identity – struggling to preserve your identity, given the situations you're in.

Would it be fair to say also, that you relished a situation where your contribution was central to the work?

Yes, definitely. Having a lot to say is very important to me. I enjoy having the bulk of responsibility for the evening. When I see the responsibility's being given to another actor and they're not taking it that makes me nuts.

Could you talk a bit more about when it's an actor's turn to take responsibility?

When I get on stage I know where I am; I feel I belong here and this belongs to me. It's about leading a company on and off stage. My mother used to say when she came to see me in things early on – 'What's great about you is that when you come on the audience relaxes. The audience thinks, we're alright when she's on because they can hear you, they know you're not going to mess it up,' and that's because I'm fundamentally at ease. I think that's what it's about.

What books have you read that have influenced you as an actor?

Howard Barker wrote a book called *Arguments for a Theatre*, in which he asserts that we are trying to make theatre sing for its supper to government agendas of social engineering. That's not theatre's primary reason for existing. Howard eloquently confirms that. The other significant book was David Mamet's *True and False* because he really values actors. He is deliberately provocative: 'the best drama comes from people who aren't feeling anything, they're just saying it' – I couldn't quite understand that. But an actor having a great time doesn't necessarily mean everyone else is: it is about responsibility to the audience first and foremost, a responsibility to story-telling, and if you're working on a good script you don't have to do anything. That is useful because when you get a bad script you think 'I'm a rubbish actor', but then you've got David Mamet prompting, 'No, no you're not rubbish, but the script might be.'

What about an influential person?

My parents. My mother was an actor from the late 1950's, before it was acceptable to have your own accent as an actor and before kitchen sink dramas. Actors, like Paul Scofield and Ralph Richardson, influenced her; she saw them as a student. My father was younger and he became an actor later in life, so he was influenced by a different generation. He worked with companies like Shared Experience, where the emphasis was on exploring emotions. My mother shows greater technique. So half my brain is always thinking 'Am I audible? Did I end that word clearly enough? Do I need to pick up that line ending?' while the other half is thinking 'Am I conveying emotion here properly? Am I being as truthful as I can be?' And they sort of come together.

What about other actors who you've worked with, or directors or designers?

Adrian Noble made me a better actor than I was. We were doing *Brand*, with Ralph Fiennes. (Ibsen makes you a better actor; it tunes you up from the inside.) I remember a particular rehearsal with Adrian when he pushed me to do something. I remember leaving the room thinking I'm a better actor than I was when I went in that morning, because he pushed me. It was a scene from Act 4. Brand and his wife are grieving for their dead baby and there's an horrendous exchange when Brand comes home and Agnes breaks down and rages at him. I was trying to limit the level of emotion I put into it. I think I was nervous of sounding too vulnerable, as well as being afraid of having to hit such an intense emotional pitch every night for the next six months. Adrian knows how subtle Ibsen's writing is, and what it needs from an actor. He has a very subtle ear. He was playing with a bit of Blu Tac, while he was listening and he kept saying, 'No... That's not quite enough...' He pushed and pushed all day, it seemed. By the end something really horrible came out, something really needy and unpleasant. He brought out something that the scene needed: that the impact of Brand on this woman was killing her; it was a sound I didn't want to make but I remember thinking how much better the scene works when you start from there, because then there's the huge journey to her salvation at the end. It has to start from this ugly place to be beautiful.

Is it useful, or even possible to consider your life as an actor in terms of a career, or can you only do that retrospectively?

When I first got into the business I just wanted to tell stories and get good parts. Somehow 'career' started to creep in over the last few years. I began to turn things down to remain available for other career options.

So you started to think more strategically as you got more experienced?

Yes.

What is your strategy?

The really great parts for women dwindle, after a certain age. There are a lot of very successful middle-aged male actors; there aren't many Helen Mirrens or Judi Denchs. That was why I started to think about the future. In my late 20s, early 30s I thought if I don't get a television part soon, the pickings are going to get smaller and smaller. There are lots of great parts for nice-looking women in their 20s. Ten years later there's a bottleneck: the actresses are still around, but the parts aren't. Once you're in your 40s, it opens again, but you need to have established yourself by then. All this made me realize the importance of raising my profile. I began fighting for greater publicity – which I'd never done, or even thought about doing, and in one production, I insisted on being featured on the poster. It sounds like a small thing – but it was about me fighting my corner, and receiving the recognition that the part deserved.

When you're preparing for an audition what is it that you do?

For that first audition for *A Midsummer Night's Dream*, I learnt the scene so I could do it better, and to show commitment. More recently I don't prepare to the same degree. If I find myself reading a script for the first time on the tube on the way to an audition, that tells me all I need to know: I don't really want the job. Sometimes I don't have to audition: I did a production of *Much Ado About Nothing* at the Crucible and the director, Josie Rourke, rang to ask me to meet her for lunch. I thought that's a weird audition, I won't be able to read in a restaurant. It was only halfway through the lunch that I realized it was an opportunity for me to see if I wanted to work with her because it was an offer.

Do you feel you can, or should, sound out the director in an audition?

I should be considering that more. I still tend to think, 'Am I good enough for you?' I went for a job recently and it was the first time I actively tried to take a perspective on a director. I'd seen some of this director's work and had mixed feelings about it, and when we met, it was the first time I thought 'What will I get from working with you?' I've started to think I have a skill that needs protecting.

Is that sense of self-empowerment you allowed yourself in that situation something you have to remind yourself of on a regular basis?

Yes, a very good friend who works in opera said you need to think of yourself more as a diva; consider the opera singer's mindset: I have this unusual skill and are you going to bring the best out of this skill? The challenge is to learn how to look after yourself in a work situation, without becoming a megalomaniac.

You say that you don't do much between getting a job and doing it. Why not?

It's partly to do with fear. When I did *As You Like It* I was convinced I was going to be rubbish as Rosalind. I didn't think I understood the play and I didn't want to go near the script again. The first read through went badly for me, but once rehearsals started, the process of building a performance edged out the fear. My father used to do a lot of research before rehearsals; he always read a lot. I remember doing that for Howard Barker's *Ursula* and turning up on the first day with pages of notes. I was just about to offer them up to the entire cast, when Howard announced 'I'm not interested in actors who do research, it doesn't mean anything to me as this is purely a work of the imagination, so don't bother.' I secretly put my notes back in my bag. I take consolation from that: what's important is the imagination.

Did it stand you in good stead, the fact that you had done the research?

Not really: Howard's story of Ursula has little in common with the traditional story I'd researched. When I was onstage, I felt aware of something I didn't need: a lot of information that was irrelevant to my performance. I've read some stuff about Ibsen before doing *Lady from the Sea*: I picked essays about where Ibsen was in his life when he was writing the play and what he was passionate about, what inspired him, rather than anything about the play, because if I hear it pulled apart from a Freudian perspective, for example, then there's a danger I'll be acting with that in mind, when really I should just be telling the story. Much more interesting and useful to me is that

Ibsen's private life was going through an upturn, so he wrote a play in which love turns out alright.

So for you it's about the other actors interacting with you and the director?

And my imagination.

Would you access external stimuli on a more general basis, going to art galleries, concerts or other theatre, etc?

I used to give all my characters a sound track. I would listen to bits of music that I thought bore some relation to the character or brought out something useful in me when I listened to it. For Lady Macbeth the music was Shostakovich string quartet no. 8. The beginning section to that is really grim and gloomy, ambitious and nasty and I thought that's her, so I would play that in my mind. I did a five-day course on melodrama once, and one day we acted to Rachmaninov. The directors of the course said 'Listen to this: the scales he's reaching, the level he's reaching – match that with your acting and that's melodrama', I loved that. I do think it works as a pre-rehearsal technique.

What do you like to do in rehearsal?

Just do it a lot. I've experienced very long rehearsal periods, where we've sat around a table, analyzing the meaning of every line, sometimes for as long as two weeks. And I've thought 'I'm going to kill myself.' Talking about it doesn't really do it for me. Sometimes, directors like their actors to play lots of games, especially if they think they've got loads of time. Those games don't help me. In fact, sometimes they can be damaging. One director, on the first day of rehearsals, got us to play a lot of games that were supposed to open us up and break down barriers, but they actually made people shy and self-conscious. Some people were still self-conscious weeks later – in performance – and they put that down to that very first day. Michael Grandage doesn't like doing a read through – I do – but he's seen actors disappear and panic at read throughs, and never recover. So we get together, have coffee, look at the set and start rehearsing. In a way I like that because it's getting on and doing it, but I also like the focus of a read through. I like that we acknowledge this is what we are going to produce, now put that aside and let's start working on it.

Do you think psychological gestures and physical gestures are related: you'll find out the psychology by standing up and moving around?

Yes much more from my body than from my head.

Would you say your intelligence, as an actor is primarily physical and instinctual?

Yes.

Can you give any specific examples of how you achieved a breakthrough in a rehearsal that was to do with that physicality or instinctive intelligence?

That *Brand* moment that I talked about before: she's been making a garland to put on the baby's grave from leaves that she collected in the summer. She shows it to Brand, but he's dismissive of it. However she's very proud of it and anything to do with the baby gives her comfort. Adrian said 'I want you to tear that garland up, all your work on it, just rip it to pieces.' I thought 'I don't want to do this', but we started to do the scene and I pulled the garland to pieces and something so horrible came out, horrible but fitting. We could have talked about that emotion for ages, but I got to it from him saying 'Just try that' and doing it.

If you were left to your own devices you would get on a tramline and go down that particular line, mining and mining, rather than going laterally?

Yes.

So it's quite linear your personal approach?

I think it is. I was working with a particular director, it was about the second week of rehearsals, and I did a speech for the first time, quite a difficult, complicated one I thought. And this director said 'Lovely. We don't need to do anything with that.' It was a flattering response, but I felt stranded. It seemed to me there was much more to find in it. I think the response I wanted was 'Well yeah, it's alright. But can you bring this into it or take that there?'

Do you just have trust that what the director sees is OK?

The director of the first series of *Rebus*, encouraged me to trust his vision absolutely. He kept saying 'Don't do anything, don't tell me a story, I don't want to see anything on your face.' It felt as if there was this huge performance going on behind a mask but he would say 'Really good, excellent.' It was horrible to do! When I finally watched it, I realized he wasn't wrong: you are very watchable, on screen, if you don't respond and just watch things yourself.

Do you ever feel afraid to say to a director 'that's a poor choice that you want me to make'?

No, it might take me a long while to do it or I might have to work up to doing it but I think most of the time I instinctively fight my corner if I think something and they've disagreed. Marianne Elliott once said, 'you're inside it I'm not, so you do what you think is right' and most directors in the end come to that.

Can you think of any example of the director as an enabler that was successful for you, that released something in you?

Several, but I'll cite Howard Barker. I'd ask what a line meant and he'd say 'I don't know, show me' and I'd think 'But you wrote it.' So I'd start to say what I thought it meant and he'd say 'I don't need to know, just show me.' That really was open and enabling because he was giving us permission to bring ourselves to it. Marianne Elliot enabled something for me in rehearsals for *As You Like It* because she allowed me to bring all my longing for love and romance to it. It was never too much, it was always allowed in. One night we all stayed in the rehearsal room late and opened a bottle of wine and lit a candle. She had told us to bring in the piece of music we associated with being in love, so we all brought in a piece, listened to it together and shared its personal significance. Whilst I wouldn't encourage that personalizing of things, that was a warm and compassionate experience and it allowed us to put something of ourselves into the play.

Why do you think, ordinarily, that a personalization process isn't a good thing?

What I resist are things like emotion memory – Stanislavskian 'method'. You tell a story of your own to get to the point where you're in floods of tears in order to start the scene. Why do you have to do that to yourself? Acting is not therapy: it's empathy.

Is your antipathy to that kind of emotional recall because it's less to do with imagination and because it's not specific?

Yes, it doesn't relate to the feeling you're telling in the play. For example, you're thinking about your dad dying and you're acting falling in love with someone and not getting them.

Are there any specific things you do to stay sharp in rehearsal or performance?

Once I'm performing something, I've mapped out my territory and I tend to try and get to those points again. I think if you go on and commit to listening, the performance will always be fresh because everybody else is different every night so you're always going to hear things slightly differently. Ralph [Fiennes] was very different every night. I'd think 'I don't have to do very much here because I just need to come on and really watch what I'm getting from you, my response will bounce back.'

With the understanding that you already had that core of preparation done in rehearsals, so that you were solid on fundamentals?

Yes, the fundamentals don't change. I'm still not confident with changing things on stage. If something goes wrong around me, I can cope but to actually think I'm going on tonight and say the line with a different inflection... I'm not very confident at that.

You mentioned earlier about knowing when you have to drive a story through, when it's your bit, so to speak, does that not necessarily require you to impose your will?

Yes.

How do you marry the apparently conflicting notions of responding to what is before you and seizing the initiative to drive a scene along?

I worked on one production where one of the leading actors wasn't happy and I remember having to shut his performance out at certain points and pretend I was getting something very different.

Do you think it's useful to compensate with your personal energy in that situation? Or are there times, when your personal energy has outweighed…

…what I can actually affect?

Or what you should be affecting?

Yes, I know I've pushed because I thought other people weren't coming up with the goods or that I wasn't: it creates a squeezed, exhausted energy.

What is your personal approach to rehearsal?

It's instinctive first and then, when the director says, 'why don't you try and do that with it?' it becomes evidential because I either agree with that idea or I don't. So then I look to find whether or not that new idea would serve to take it to a different level or direction that I hadn't thought of. There's also a structural aspect of identifying how the scene works: the movement through the scene, where it starts and where it ends. Crucially, you respond to what you're being given, although I have to say I can sometimes disappear into a bit of a bubble.

Do you actively try to avoid that, when you feel confident and are surrounded by generous people or does it surface even then?

I remember reading for Michael Grandage when he was auditioning actors to play Ferdinand and I was playing Miranda; we did the scene where Ferdinand is carrying the logs and Miranda says 'Let me help you.' When Sam Callis auditioned, he went to pick up an imaginary log and I instantly went to pick up the other end of it because I could see the log, when he imagined it, I could see it. I instinctively stepped out of my bubble to act with him, because I believed him. I go into the vacuum when I think I'm not going to get what I need, so I'm going to have to imagine I'm getting what I need.

How do you use your time during technical rehearsals?

The tech is very important, a massive hinge point when everything you've done in the rehearsal room – in privacy and in your own clothes and your real hair – turns into something else, when everybody's vision has to come together. And you might not like what the designer's done, you might not like the set, suddenly you can't see someone's face because it's lit bizarrely, or you can't be as intimate as you were in a particular moment because you're now in a much bigger space. There isn't really anything you can do – it is quite brutalizing, that's part of its function, and all you can do is be aware that you've got this intangible thing, and you've got to get it into its new home.

Do you put your rehearsal process into suspension, or is the tech another rehearsal opportunity?

I regard it as a necessary aspect of things. I think it should be as creative for the actors but somehow it isn't. We can't use it as a rehearsal though, because you can't get a flow on things, you get interrupted.

Is that not also true of rehearsal – you run a scene, or segment of a scene, stop and analyze it and then try again?

That's true but in a rehearsal you can count on the undivided attention of your director – in a tech you haven't got that. So it's not quite the same.

Does the move from rehearsal room into an auditorium affect how you view your character and the story-telling process?

It really does. I've noticed it most when moving a production into a really big theatre. On a few occasions, it seemed as if the atmosphere we'd created in the rehearsal room had just drifted away and never quite came back as it was: we developed something else. The Olivier in particular can do that – there's stuff that might work in a rehearsal room, that the Olivier doesn't want, if that makes sense. The space is not interested: it wants something else. All the things you found in the past, stay under the surface, but you're not able to show them in the same way. That's why it's so important to concentrate during the tech, because you have to try to hold on to things.

What do you do in order to retain a sense of ownership or to not lose the play during the tech?

I tend to watch techs, I stay in the space, so that I get to know it. I like hearing all the different layers being put together. When you sit in the auditorium, little of what the actors are doing at that moment is relevant... the conversations are about lighting or changing something on the set...the actors are like unobserved children.

Are those conversations about how you light and therefore help the actor, or is it that the actor has to fit in?

It's all support, it's all about heightening an actor's effect. But I don't think I've ever been in a show where I haven't had to modify something because the stage has been lit in a certain way.

How do you feel about that?

It's a marriage isn't it, a compromise. You have to relinquish control in techs – previews and performances are about getting the control back for yourself, making the changes feel like your own. But you still can be left with a wig you hate or a dress you think is wrong.

What do you do in that situation?

I argue my corner. There was only one production where my vision and the director's were completely different and, in the end, I had to accept his vision over my own.

Did that adversely affect your performance?

It made it different to what I'd imagined it would be. I had a strong image of how I wanted this character to look and why. I saw her as one thing, the director saw her as something completely different and there wasn't really a compromise. It still worked; I just didn't get to tell one of the stories about that character that I wanted to tell.

What distinguishes previews from the rehearsal or performance period?

I never think of previews as different from performances. I suppose the previews are when I start to take it back for myself, because it's the point at which you know nobody can interrupt you so you can get a flow.

What does that mean, 'take it back for yourself'?

In techs, it's almost like I hibernate: I get on and do it. The previews are when you start to get the play that you rehearsed back, as much as you can, and put it on stage and give it to that dark space.

So you don't see the possibility of accelerated, creative development in tech time but you do in preview time?

Yes, it's partly because you get the director's attention back – you're under scrutiny during previews. There's a hiatus, then quite a lot happens very fast doesn't it? *The Relapse*, over four or five previews, changed beyond recognition, we cut out nearly an hour.

How do you make that adjustment, working at that speed, in previews – for example, cutting an hour of performance in four days that you've spent six weeks facilitating? Is there a strategy you employ to enable you to do that, or do you even think about?

That was a radical one. Trevor Nunn, who directed it, said, 'We've all got to be very brave, we've all got to let go of something.' Then he went through the cuts. He did it in such a way that we all just came together in the spirit of it, we all gave something up and got on with it. But there have been other shows where I've been given notes during the previews that my performance was suddenly lacking something, or not getting up to the next level. That can be distressing and I've sometimes panicked and thought I'll never be able to give a director what they're after. But then things have started to click into place.

Can you identify what it was you did that made that possible?

I practice a lot at home. Life stops during previews; I don't return calls and the day is all about building up to the evening. It's very concentrated. It's like a rollercoaster ride; it's hurtling towards a press night that you have to be ready for. And I suppose I try to let go.

Let go of your own perceptions?

Yes and just be willing. A critical note from a director at that time can be really discombobulating, but I can see later that they're just pushing for another level. But because you don't have that concentrated rehearsal time any more, and it's a note given out in front of 30 other people, it doesn't feel so safe.

How do you retain your sense of purpose, as an actor telling the story through your character, on press nights, when the play can feel secondary to the event itself?

I used get into terrible tizzies, so I developed lots of superstitions and rituals to try to counteract the nerves. My mother said to me once, 'When you're an actor of a certain quality, there's a level below which you won't fall, so it doesn't matter if a performance wavers a bit, it's always going to be at that level and that level's good.' So I always try and hold on to that. I don't know, really, I just get through it. I stand in the wings and try to feel my feet on the ground, then walk on stage and do it, that's all you can do.

Do you think actors cede creative authority, before they've even entered a rehearsal room?

I'm not sure. When I read a play, there are some points where I think 'I know what I'm going to do there, how I want to tell that story'; then, if I feel that I'm not getting what I need for whatever reason, I know I can come back to those points, because they came from my own instinct and imagination and I anchor myself in those. However, there are directors who get something new out of you, something you hadn't thought of or didn't think you could do. So I don't think I cede authority; it should be collaborative and it's about earning trust.

Is it useful to have a sense of purpose and to have that clearly articulated for you?

Yes I think it does help. For all I say though, it's very important for me to please a director, which is a child/parent thing; it's very important that I can see on a director's face they've got something out of me that afternoon in the rehearsal room. I'm thrilled when a director comes over unprompted and says 'Good work'. There's a slight contradiction here: you can be quite certain but still have the child in you, willing to work to please somebody and be thrilled when you have. So yes, a purpose does help. But not necessarily a concept; I worked on one production, where the director could see the play conceptually but didn't know how to bring out from the actors the intricacies of the relationships and feelings within it.

Because their understanding was essentially cerebral?

Yes exactly. In which case, being told your purpose in a play is of no use because you can't act a concept.

What for you is a good performance and what's a bad performance?

The difficult shows have been when I didn't feel supported on stage.

How does an actor fail to support you on stage?

If they change a move or try to upstage, if they get seduced by a laugh or start chasing for a laugh. Dropping a figurative ball because they can't be bothered to catch it, not because they were distracted or meant earnestly to catch it but just didn't. I've often noticed that when a production is a critical failure, or the rehearsal process has been very painful, the actors really bond, on and off stage. Some of my happiest times, socially anyway, have been on a grim tour of something, when the actors have nothing but each other to get themselves through the experience. One director, who's been an actor himself, once said something very interesting to me about actors and how they bond. He never joins his cast in the bar after rehearsals because he says it's an important time for the actors to get together to let off steam, about the day, about the process, about him. He appreciates that separation between director and cast, is part of the cast coming together.

Why do you think that companies are more likely to come together in a failure than a success?

When a production is successful, the actors can't help but compete for a share of it, particularly if it's a very glamorous production, and you know your audience might be high-powered and influential. Whereas in a show that's a failure, it doesn't matter, you come together because it's just you.

Do you think those performances of celebrated or successful productions suffer because they cease to be team play?

They can do, yes.

How important is confidence to being creative?

I make a distinction between courage and confidence. Confidence is what you need to stand on stage and for it not to matter when something practical goes wrong – a bit of set doesn't move when it should, or you're standing there in darkness. You acknowledge it to the audience, they laugh with relief because you're not going to lie to them about it and then you carry on. Courage is what you need to come into a rehearsal room and not hide behind a cup of tea for half an hour so rehearsals don't start on time. I did that for years. One actor pointed out to me how many people had come into rehearsals on a particular day with a cup of coffee – he said it was a little shield that says, 'Don't ask me to do anything I'm still drinking my coffee'. So courage is coming in ready to go; and it's hugely important for creativity.

Have you ever experienced a loss of that courage?

Many times I've been in tears in my dressing room, or on the phone to my mum, saying 'I can't do it, I've not got it, I'm going to be rubbish.' I used to think that if you suffered enough as an actor you'd get rewards; people would see you cared about it more than other actors and you'd get better parts. Now I understand that's not how it works, it's not about justice or deserving.

Have you ever felt blocked; 'I don't know where I am/what I'm doing'?

Not a feeling of blockage so much, as a feeling that I've run out of territory. If I haven't taken the time I needed in rehearsals, really asked all my questions, if I've worked at someone else's pace, I can suddenly find, three weeks later, in the middle of a run that I've nowhere left to go. I'm just repeating and that can be agony. For example, I don't learn a part before rehearsals because I think something important happens when you're holding a script. You can start to mark things and try things out, and you don't have to quite commit to each other yet because there's this script between you. If I learn something cold off the page before I start, then it can't go in at the same time as my mind is mapping out the emotional connections in the play. The words are already in and the feelings get tacked on to them afterwards, and it's not the same.

And is there something there for you about seeing a word on a page that releases your imagination? The physical sight of the word?

Yes and the process of having to read it, having to read the line before you say it – then you get to absorb it, understand it.

How do you define presence?

I think it has something to do with the audience relaxing when you come on. Michael Gambon came into my mind when you said the word presence. He's unapologetically and unequivocally himself. That's not to say he isn't different with each part; there's just something defiant and authentic about him.

Your eyes are drawn to people with presence, but how do you distinguish genuine presence from upstaging?

It's taste: I might say one actor has presence and another is just showing off, and somebody else would disagree.

Are the best actors those that are most comfortable in their skins?

The actors, who are most comfortable in their own skins, when on stage, definitely. Those are the interesting actors.

Has your best acting been when you've been most comfortable?

Yes, with each performance, I give something up, I stop doing something that I think is good and the performance gets better and simpler. Ralph Richardson, one of my heroes, once said that – let go what seems like a good idea or a good choice, and try to give up one thing a night, and in the end you might have a good performance. As a young actor I thought that if I hit certain emotional points that I could tally up at the end of each show, I'd be able to say, 'I got it 97% right this afternoon. But only managed 67% in the evening.' But that's a kind of arrogance really, a desire to be in control. Once you let go of self-consciousness, you start to actually react to things, and the writer can speak through you. I think that's what happened on *Brand*: it was the beginning of quite a big shift into an actor who's much less controlling, not trying to hit emotional high points, just being open, and trying to be more authentic, I hope.

What is an actor's responsibility in rehearsals?

To be brave. To do what's asked of you unless you really disagree with it, in which case stand up for why you disagree – because that's another form of doing what's asked of you actually – and respond, collaborate.

What's the best direction you have ever been given?

Probably something really basic: my mother said to me that I had 'starfish hands', because I acted with my hands spread out. She also pointed out that I tended to lean forward when I was trying to make my point. She said just be aware and don't do those things – it's basic but fundamental – because it's all about physical expression – your body and your voice are all you have.

And what's the worst direction you've ever had?

When a director did something that felt destructive. It was about restraining an emotion and I think it was because of taste, not because the emotion was too much or inaccurate. I thought 'You're not saying this because you think I'm not serving the story, you're saying it because you don't like seeing women angry and that's about you.'

Does the chronology of the employment process affect the status of the actor within the creative hierarchy?

I do find it intimidating when you turn up on the first day and there's a little box set and drawings of what you're going to look like. It's very curious: you're the most visible aspect of the whole thing, but the least involved up to that point. The four weeks' rehearsal focus on the actors' needs, then the tech when it's not about you at all and then the performances when you get it back. The power constantly shifts between the management and the shop floor, so to speak. In television you see it most clearly – your performance is like cloth from which editors, directors and producers cut a suit.

How do you view the distinction made between the creative teams and the cast?

It's another aspect of us being a bit like children – the children are allowed to play, whilst the adults go away and make the big decisions about what the children will wear, and how they'll be lit.

Where do you as an actor feel that you currently fit into the creative hierarchy and where do you think you'd be better placed in order to make theatre-making better? Do you feel you should be party to those key artistic decisions of design etc. or do you think, no my realm is in acting?

I'm not sure how far actors can be involved in the design process. When I did *Much Ado About Nothing*, I didn't like the dress because I thought it made Beatrice plain and I fought to change it: Beatrice should be beautiful; her singleness shouldn't be for any obvious reason, it's because of something inside her, a choice. And in the end they changed it and made it very pretty and lovely. I put it on and thought 'Oh no, this isn't right, I shouldn't be in this', and the only negative comment I heard about that performance was that I looked too nice. But I never had the courage to go to the designer and say 'You were right, I was wrong, I'm sorry' – partly because I didn't want to admit that to myself while I was still doing it. On reflection, that was a moment when my vanity got in the way. So I'm not sure that actors can be involved because they're not always the best guardians of their own vanity. Who is? If an actor comes into a production and wants to tell a certain story, that's different – if it's really about an actor's particular understanding of a character, something they're bringing that no one else would. Ideally, it should be more a case of listening to your child when they have an interesting idea but not necessarily letting them have all the sweets. It's that balance, I suppose.

What are the essential ingredients of art?

Art is something that is unapologetic and true to itself. And its effect should be profound.

And would you say that as an actor you are an artist?

We're not quite accorded that status are we? Acting is a conjuring type of art. In that extraordinary film *The Seventh Seal*, one of the things that moves me the most is that the actor lives. Everybody else dies, but the actor gets away because he has an imagination. He sees things, so he knows tragedy is looming before anyone else does. I think Bergman is saying that an actor has kept the child eyes in his head, so when he looks at something, he sees the spiritual in it. And imagination means you get to survive.

What do you think are the artists' needs, of their art?

I've grown up with actors and it's all I've ever done. I can't imagine a life where you don't get to go and work your feelings out. And I mean in both senses of that – work them out and work them out of you. So I think the actor's need must be to express something truthfully, to express themselves whilst pretending to be someone else.

Do we do it for ourselves or do we do it for other people? Is it an act of selfishness or an act of generosity?

It's both. Our culture, our plays, are like waking dreams. They're the stories we tell ourselves to make sense of things. An audience watching a play is having a collective dream experience. Actors perform an important function because they act out those dreams. And on a personal level, the actor is doing something for themselves.

Do you feel comfortable with that?

I do. I remember a debate in drama school in which I asserted that being an actor had a social function, a responsibility. Another student said that anyone who says they're doing this for anyone else is lying; actors are just in it for themselves, because they're vain. I really didn't agree: to do something that doesn't give you much money, where you're always worried about the next job and you're always being judged – that's a difficult way of life. And when you get a job, it's hard to stand up and offer something up from your own private feelings: that can't all just be an ego trip; I don't buy that. As I've lived it, done it and had to protect myself from all the negative things you face as an actor, I'm much more comfortable with that duality. Nobody really wants to entertain the selfish aspects of it.

Why do people come to the theatre?

It holds a promise of something, and that promise is very old. It may be to be entertained, scared or really moved, or because the play is on the syllabus, or someone really likes a particular actor, or 'I do this every two months' or whatever it is. But underneath that, the reason for going is ancient, and it's because you don't know what will happen. Because to me, the theatre is still magic, weird and spiritual, but we don't like to talk about magic now.

What's the best thing about being an actor for you?

To get to express a feeling that in real life I might have to restrain. To get on stage and think, 'Oh, I know that feeling of confusion or terror or rage, I've been there' – and to show it. A sense of freedom then.

What's the worst thing about being an actor?

The pressure on me as a woman to be a certain size.

How do you define success for yourself as an actor?

I used to define it specifically as having an Oscar. When I was a child, I imagined success as a life in LA, making films. Now I'm actually an actor, the things that satisfy me are plays, being on stage. Having a bit of money as well, that's a big thing. Becoming VAT registered (I remember thinking I'm like all the men I know). That makes me feel successful, it's as simple as that.

What does it mean to you, Claire Price, to be an actor?

The first thought I can remember having was that I wanted to be an actor. I've been an actor now for fifteen years; it's still the only thing I'll ever want to do.

RUAIRI CONAGHAN

Ruairi has appeared in world premieres of the plays of Owen Mc Cafferty, Gary Mitchell, Debbie Tucker Green and Georgia Fitch at the National Theatre, the Royal Court, the Bush Theatre and The Lyric, Belfast. He has also played extensively in Rep and Fringe venues in a variety of classical and contemporary roles. He has appeared in British and Irish TV and film productions over the past 15 years, including *Waking the Dead*, *The Catherine Tate Show* and *The Suspicions of Mr Whicher*.

POK   *What was your first encounter with theatre?*

RC   My mother and father were amateur actors; my earliest memory was of my mother producing a version of Brian Friel's *Philadelphia Here I Come*, in which she was also playing Aunt Lizzy. I was 7 or 8 and I helped her learn her lines; I loved the characterisation and I loved doing it. I can't remember anything about the production, but I remember those rehearsals with my mother very, very well.

Was that what sparked your interest in theatre?

I'd done page-boys, carried on pillows and worn tights in little pantos. I hated that, but what I loved was that development of character when I was learning it with my mother. I began to love text; I was learning it and getting the gags; it was a sophisticated scene but I was still getting the gags.

What made you want to become an actor?

I must have been about 11 or 12. We used to holiday in Donegal; Ray McAnally, a fantastic actor, would play golf there and my mother had a vague connection to him, so I caddied for him. He'd talk about theatre and I loved it. I confessed my desire to act one day and he said, 'don't go near it, it's a ridiculous thing to do; be a lawyer, be a doctor'. Subsequently he came to Magherafelt, my hometown, in the original Field Day Theatre Company production of *Translations* with Stephen Rae and Liam Neeson – he came to my school. It was brilliant. I met them all afterwards and I talked to Liam about what it's like to be an actor and he had a very down to earth approach to it all – and was very happy to talk to 11 year olds about it. It sounded fantastic – going from town to town doing a play, going out for a drink afterwards. I didn't look beyond the realms of Northern Ireland; I didn't think about movie stars, I just thought the life sounded great.

Once you'd had that experience, did you then seek it out?

In school I did and because I was OK, I was picked to be part of the adult amateur company – I was only 15/16. It is a cliché but I was a disaster at school and what saved me was acting. It gave me something personal, an enjoyment really; I think I just liked it and there were lots of nice girls around!

When did you decide to pursue it professionally?

My father was a solicitor and the natural progression for me was to move into the business, but I left home when I was 17 so there was no longer pressure on me, as a middle-class Catholic boy, to follow my father's profession. I signed on the dole and did acting with the College of Business Studies and the Circle Theatre Company, in Belfast. I did stuff like *The Playboy of the Western World*, I played Christy Mahon; it was wonderful to get hold of that text.

Did you receive encouragement there to keep going?

If you were a certain age, looked a certain way and had a modicum of talent, there were a wealth of roles for you in that world and there were a lot of people encouraging you to continue. My parents were dealing with their own issues but they also encouraged me, saying, go the path you want to go, but get a degree.

So you went to Liverpool University?

Yes, I didn't bother with drama school auditions and one factor was financial considerations – I literally couldn't afford to go to London – but I was also scared of the rejection. It also seemed like a world away. I'd hear about some of the Ulster Youth Theatre guys like Conleth Hill and Jimmy Nesbitt, going to drama school, and I found that extraordinary. I decided to do a degree in drama. Paula McFettridge, (recently artistic director, Lyric Belfast), was very helpful and Dorothy Whiley at the Circle Theatre, also gave advice and encouragement. So I sold my guitar and bike, I went to

Liverpool and I copped off on the boat over which was an encouraging start. I arrived in Liverpool, in 1985/86; it was the time of Militant and Hatton, it was impoverished, but it was great. I had an interview with these longhaired hippy types and then we did a group audition. There were two things that could have happened to me that day; I could have gone into my shell and walked away, particularly the group thing, but for some reason I thrived and was accepted.

Was that an entirely academic course?

Overall it was about 60% practical and 40% academic but I had an understanding of Brecht and Stanivslaski, Grotowski, Artaud, European theatre, Dürrenmatt, the history of the Royal Court, the National, Glasgow Citz, about Brook in Paris and the RSC; the only thing that it lacked was actor training. I did lots of acting, saw lots of plays and got a really good knowledge base but little training that was of use. Very few actors graduated from that course – lots of directors, producers, teachers and people who work in arts administration or in television – only two or three actors though.

What impact did that training have on your career?

When I would first look at a text I wouldn't count the lines, I'd read the play, look for the dramatic function of my character – then I'd count the lines!

Do you make yourself conversant with the idea of the play first, before you start focusing on your particular function as an actor and a character within that?

That's correct.

Do you think that distinguishes you in any way from other actors?

It did at the start certainly.

Were drama school actors not encouraged to think contextually like that?

The first play I did as a professional actor was a season at the Northcott in Exeter – two Orton shorts *The Ruffian on the Stairs* and *Funeral Games* and two new plays, one called *Box* and *Rough Justice* by Conall Morrison. I played the lead in *Rough Justice*, a great part in *Box* and the title role in *Ruffian on the Stairs*, brilliant parts. There were three other lads in it who'd gone to RADA and one lady who'd gone to Drama Centre. At first I was a little intimidated by these trained actors. As the process developed and we became more friendly, I discovered they'd been intimidated by me and my understanding of text and my process, simply because I had a degree. I did have a certain way of looking at text, which was different to their approach – not so much nowadays; lots of actors, old, young, work in that way now.

Would you say your training, your degree, stood you in good stead?

It did. I didn't learn how to be an actor until two or three years later though.

What were you expecting from your first job?

It was one of the best jobs I've ever had – playing leading roles at the very start of your career was tremendous. I also learnt a lot about working with other actors, proper actors; particularly from Roger Llewellyn who's still a friend of mine, he was in his early 40s then. He was very distinguished, he'd been to RADA and he'd won the Shakespeare prize there. He'd had a tremendous regional theatre career, playing lead roles, been to London, been to the West End. His rehearsal process blew me away; he learnt his lines very quickly, he was playful, he would try things to make it new and fresh. I had thought once you got it sorted, that was it. He would really look you in the eye, and you had to maintain that eye contact, which was quite a challenge. He became a mentor. He's very good at developing the business aspect – he'd say look, you've got to move to London, you need to get an agent, these are the people you need to talk to; theatre auditions go like this, TV auditions go like that – he was brilliant at that. He said something to me once that has stuck: because I push naturalism, he said you can be big and be truthful as well. It was a very sophisticated thought for a twenty-something actor who hadn't been to drama school, because I didn't really understand a lot about dynamics; I was a musician, so I understood the musical aspect of it, but that idea was hard.

Did that job at Exeter establish any patterns for your career as an actor?

I didn't play leading roles again for another ten years! It set a pattern in that it made me realise that you're not the finished article when you arrive in the rehearsal room for your first job – there is a real journey to go on. I was

39

genuinely willing to learn. I thought I was good, but I didn't think I was the finished article; nor did I think I was the best either; just as in sport, I knew that great players didn't start out as great players, they became so because they were guided and were around other great people. For the most part I didn't start working with really great practitioners until about 2000/2001 and that's when I really took a leap.

In those ten years, what were the key events that changed the way you saw both yourself and the business?

I really started to develop as an actor when I became part of a permanent company of eight actors at the Liverpool Everyman, on a one-year contract – four classics: *Othello*, *School for Scandal*, *The White Devil* and *Alice in Wonderland* – we were all young except for one or two. They brought in telly faces and more established actors to play the leads, so I would play some of the good small parts. I really began to develop technically as an actor; I learnt about voice, presence, being physically fit and the need for stamina.

Was that peer-to-peer learning or did you take classes?

There was a lot of further development organised by the theatre: lots of workshop development, community involvement, voice work and that classic rep system of rehearsing by day and performing at night, that leap from one character to another. I learnt about the impact of small parts as well; when young actors get a small part they can be filled with resentment and anger – I have been at times – but I learnt that you can make a tremendous impact with those parts. For example, the mechanicals in *A Midsummer Night's Dream* – extraordinary impact, steal the show. I learned to understand and respect that as well – get rid of the resentment and get on with the job!

Did the community involvement provide context for the role of theatre?

It did. I got very friendly with Andrew Sherlock, a great community practitioner; he devised a show called *Fall from Grace* about the Irish impact on Liverpool, which I helped develop. I saw a dress rehearsal of the original production and it was probably the best piece of theatre I have ever seen. From the moment I stepped into that theatre, I was enthralled, amazed by the spectacle, affected – it made me think. I'd studied political theatre, Brenton and Bond, the Royal Court, its historical impact and its role in new writing, but I thought it played to middle classes. I'd only ever played to people who were middle class – when I did plays about Northern Ireland and I had to wear balaclavas, it was to middle-class people who would come up to me afterwards and say it must have been a terrible thing to be brought up in that kind of environment, 'Aye that's right. What's your name sweetheart, what's your number…'

Did the technical development of your professional skills come in the course of doing the job?

On the job, simple as that.

Where did you learn how to act?

On the job.

Any other significant people or events in that early period?

Dan Crawford, lovely man, a real radical, maverick guy, directed *Philadelphia Here I Come* – the play I talked about with my Mother – at the Kings Head, Islington, a brilliant theatre. We got £120 a week, all the beer you could drink and all the food you could eat – I still have a bar tab there – you felt like a rich man. Then we transferred to the West End and they paid us properly but I never seemed to have any money! There's a scene in the play where a group of boys have come to say goodbye when Gar's emigrating and I played their leader, big brusque guy, a bully – he cast against type for I was a skinny wee guy – and they cast big George Heslin as the soft sensitive one, and Aiden Dooley as the fool. Dan was hands-off directorially, but he sent the three of us to see *Run for Your Wife* at the Playhouse in Northumberland Avenue. We were ambitious, sensitive, young Irish actors interested in culture and art – why are we going to see this farce bullshit? We went in, sat down, the curtain pulled back and we started laughing and we didn't stop till the end of the show. The technical achievement of these actors was phenomenal. I wouldn't rush to see another Ray Cooney farce, but I understand what Dan was doing – he was saying to us, there are elements of farce in your scene, elements of timing, playfulness, that the scene needed real levity for the seriousness of the denouement to pay off. George, Aiden and I became very good friends, we were very playful, we must have done it about 180-200 times, we understood that we needed to make it as fresh as we possibly could every night so we would constantly find new things; the three of us were in agreement about that and we trusted each other. It was one of those key jobs.

What's the next landmark?

I went back to Ireland to work. I'd never felt properly like an actor because I hadn't worked in Ireland – the emotional stuff – and even though I had a really great start to my career nobody in Ireland had a clue who I was, so I went to the Lyric, Belfast, to do a light comic farce about the blitz in Belfast in the Second World War. Two significant things happened on my return home. I met my beautiful wife Caitriona and *Philadelphia Here I Come* came back again; this time I played the lead. I had an extraordinary, emotional time playing that part; it was very successful, we took it to America and toured with it. But the most significant thing for me, career-wise, was meeting Gary Mitchell. I auditioned for Gary and Brenda Winter, who was directing Gary's TIE show, *That Driving Ambition*. It was brilliant stuff about punishment beating, it was going to go around schools and I went up for two fantastic parts; one was the UVF leader who had a conscience and thought he was trying to drive the community but was brutal, and the other part was a young, mad, crazy renegade guy; but it was a TIE job – five months before that I'd been in the West End! My initial thought was there was no way I was doing it but I was in love with the play. I'd picked up an agent by this point as well, so those influences were there. I met Gary on the set of a television job and he said, 'how are you doing Ruairi, you will be doing my play won't you?' And I said well, lots of things to talk about, and he said, 'no, you will be doing that play.' So I said OK – I liked his bravado, I loved the fact that he really wanted me to do it and it turned out to be brilliant: we toured schools and a couple of borstals and it had an impact.

Are the influential people and events in the early part of your career defined by
a political or at least analytical consciousness and did the key theatrical events
have a social impact as well as a personal impact?

Roger was about me as an actor. Andrew and Gary were about the power
of political theatre to affect you. Dan was about the idea of actors as
community.

Does that still inform your view of the theatre and your view of actors and
acting?

My opinions of theatre are just different now; I'm not as romantic about it.
I have had a progression in my work in theatre and I've done some brilliant
work and I've done some shit work. I've worked with too many directors
who shouldn't direct, with some OK directors and with too few inspired
and brilliant directors. I've worked with some fantastic actors and I've
developed, travelled and experienced great things, had tremendous highs
and tremendous lows, but now my challenges are in camera work and the
development of that side of my career because of the practicalities of being
a father and having a mortgage, but also because I just don't have that same
love of the practice of it any more.

Can you identify when and why you fell out of love with that?

A lot of people are trying very hard to get very small amounts of money to
practice their art and that creates a lot of tension. I still have an optimistic
opinion of artists and the creative process and I still feel that we're in it
together, but when it gets down and dirty, too much work that I've been
involved with has been about everyone slagging each other off, and about
finding your own little grasp, your own little place within that.

Why do you think people do that?

Because they're desperate and it's hard, it's too hard; it should be easier. In
Germany and France it isn't as hard as this. In France you can work for nine
months and then sit for six or seven months and develop creative ideas and
you can earn a living doing that; you can set up with another project and
spend two years on it – where we are here, you can't do that.

Why not?

In my experience, a lot of the people with control and power are not the people that should be in those positions. So you walk on to the set of *Murphy's Law* or *Waking the Dead* and you know you're in television land; you know where you are, what the structure is and you make your way within that, you can go on learning about your craft and very, very occasionally in that world you get work that can really create an effect like *The Street* – McGoverns' piece, you get to work with Paul Greengrass, you're suddenly in this extraordinary world. And in theatre, apart from the work with Andrew in *A Fall From Grace* or maybe some of the early Gary Mitchell work or apart from *Scenes from the Big Picture* at the National Theatre or my work at the Court and the Bush, I've rarely been in that place; the rest of it, the good times, have been about enjoying the wonder of acting and having a brilliant acting experience, but not really having an impact.

What do you mean by impact?

We're not effecting any change, we're not changing any minds. When are the times that I've had the effect that *Field Day* had on me and my career; I think a couple of times it's happened, but I've done over thirty plays.

Is it your responsibility to find out the level of impact your work has had?

No.

All you can hope to do is offer it up?

Yes I suppose.

What, in your view, is art and what is art for?

It's up to the individual viewing it. I love the story about the presentation of the rubbish in the corner, at Tate Modern – one of the cleaners cleaned it up. But I love the wit of the artist as well. I can't stand somebody saying that's not art; it is, it's either just good or bad or it has an effect on you or it doesn't.

What effect has good art had on you?

It's moved me emotionally, it's driven me, it's made me change my mind, it's made me strive to create something like it, do something positive or re-look at my relationship, attempt to achieve something good.

So it transforms you on all levels of consciousness?

Because I don't particularly have any religion, art can really move me in that way.

Do you think there is a spiritual component to art?

Yes; whatever spirituality is, whatever the real beauty of religion can mean to people, you can get that from art I think.

So it has to contain beauty as well?

Oh God yeah.

How do you define beauty?

Sean O'Casey would write a line that would be both moving and funny at the same time and you would have both those reactions simultaneously and I think that's incredible.

What is an artist?

Artists are people who try to create some expression of their own personal, emotional, societal or political feelings that can have an effect on someone else. I don't think you create art for yourself do you? You really do want someone else to see it or else it wouldn't be art? But that's a good definition of art isn't it? Someone else has to see it before it's art.

What do you think the specific role of theatre is, within the context of art?

I used to think it was a means to influence people, to effect some change in both their individual lives and in society.

So you don't think it is any more or you don't think it can be any more?

I don't think it can be to a large group of people, it can be to individuals.

More people go to theatre than go to football matches, why can it not have an effect on a lot of people?

It can, but it's rarely as dramatic as football and secondly, because if it did and had managed to achieve that, why are we in the position we are now – scrabbling for funding, an extraordinary amount of people out of work, a society in which the means of art and creativity are controlled by a few and therefore the majority of what we see creatively is of a particular genre and substandard, that you have to seek out the good stuff, that the majority of art and creativity is bad.

Why do you think that?

One reason is that people control how you create it.

Is it being used as a social engineering tool?

No, it's just because people are a bit lazy; I don't think there are enough people out there who are really driven and work and strive as hard as they possibly can, who are theatre animals that wish to effect change, who believe you can still do it. I admire these people fantastically, but I wish I was one of them.

What's the greatest threat to theatre?

Financial impoverishment of its artists. I've got to know a lot of stand-up comics, actors, artists and writers; after a while they get pissed off with having no money and because of that, their initial rawness of creativity gets hit hard, they consider other options, and they either make concessions or they move away from this life. How do people think they can cast a 45 year old to portray a man of some influence and power, who can create some effect in a play and they want the best; let's say they want to do it at a fantastic venue like the Bush and they pay them £350 a week, which, after tax and agent's fees, becomes £270; at the same time his wife isn't working and they've got two or three kids – you can't do it. I have survived as an actor because I've been able to do corporate role play – that has enabled me financially to be available to act in the theatre and I'm over forty; if I hadn't had that, I couldn't have done it. Of course there are actors who work continuously, but most of us don't. In answer to that question: if you properly fund the arts you will gain the best creativity and the best work.

Why should I fund the arts when hospitals are...

That's no argument; you can counteract that with the other cliché – don't invade other countries and don't kill lots of Mulsims. Don't gamble our money up the swanny. It's a ridiculous argument – they're all intertwined. Art is a crucial part of identification.

So if you want great art you have to pay for it? A lot of the general public would not agree with that, and think that art is a trivial thing, that artists are trivial people. Do artists' needs and expectations of art differ from the public's?

If they think art is trivial, why are there fifteen million of them watching soap opera? They clearly don't think it's trivial: they think it's important, or why would so many of them buy a particular pop album? Theatre is a branch of those pieces of art. If you want to make great art, pay for it and don't make it so expensive to see.

For you, is it a vocation or a job?

So many aspects of my life have changed since I had a child. The whole idea of vocational employment is changing now anyway, it's very hard to find vocational employment. You knew you were a nurse because you had a vocation, a priest, a doctor, a teacher; it's not really about that anymore and I suppose being an actor was about vocation.

What do you understand by vocation? A calling?

Yes; you're not necessarily doing it for financial gain or careerist ideal.

Did you have a compulsion to act then?

Yes, a need. Also vocation means something about aspiration, about aspiring to do some good as well, I have this vocation to do this therefore and to have an effect upon other people.

How much does that aspiration, to do some public good, relate to the quest for personal enrichment, for self-expression?

Apart from the birth of my son, practising my art has created the most fantastic moments of my life. As an actor there is a moment of direct communication of feeling: I'm so embroiled in this and what I'm doing is really telling the story and I'm really in the moment here but despite the self-involvement, you sense that you are having impact.

Do you ever get a sense that we're just doing this for ourselves?

No, I don't think I've ever thought that. Sometimes people say in the rehearsal room, let's do it for ourselves and it's usually associated with a show that's not working so well. The 'ourselves' is not about ourselves, it's about the community of it. That's primarily what we are as actors: we're story-tellers.

Do you think you make many sacrifices?

Some kind of secure environment – it's not just the financial aspect that makes it hard to achieve. It's the reason why I've had a child so late.

Does the job, the actual acting – rehearsing and performing – does that make emotional and, dare I say, spiritual demands on you?

Sometimes the best work and greatest moments are achieved in the rehearsal room. It's not that what we produce after that, in performance, is worse, but there are moments in the rehearsal room when you think that's just been extraordinary, what's happened to us here.

Because it's the original point of creation?

Definitely. It's one of the reasons we do this job: that moment is as good as sex – it's an orgasmic moment isn't it? Everyone's doing what we do because everyone wants to get those moments again, don't they? It's a real rush, like a bodybuilder's steroid rush: you know something has happened and you strive to achieve that again.

How does that tally with the generous impulse of giving over a story to an audience?

You can get it in performance but it's different – you get a reaction, that immediate reaction, you can feel it. If you're in a tense drama you can hear a pin drop, the coughing stops, the shuffling stops, there's utter focus on what you're doing and the story you're telling. With a comedy, you get that comic reaction.

Is that about power, about having everyone looking at you?

Yes, certainly there's an ego thing there sometimes: look what I can do. I can also think, look what he/she can do and get as big a rush – particularly when I'm on stage with them because when you see someone else do it you want to be a part of their brilliance because, one, it's your duty and your job to do so, but two, because it's fantastic: it's a great thing to happen and to do.

What is your relationship with, or awareness of the arts/theatre institutions and funding bodies?

I'm a freelance actor, I've never been a producer or applied for funding from the Arts Council, but I have worked at the Bush and I have worked at the Northcott for example; both were reprieved from recent funding cuts, the Northcott my first job, the Bush very recently, so the thought of those two going personally impacted on me and I was very pleased when they were reprieved.

Do you think there may, could and indeed should be a way, where there was a channel of communication between individual actors and the Arts Council?

The petition against the Arts Council cuts was brought by actors, so there was some kind of relationship there.

That was organised by Equity.

How can I do anything, apart from being a part of my union and supporting it?

Do you think your union represents you effectively?

It's easy for me to criticise my union when the only active thing I do is maintain my membership; I think the people that are involved in it are good people but I don't think they're as effective as they could be; if they were, we wouldn't be on £350 a week, or we wouldn't be screwed over by commercial television rights.

So they're not an effective lobbying group?

There have been successes over the years and they have that battle further down the line that the American writers are having currently with new media and how that's going to affect us, because we are there, we're online, just you stick your name into YouTube and something will pop up; are you going to get paid for that – that is your right, that's you there, that's you practising your work.

Do you have an artistic responsibility to the broader public?

It depends where you work doesn't it? I knew when I was doing *That Driving Ambition* in a borstal in the middle of Bangor that I was doing the right play to the right people at the right time.

How do you feel about the post-show discussion?

I enjoy any interaction; any feedback you get is usually a positive experience but it's also challenging, depending on the kind of work you're doing.

Do you think actors are enabled, in the course of the preparation for the play, to participate in post-show discussions effectively?

If an actor has a problem with a question, they could simply respond, 'I think it would probably be better if the director answered that question because I'm not sure if I can really answer that for you'.

Do you think that's a fundamental flaw in the creative process?

I can't recall that happening in post-show discussions in which I've been involved, although maybe that's because I've been amongst actors who are happy to talk about any subject whatsoever! Often people want to know story issues, actor issues: how did you prepare to achieve that or how did you feel doing that in the story, or what impact do you think this will have on such and such? Those are questions that you should be able to answer.

Do those discussions, in your experience, take place in the rehearsal room?

Sometimes yes, sometimes no, it depends on the work process doesn't it?

In the course of a performance, is it ever your role, to lead the audience, to guide them, or to dictate to them?

No, I think our objective is always to serve the play, always to serve each other, but I think you can respond to the energy of the audience, absolutely. You want to make it the best you possibly can for everybody on stage and everybody watching it.

Do you feel that your status as an actor in the creative process is reflected in the chronology of the employment process?

Yes and no, it really depends on the theatre and the director you're working with; I have worked in situations and with directors when you absolutely feel on the bottom rung of the creative ladder. However, I've been involved in lots of work, in lots of buildings and with lots of directors when I've felt intrinsic to the fabric of that building and to the creative process and therefore I've felt a real love and understanding and sense of belonging to that building.

What happens when you feel that you are on the bottom rung of that ladder?

It makes the process suffer and the product suffer.

Where do you feel actors currently fit in to the creative hierarchy?

It depends. Commercial theatre cannot survive without the star and the star therefore has great influence and control over the artistic process there. If you're working at the Royal Court or the Bush, where you're doing new work, you really do have influence I think; you're the first people to approach this and there are always changes made to the text so actors really do have an influence.

Do you think it depends on what part you're playing?

It would be brilliant if that wasn't the case; if it were the purest form of ensemble theatre. The actor, who drives the play forward and has the weight of the play upon on his or her shoulders, needs support; at the same time, they have a responsibility to understand that the contribution of those around them is no less significant than theirs. When you understand that, you're in a good place to produce something special. My favourite plays are not lead-actor driven.

Does every team not need a captain?

If someone said – it's happened to me once – 'don't you understand I'm the leading actor, therefore I need…', you just want to kick them in the balls because of the self-indulgence. 'Don't you understand it is a privilege what you do, you are a very fortunate person to be doing what you're doing and to be in the position that you are in'. The best practitioners understand that and never forget it.

How do you prepare for auditions?

I focus on certain speeches because I identify what I think I'm going to be asked. I think there are jobs out there that are not naturally your casting, but you can convince the director into casting you purely on the basis that you did the work to get the job. With thorough preparation you can shift a director's perception of both you and the character.

Do you do any further work in advance of rehearsals or do you let it sit?

I will do some research; for example, when I was doing Conor McPherson's *Port Authority*, about the depths of alcoholism, I needed to go into certain aspects of drug addiction and dark, dark places. I also had to get my head round the geographical aspects of Dublin and familiarise myself with that. But you mustn't have made any firm decisions; if you walk into the first day of rehearsal saying you know how to play this part you're in trouble.

*About research, for example, if you're doing a Frank McGuiness play, do you
read other Frank McGuiness plays, or do you go to art galleries to look for a
visual image that might stimulate you're imagination?*

I've never done that but I know actors who have: Ray Fearon, when he
played Othello in Liverpool, went to the zoo and looked at the lions. I
thought that was an interesting way to access your character and that was
his instinctive idea to do that. I went to an art gallery once, for research,
because I was playing a war photographer and I wanted to learn about
image, process and shape.

*Would you listen to music as a way of kick-starting something, if you were stuck
on the meaning of a certain section or scene?*

Sometimes you try and put your own cinematic score on a character. It really
worked for me in *Someone Who'll Watch Over Me.* I had a real breakthrough
with that listening to a piece of film score.

Do you ever learn the lines in advance of rehearsal?

If I was asked I would. I try to have it sorted by the end of the second week.
I prefer to hold back and make discoveries in rehearsal.

What do you understand rehearsals to be for?

To create the most clarity you possibly can in the story you're trying to tell.

Do you learn lines or thought processes?

I learn lines first; if you start going into thought processes while you're
learning lines, you're in danger of starting to direct your own performance,
so I try to learn the lines first and then inevitably you start to play.

What is your preferred rehearsal process?

I enjoy sitting round the table and discussing the work and the writing.
That's pretty essential with new work. It's a fantastic privilege of new work
that the writer is usually there.

Why is sitting round the table useful?

For achieving clarity; you get an idea of the overall picture and your place within it. We are discovering the story but we must be absolutely clear about the text and that includes punctuation and the clarity of the writing.

Would rehearsals for a classic text, like Hamlet, *be different to rehearsals of a new play?*

In terms of the Shakespearian experiences I've had – about four or five plays – there's a tremendous intellectual and technical challenge: I've adored the idea of getting into the understanding of the text and finding my way through the iambic pentameter; I really began to enjoy the storytelling of it.

Do you think that the focus on intellectual comprehension overrides any other form of comprehension of language?

Because of my training, I do have an academic sense of text and I enjoy working in that way. I know there are good actors that haven't had that kind of journey, but I think it can only benefit them eventually, to develop in that way.

What is your responsibility as an actor in rehearsals?

It's important to arrive with some work done, but to bring out the best in the story you need to work through consensus and when conflict arises, which it often does, to work hard through the consensus, to get something creative out of it. It can happen sometimes.

Is the primary responsibility of an actor to be generous?

I think that's absolutely right.

Or is it to defend your character?

Do you know, and at what stage do you know, who your character is to defend? 'I think my character would do this' – well do you actually know what your character would do at this stage?

Does the work on your character go into suspension during technical rehearsal or does it accelerate?

I love techs, I think that we all make a leap when we get into that world. There is a stop/start system to it, that's fine. The pressure is really off you in technical rehearsals because the director isn't really looking at you at that time and that really focuses the work; really good directors can be aware of both technical and performance demands during techs, but I don't expect them to do it. It's a real opportunity for you to really step up and find things; I find lots of great stuff in technicals. There's definitely a benefit that you are not necessarily being watched for performance or acting at that stage.

Are you aware of the auditorium – that those seats are going to be filled with people in three days' time?

Everyone has got to try to play that auditorium; particularly its size – your performance has to shift, from what you've achieved in the rehearsal room, to make its link to the level of the auditorium, or step back to the level of the space, in some cases, if you're in a studio theatre.

What about costume, lights etc., has that ever utterly changed your understanding of your character when you put a costume on, or a pair of shoes?

It can cause some damage. I played Lysander in *The Dream*; the costume designer put me in a pair of silver trousers. It was like being back at school: I suddenly went into 'I'm in a pair of fucking silver trousers' and for me it was destructive. I fought it, but I wound up wearing them; I was persuaded that the image of the silver trousers was what they wanted to see with the character!

What were your objections to the silver trousers?

That the audience will not be listening to what I'm saying: they'll be wondering why this silly fucker's wearing silver trousers. Nowhere in the rehearsal process did I get a semblance of an idea that he would wear silver trousers: there was no consultation. The best costume designers are prepared to listen to your ideas; they could be tiny and small – I don't think you should be trying to radically change things.

What happens for you, in terms of your creative journey, during previews – is there another significant gear change? Do you differentiate between a preview and a performance?

It's a performance but it's not finished, everything's a work in progress but it's not something that should necessarily be judged yet. I try not to go to see previews, or if I do, I try not to go with that kind of attitude, because the performance can radically change, over the preview period, because of the relationship with the audience. Even though you may think you are totally involved in the world of the play and are not aware of the audience being there it is a different experience: you've got to make yourself heard, you've got to make yourself seen – do proper storytelling.

Are you ever so completely in the world of the play that you're not aware of them, or is that wishful thinking?

You can only ever analyse that once a performance is over. I've never had a 'Daniel Day-Lewis moment', when he reportedly saw the ghost of his father. My father died in the middle of a creative process when I was playing a grieving son, burying his father and I remember thinking to myself when I was in the play – and it was also at the National – what if I do see the ghost of my father? Unlike Day-Lewis's reaction to it, I thought the bastard will make me corpse or make me forget a line! So in answer to your question I suppose you can't be completely.

How do you cope with the pageant of press night?

I've come to the conclusion that it's something to be got through. I've never ever – once I think I was happy – been happy. I don't let anyone near a press night.

Is that because you feel the pressure of judgement?

Yeah and everybody does, and people that say that they don't are liars. It's not just the actors: everyone feels it.

Do you think that's a good thing?

No, it's a necessary evil, a marketing tool.

Is there scope for change in that relationship with the advent of the blog?

The blog is exciting. Only recently it had an impact on what I've been doing – at the Bush; we got fairly good reviews, not great but fairly good, but the blogs started and they were all real raves. It really had an effect on audiences; people came to see the show because they'd read blogs – that's tremendous.

Tell me about a good and a bad performance that you can remember.

The whole process of *Peer Gynt* at the National was bad because I was trying too hard, on stage.

Was there an element of will that was stopping you from being present?

Within the realms of one performance both things occur; as an actor you continually think, 'I wish I hadn't done that', but you have the opportunity to retrieve. It's usually about the energy, sometimes you arrive with the wrong energy and you need to find a way of creating the right energy.

How do you do that?

If you're aware that it's the wrong energy then you can go about trying to change it. I play with the idea of being as truthful as I possibly can.

Is 'truth' a strange notion given that what we do is pretend for a living?

It's the one word that has driven me – truth: to the character, the play, to whatever you're trying to achieve; it's about honesty, about not being hypocritical. So if you're in a naturalistic play, to try to be as real as you possibly can and really understand your character, your text, the interaction you have with the other actor, so your reactions can be as truthful as possible. Surprisingly, my corporate role-play work really helps that because you have to be instantly real and truthful. People ask you to be like this person, this person is a, b and c and you have to instantly be, to express some kind of behaviour.

Is immediacy of response an essential ingredient of truthfulness?

Yes, because it is unmediated.

How do you keep performances alive over the course of a run?

I try to effect some change, pretty much nightly, in the performance, in the interaction with the other actors, some differentiation – but always within the boundaries of what we're trying to portray. Olivier, in one of his biographies, talks about comedy: he said if they laugh, change it, which I thought was dramatic but once you get the laugh you think that to recreate it, you should do it exactly as you have done before, but then the truth of it's gone, because you're applying a technical process to get the laugh. You can't help seeking the laugh, but keep it truthful, keep it real; trying to recreate technically the intonation, the timing, rather than the truth of the moment that got you the laugh, is where you're going wrong.

How do you avoid things becoming stale?

It's to understand that there's always a wealth of creative ideas that you can bring. We did *Philadelphia Here I Come* maybe 200 times; with that boys scene, all three of us would agree this is getting a bit tired, let's try something different; we really trusted each other on that and it really kept it fresh for us.

How do you feel about the curtain call?

When I was at college we all felt the curtain call had no bearing on the story and that it created hierarchy, therefore it was redundant and we got rid of it. As an audience member that's very unsatisfying: you want to reward. I remember seeing the McDonaghs *Leenane Trilogy* all in one day. It was a really hot Saturday in August, in the Duke of Yorks and at the end of it all we started applauding, I mean really applauding and they started applauding us: I really felt we deserved that as well, the amount of applause they gave us.

And after the curtain call, what happens to you, are you on an adrenalin high or not? Some actors talk about a feeling of loneliness.

People do get melancholy. I don't; if I ever do, unemployment brings that out much more than ever being at work. I like to have a drink and a chat. I don't like going home straight away; I like to be around the building, to have some interaction with the audience.

How do you cope with unemployment? Do you employ certain strategies to maintain your acting skills or do you sit and wait?

With the corporate training, I'm always working; I'm always acting, so the muscle is always being used, improvisationally. Financially, it keeps me alive during unemployment: I earn more money doing that than from acting. In terms of seeking out work, I've always been fairly poor, specifically now, because I'm trying to develop my television career rather than a theatre career. So I'm getting a showreel together, trying to push casting directors.

How do you cope with rejection?

I don't have as much of a problem with it now; as a young actor, it would really hurt. I know I work really hard for the casting and therefore I'm usually acceptable, I'm never bad. They'll make a casting decision, which is beyond my control.

Is fear, both personally and within our industry as a whole, an enemy to creativity?

If we're frightened on stage we're not really in the moment, in the truth of the character, so we're not telling the story as best we can.

Is there ever an instance when it can open creative doors?

There's a connection between fear and danger; there are moments in the rehearsal room, where there's been danger, could be physical or mental, or truthful, and when something goes wrong, boy can it go wrong, but some really good creative work can come out of that danger. Fear, itself, is negative. I had a period where I went through a crisis of confidence and it was crippling.

Confidence is crucial: why does it go sometimes?

For me, I was given a big responsibility and I was frightened of it. Was I capable of giving this to people and having so many people relying on me? 'I don't know if I can cope with this responsibility. I'm frightened. It would be quite good if I got knocked by that car so I could leave this with dignity; ah Ruairi, you would have been great but you had that accident so we had to replace you.'

How do you then retrieve it, do you employ any specific technique?

I know of an actor who went to see a psychologist. One reason why I was fearful was to do with drinking, so I pretty much don't drink in the rehearsal process now. Other things in your life impact on you like the death of parents. It hasn't ever particularly been about unemployment, because I accept that, that's been my career. There are actors who are hot and wanted: I've never been that kind of actor. I've worked pretty consistently so when unemployment comes, I think, well I worked for this time, has my confidence gone? – not really. I still think when I walk into a rehearsal room that I'm good and I'm going to be fine. The problem is when someone as good as Toby Frow says, 'I could have cast…but I didn't I chose you and I want you' and I realise someone's taken a real risk. It's a burden of responsibility, but that's mostly passed now. Now I crave the responsibility.

What about blockages, such as, 'I don't know who I am, I don't know where I am, I don't know what I'm supposed to be doing': how do you overcome those?

Well, you first broach it with the director, but it could be that the blockage has occurred because there's nothing coming from the director. I think actors being mutually supportive of each other is a really great thing, but you've got to be subtle with it – I teach feedback now, I teach how to give positive, supportive feedback and it's important to deliver the message in a positive way. Some directors should learn this.

What do you understand by presence? How do you quantify it? How do you identify it?

I think a lot of that is to do with stillness isn't it and a lot of it is to do with peoples' physicality, but it transcends the physical dimension: it's about being utterly present in every dimension. For something like *Hamlet* for example, even when you're not talking, for the vast majority of that audience, the story depends on how you are reacting to what other people are saying.

Is that about being in a state of readiness?

Absolutely.

What's the difference between presence and upstaging?

It's about the honesty of the performance: if you're upstaging you're not telling the story, you're not even in the world of the play. If someone's upstaging, I'm pushed back, I'm losing the story.

What's the most crucial relationship for you when you are creating your character?

When it's at its best, between the actor and the director.

So what is it you seek from a director?

Support. The ability to recognise the generosity of what we offer them, to be concise with it, to not push their ego upon you or, if they are pushing a creative concept or idea, that they do it in such a way to make it look and feel like you're creating it, because you are. Actors are terrified by the word conceptual – we think that it will not be creative for us and, often, that is the case.

What's the greatest influence on your career as an actor so far?

I talked earlier about *Fall From Grace* and the community aspect. I remember seeing *Closing Time*, by Owen McCafferty and it dug deep into me, I suppose because it was about alcohol. In terms of changing my career: Gary Mitchell and my Royal Court work. As a theatre artist, it's always been about the writers.

What's the best and the worst thing about being an actor?

The best thing is being able to be so creative; not just with your hands and your head – it's with everything, your lungs, your guts…

And the worst?

Lack of control, the business itself.

What does it mean to you to be an actor?

Well I think now I *am* an actor, I didn't think I was for a long time, but I am now and I always will be. The business might leave me for periods, but I'm never going to leave the business or the art of it. It is a privilege still, I do feel that, it is a privilege to do this. I have been incredibly lucky in my career, particularly in theatre – to have done the new work that I've done, I've worked in pretty much all the buildings I wanted to work in, to have worked with some of the practitioners I've worked with, some of the actors, it's been a real privilege and exciting and exhilarating and it's kept me going; I'm in my early forties and I'm still in the business. I live in London, I have a family here and I own a house; all that has been brought about by my being an actor. The whole diaspora of it all, the difference of it all, the extraordinary wealth of people, and actors – 90% of actors – are extraordinary people; they really are fantastic people and when they're in it for the right reasons, they're the best people.

MOJISOLA ADEBAYO

Mojisola began performing as a street rapper in the 1980s before embarking on formal education and training in theatre. She trained extensively with Augusto Boal and is a specialist facilitator in Theatre of the Oppressed, working particularly in areas of conflict and crisis. Mojisola has worked professionally in theatre, television and radio, on four continents, over the past two decades, acting in over 40 productions, devising and directing over 30 plays and leading countless workshops. Mojisola is also a produced playwright. *48 Minutes for Palestine* is currently touring internationally and is published in *Theatre in Pieces* (Methuen). Her other publications include *The Theatre for Development Handbook* (Pan Arts, written with John Martin and Manisha Mehta) and her first collection, *Mojisola Adebayo: Plays One*, also with Oberon books.

POK   *How long have you been an actor?*

MA   Eighteen years.

What would you do if you weren't an actor?

Whatever I imagine I might be, is somehow always connected to theatre. Theatre is a complete art form; it encompasses visual art, singing, dance or movement, writing or teaching and all those different roles are so multi-layered.

What was your first encounter with theatre?

I remember, as a child of about four, being in absolute rapture, screaming at the stage during what must have been a panto. It was physical: I was on the edge of my seat, my whole body shaking with absolute ecstacy, screaming with all of my body and all of my voice, probably, 'he's behind you'. I was an interactive audience member; I didn't have any notion that I was somehow separate from all that was going on, on stage, I was part of this incredible event. That understanding of what theatre is, or can be, has stayed with me. I don't get it when there isn't a sense of relationship with the audience and I don't get it when it's not embodied in some way; it should have a physical impact, whether it's within a performer, or in the relationship between the audience and actors. Theatre can and should drive someone to the point of wanting to jump from their seat! Be it to jump from one's seat in outrage, or to fall on the floor in laughter, or sink into the seat in despair, it should have a physical impact on the audience.

What do you think causes a breakdown in the connection between audience and performer? Can you think of examples of when or why that relationship is broken?

Probably the majority of what I see, I'm surprised to say. I went to see a production at the Barbican, which was incredibly slick and technological and the images were striking and it was all very expensive and multicultural and the theatre was packed, but it felt like I was in some swish bar in Kensington where the design was immaculate and all the right people were there having the 'right' conversations, thinking the 'right' thoughts and actually no one gave a damn about anybody. I didn't feel any connection with any of it. I fell asleep because it was so involved in its own slickness and presentation. It didn't really care about what it was saying. What is crucial, for me, is the story: what are you talking to me about? If you're so involved with how slickly you've put it together, you've forgotten what you're saying. I knew I was supposed to like this contemporary performance but I just thought, 'Hello! I'm here.'

Was that because you were made aware of the brilliance of the performers or the artistic idea, rather than the idea itself?

The performers were merely placed within the design. There was no sense of who they were, what they wanted, who was speaking, what they were playing or what they were asking; nothing. It was an uber-neutrality, so neutral that I felt, 'I don't care about you, I don't care about anything, I'm not required to care'. It's the human relationship between those human beings on that stage and me, the audience that one can't do without, it's the people! There was no sense they were people, why have actors, why are they not puppets?

Who or what were the most influential people or events in the early stages of your career, which helped form your artistic sensibilities?

I was in a born-again Christian cult and part of its youth group. One of the means of expressing your faith was through being encouraged to perform and I loved it. I've always loved poetry and music so I started to rap and I was a rapper for Jesus! – on the streets, Leicester Square and Piccadilly Circus and various shopping centres and in church as well. We tried to make it all very cool and used to rap to instrumental versions of Neneh Cherry songs, Salt and Pepper, all that 1980s hip-hop. That was my entry into performance and probably why I'm hesitant to use the term 'actor'; I've always thought of myself as a performer because of all that reggae music and rap music. I'm very wary of my tendency towards a kind of theatre evangelism, I'm not preaching Jesus anymore but I am very politically driven so I need to be careful of my attraction towards evangelism.

What are the dangers of that?

The work ceases to be a dialogue, it ceases to have questions at its heart: it has statements instead. When I'm writing or performing/acting, I try to make sure that my mind is always going towards the questions rather than answers, whether I'm acting, reading a play or in the rehearsal room or writing. I did a Drama degree; I remember the very first role I ever had on this drama course was in a Galsworthy play. I had to do this two-hander scene between an 88-year-old gentleman and a young maid. I was taller and had a deeper voice so I was the old guy. I'd never acted before, and on the day we presented it to the class, my debut, I put on one of my Mum's 1980s suits, with big shoulder pads, drew a moustache and slicked my hair back. I'd heard something about Marlon Brando putting cotton wool in his mouth to give himself some jowls so I put cotton wool in my mouth – this was acting, for me. Obviously I was awful but what amazed me in the feedback facilitated by the teacher – and I was the only black person in this class – was that the class was really angry about what I'd done: not because I was female playing male, not because of my atrocious acting, not because I was an 18 year old playing an 88 year old, but that I was a black person playing white. In this class, in 1989, most people were very animated that it wasn't appropriate that a black person should play white in this way. I remember sitting there thinking, fucking hell, is this what's pissed you off, that I'm a black girl playing white? That was a defining moment for me because that was the moment where I was either going to give up this ridiculous drama degree that I'd blagged my way on to, by virtue of being a lazy bastard, or

65

whether I was going to say, 'well this is really powerful, because if this can fuck you up so much, that I'm playing a white person, then this stuff is really, really powerful'. It was either leave it or do it and I thought I'm going to do this. I suppose acting is a kind of provocation.

Theatre as a forum for ideas?

Absolutely. To see the class so animated in ways they hadn't been before – and also the potential for us to play anything and anyone – was really exciting. To have that kind of response, even if it is a negative response, is exciting, because it means that people are thinking and questioning. I spent those three years being shocked at the level of racism and how narrow people's ideas were about casting possibilities, how exclusive it all was, how sexist it all was and how irrelevant most of the plays that we did were – they didn't seem to speak of anything out there on the street, in New Cross, where we were. In my final year we had an option to go off on exchange to a different country for three months and do our own special project. There was an option to go to Italy, Holland, or Dublin and although most of my experience was very negative, the only area that particularly excited me was Irish drama, because I loved Synge. Even though it was written 100 years before and, for me, as a young black South Londoner, it was a very foreign work, all I knew was that there had been riots at the premiere of *The Playboy of the Western World,* so as far as I was concerned this was worth reading and I found it exciting and moving and political. I was fascinated that that work had been so important in terms of Irish independence, so I decided to go to Dublin, to Trinity College. I was going to write a play about oppression and sit by the sea! However I didn't particularly know what this play was going to be, so I went to the library and I thought I'll get a book that'll show me how to do it: I found *Theatre of the Oppressed,* by Augusto Boal. That book completely shifted my understanding of the possibilities of theatre. His argument, which I question now, that theatre was of the people by the people; that the heart of theatre was in carnival; that it's a collective experience, really connected with my very first experience of panto. It asserted that theatre had a potential to speak of peoples' lives and to question and to ignite revolution – all of the stuff that I was interested in with Irish drama. His ideas of Forum Theatre, the possibilities of interactive theatre, opened my mind really. It was a sheer blessed coincidence that Chrissie Poulter, who was a big influence on me, was lecturing at Trinity and had organised for Augusto Boal to come to Dublin to teach for a weekend: I went along and that was it: I was totally sold on it! When I returned to England, after my three months, by pure coincidence, Cardboard Citizens, through London Bubble, had arranged for Boal to come over to teach for two weeks, so I went on that course as well. At Goldsmiths, Boal became my 'specialism': I got a team of actors together and I literally had a Boal book in one hand, directing the actors improvising together, putting on shows, which loads of people came to see. So Boal was the major influence.

After Goldsmiths University you did an MA in Physical Theatre?

That was quite a while after the degree; I'd been acting and leading workshops for some time, getting more into movement-based work and devised work, but I got a bit stuck in my career. I wanted to be nourished; I was a bit exhausted, devising, improvising and teaching, so I decided to do an MA in Physical Theatre, in 2000. I did that part time over two years. It gave me a lot of technique in terms of physical awareness, alignment etc. I did yoga and T'ai chi and Indian martial arts with the brilliant teacher Phillip Zarrilli, and a massive influence on me was a choreographer and teacher called Emilyn Claid. I worked with Emilyn and started to collaborate with dancers. I'm still really interested in that meeting point of actors' work and dancers' work. Strangely, although the MA was in physical theatre, it sparked my move into writing – writing for movement-based work: the first draft of my play *Muhammad Ali and Me* came from that.

What were your expectations of those BA and MA courses and where they met?

On the BA I expected to be trained in how to act and technique and it wasn't a training; I still feel like an untrained actor.

Do you feel disadvantaged in that respect?

I feel a mixture of advantaged and disadvantaged. Disadvantaged in that I still struggle when it comes to text work and the idea of building a character. I still feel I don't necessarily have any techniques or routes into those things that I can call upon. I feel advantaged in that both courses – even the BA, through the Boal work – encouraged rigorous thought and investigation. Both courses encouraged the students to think about the purpose of the work, what the influences on it were, what the historical context is, etc. I've never been to drama school but I don't always get a sense that the students are encouraged to think about the social context and meaning of the work.

So for you, there's always been a consciousness of the function of theatre?

Yes, what we are doing this for, absolutely.

Looking back on it now, is there anything you would change about your training?

If I had my time again I would have trained in dance, in order to have some grounding in a performance technique. If I felt stronger and fitter I might even approach a dance course now because there's something about applying oneself fully to a performance discipline. Even a formal technique, like ballet, would be some kind of reference point from which to work. I feel my references, in terms of acting and performance, are fragmented and random. *Theatre of the Oppressed* has overall structures for how we make theatre, how we present theatre and involve the audience, but it doesn't teach you much about acting and I don't feel I have any kind of reference. So I would have started with dance from a purely physical point of view, but then, having done a dance degree, I might have even had something like a Strasburg training – to give me something to resist, even. I don't have a strong enough discipline in my training that gives me anything to either work from or resist.

What prevents you from seeking that out and doing it now?

Just time, I think. At some point, I'll take some kind of 'Method' course, just to understand it more. I'm often in a rehearsal and I don't really understand what processes people are using. I watch other actors and think, 'what are your references here, how are you approaching this, is it purely instinctive or is it somewhere deep in the back of your mind, giving little sign posts as to how to approach your role? When you get stuck in a role, what do you call upon, what are you doing?' I always feel I'm blagging. Maybe that's inherent in the acting condition: we all feel like we're blagging! Certainly with naturalistic work, I feel the other actors have certain reference points that I have no knowledge of and I feel that I ought to.

Does your writing not inform that? Is there no crossover between those two disciplines?

It probably is informing it. A lot of what I've written has been scripted from devised work, so listening to and being involved in improvisation has informed that: listening to rhythms of how people speak, how relationships are formed, that kind of microcosm of real life. I directed a couple of plays that emerged from improvisation in the Palestinian Territories; people were improvising in Arabic – I don't speak Arabic – and I was directing and editing the improvising. I had one person in one ear, another in the other ear translating while the improvisations were happening. I would write what I heard as quickly as I could, edit it and shape it into scenes, then those scenes would be made into Arabic and then I would start directing. I knew what the words were but I didn't know what every sound meant that they were uttering, so I started to direct, instinctively, by listening to the music of how they were speaking. Things like that have influenced me as an actor; thinking about the music of language, rhythm, etc. – things that I've never read about in a book, but have come through being in a workshop situation or a rehearsal room.

Do you feel you need a formal training?

There's certainly desire there, I don't feel a need: it's a sense of responsibility, in terms of constantly being open to educate myself, especially when it comes to naturalistic text and naturalistic approaches to acting. I know so little about it but it's such a huge part of the European tradition and the industry I work in, that to not know about those things, in practice, is ignorant and I ought to find out about it. I have no interest in ballet, in terms of movement, but I think if you live in Europe and you're interested in movement, dance, then you should know something about ballet and should put your body in that place to try to understand something of it. I've always thought it was important that one should know one's place in a cultural history, the long journey of the Stanivslaski way to its disputed version in Strasburg, such enormous influences on the approaches to acting.

So context is crucial?

When I come to a play, writers may also be coming from certain traditions and influences; they've read the traditions and it feels important to know what some of those roots/routes are.

And it enables you to know the power of gesture, or a certain turn of phrase etc.?

Yes, absolutely. It is also important because we borrow things from each other: you see something and you think, 'Oh I like the way he does that, I'll have a go' and you don't quite know what, how and why that actor's doing it. One can easily be seduced by other actors' techniques.

Is there anything wrong with that?

Only that one can become clichéd and by taking on board somebody else's habits, you can end up presenting, rather than inhabiting your own creation; when you're in role you're doing, 'being an actor', as opposed to telling the story. For example, everybody's voices sounding the same: you go and see a show and you think, 'what are the actors all doing? They're all clones of each other because they've all thought, the way he uses his voice is amazing, I'm going to use my voice like that, so they end up all sounding the same. It's not that what that other actor is doing isn't wonderful and it's not that one shouldn't be seduced by it – an audience might be seduced by it and that's fine – but unless you know where that technique, vocally for example, is coming from then you end up doing an impersonation of someone else and you don't know what the root of it is.

We affect each other, constantly: you take what you like and leave what you don't like generally, in life, so why not do that as an actor as well?

It happens anyway doesn't it? I constantly interrogate the manipulative power of theatre and also its potential for subversion: I always want to know where things come from. Boal talks about catharsis, how it's a technique used to pacify the masses, an acting that drains people of emotions and allows one's audience to get it out of their system and to cry with you and to feel with you and to feel your pain, I haven't gone through that kind of route but I feel I ought to. At the same time, given I've been influenced by Boal or Dario Fo not to go down a pacified route, by not understanding what the route of another approach might be, then perhaps I'm being just as passive. I ought to be open to a constant state of training.

What is the function of theatre? What does art mean for you and why do we need it?

A bird needs to sing, it's part of its make up as a creature, part of its communication, of how it exists. Do we need to sing? No, but our desire to sing is part of what defines our humanity and not necessarily just to sing, but our desire to imagine, to create, to recreate, to enjoy a creation, to enjoy a song, is part of our humanity: it's not the need for it but the desire for it. The want is an absolutely necessary part of one's humanity, so the right word is not, 'necessary', but, 'essential'. It's not that I need to sing, but my desire to is what makes me a human being in the first place and not a bird. It's essential, it's not something extra, it is integral to my humanity. My enjoyment of that song is not whether I need to enjoy it, I just do enjoy a song and I can differentiate between a song and spoken word; it's not just a reflex, it's a voice.

Is that relationship to art different for a member of the public?

I don't think so, no. Human beings do want to express or enjoy another's expression of creativity. The desire for beauty, the inevitability of imagination, the impulse to order and, in the ordering of things, to be creative, to invent, to solve – all of those are creative impulses. Some people define their job by it and get paid to do those things and some people don't, but I think it's just humanity, so we can't help it, we can't help creating art, enjoying art.

If it's a fundamental human characteristic, to create and receive art, where does theatre fit within that understanding of art?

The theatre is unique in its encompassing of all those individual art forms. It has the potential to incorporate design, sound, music and text. It has an overarching holding mechanism for many different art forms, yet it's also incredibly detailed, or minimal, in that you can strip all those things away and have one person speaking to one person, one person on the stage speaking to one person in the audience.

So a transmission of ideas?

Yes, to transmit ideas and to engage in a dialogue, a passionate dialogue.

Does it have a transformative power?

Yes, for both the performer and audience it has the potential to move beyond the normal, to have a different experience of life, to be cathartic.

Can you give an example, either as a performer or as an audience member, of just such an experience happening?

I'm going against my guru, Boal, somewhat: I was in a play, *The Almond and the Seahorse* by Kaite O'Reilly, during which I had a cathartic experience. I played a doctor who deals with patients who have memory loss. I was delivering a monologue directly to the audience – it's a lecture which is both an external lecture and the doctor is also making mental notes about how she's going to approach her lecture. During this monologue it's revealed that her own father had lost his memory and she breaks down. I looked at a man in the front row and he was weeping and then I wept. I hadn't had that moment ever before in this role, partly because the director's approach had been one of emotional containment, but at that moment this man was weeping and then I wept, in character. His response to what I was doing enabled me to find something in that role that I hadn't found before and that was a departure from the direction I'd been given, but I'm sure the director would accept what happened in that moment, any director worth their salt knows you can't plan for everything. It transformed how I approached that speech thereafter. I don't know what he was experiencing, but I suspect it was a recognition of his own experience, or the experience of someone in his family. There was a big group in that night associated with Headway, a charity for people who experience brain injury, so at the very least there was an acknowledgement between us of the subject. For two human beings to acknowledge this pain together – me from the side of fiction, him possibly from the side of fact – was a transformative moment.

Is that what differentiates art from entertainment, in your view?

Possibly; entertainment may change a moment for the period of time in which you experience it, but it probably won't change how you speak to your wife or raise your kids, etc. And it doesn't endeavour to. I think the aim of entertainment is to generate pleasure.

And art is to ask questions as well as generate pleasure, hopefully?

Yes, to ask questions which have an importance or significance. So for instance, with regard to *The Almond and the Seahorse* again, I don't have anyone close to me affected by memory loss, but the play is making me consider whether life is all about what you can remember and if you don't remember anymore, if you don't remember anything, are you human? What are we if we don't remember? Did it happen if I don't remember it? As a result of my engagement with the content of that piece of art, I am considering all of those big questions.

If art is to ask those types of questions and theatre is a discipline within that process, where does an actor fit in? What does an actor do?

What does an actor do? I've got all kinds of words going on in my head and I'm resisting words like 'vehicle', because a vehicle is inanimate until someone gets into it and makes it alive, whereas the actors themselves are alive, so I'm resisting it because it's not like something enters me. I suppose that common cliché of an actor being a vehicle, or a tool, and that he has to be used like a tool: 'a script enters me and then I'm animated', well no, I'm animated anyway! An actor delivers, perhaps, a story, or elements of a story, or character, through which questions are raised and people are provoked to think about things, sometimes pleasurably, sometimes not.

How do you marry the desire for self-expression with the discipline of delivering a classical text or any text in fact? Are they ever in conflict?

Part of the actor's art is to find a presence within a classic text, to open it up, to reveal it, to enable people to hear it, see it anew, so that what is potentially ancient can be, absolutely, in the moment.

Can you give a specific example of how you married your desire for self-expression, what you brought to it, and the discipline of the text, itself?

I'm a Danish, Nigerian, urban woman, born and brought up in the cultural climate of Britain in the 20th century. I played Oberon in *A Midsummer Night's Dream*: how was I, as a female, going to approach this male role, this mystical role, this text that's 400 years old? In the rhythms of the language, what could I bring to that in a fresh way? My way into that role was the word 'herb'. Oberon uses magic, he uses herbs. When I think of the word herb I think of weed – so my Oberon became a Rastafarian, mixing his herbs, making a potion, changing things, altering perceptions, a Rasta mentality.

So that interpretation came from one word and how you personally responded to it?

Yes, herb, or 'erb as I used to say it. I also had dreadlocks at the time, I'm black, I'm a woman: what will you see when you look at me? Let's not deny what you'll see, you'll see this woman with dreadlocks: you see something and I take it further. It's not what is, that way. I always think there's no point in pretending: the body of the actor is part of the performance. If you're a sighted person you'll see a person with dreadlocks. I was not necessarily going for a type, or typecasting; I was naturally going to have some fun with that role and not ignore my appearance and the perceptions associated with it, but I didn't have to.

Are you constantly aware of your ethnicity? How do you feel about the concept of colour-blind casting, is there such a thing?

The company I did that show for were very proud that they were one of the first colour-blind casting companies in Britain. When, many years later we went to tribunal about racial discrimination, their use of the term colour-blind casting formed one of the many bases on which I argued my case. Blindness is an impairment, so why approach this idea of casting as a kind of impairment? It's a falsehood that we are visually impaired when it comes to casting, it doesn't happen. I don't understand the analogy, I don't think it quite works.

Presumably they were well-intentioned. They were hoping the use of that label was going to be a positive one, that it was going to open up casting opportunities for people of all ethnic backgrounds?

Yes.

So given that that is generally the vision behind that term, what are the problems associated with it?

It makes us all a kind of grey and is underpinned by the idea that we can pretend that we're not different, we're not diverse. Colour blindness, or colour blandness, is not about neutralising us, it's actually about conforming to a notion of whiteness, white Englishness or white middle classness.

Why do you say that? Has there been a specific experience, either for you as an audience member, or as an actor, where that has transpired to be what's really happening, rather than, 'we give it to you because you're the best actor who came through the door, we didn't look at your colour in that respect'?

Almost everything I seem to audition for or end up getting is heavily influenced, in some way, by my ethnicity, or I might be upping the 'ethnic numbers' in some form-filling way.

Currently, within theatre, we seem to be continuing to plough the furrow of colour-blind casting, but it doesn't seem to be responding to a real debate that is going on in society at the moment about what ideas of assimilation, integration and diversity mean.

It feels to me that we get caught in knots. For example, one of the many amazing things about the production of Macbeth that we did at the RSC, was that it was a very culturally diverse cast, but that was an example, for me, of something that was ambitious, well-intentioned and noble in its resolve, but in many scenes, distracted from the thing that we were doing: telling the story. For example: two actors, one is Irish one is Nigerian, speak in Irish and Nigerian accents, but they're brothers – it brings up more questions than you need. In its ambition to cast as many black people and as many white people together, it embraces that people have cultural traditions, cultural heritage and we're going to articulate that cultural heritage and accent; so much so that you confuse the actual play.

75

So the problem is that things are not rigorously pursued to their logical end?

Absolutely. If we decide to do plays, texts that are already written, let's work from that outward. Sometimes we almost overcompensate cultural diversity out of embarrassment and we layer things on to tick other boxes: we need to be looking at the play, like the play. For example: there's a play set in Wales, there are two couples, in relationships, two married couples and a doctor and in each of those relationships one of them is a patient and one person is the partner/carer of that person. I play the doctor and I was told by the producer (and not the writer I hasten to add) that this character is an outsider and that's why I wasn't going to be Welsh and that's why they were only auditioning black and Asian actors. The other characters are white Welsh, but for me, if I look at the play itself, by definition my character is an outsider because she's the doctor! I was happy I was cast but one doesn't need a black person in order to say this person is an outsider. Get a black actor if you want one, but the doctor is the outsider, by virtue of her professional position and her relationship to the other characters, it's in the play, let's do the play and everything else will fall into place. If you want to use the casting of the doctor as an opportunity to fill in a report at the end of your financial year to the Arts Council saying how many people in your building this year were black, Asian, disabled, if I'm actually there so you can write a one when there would have been a zero, let's have a real conversation about that and don't portray me as the outsider, when I know why I'm there. But it's a constant tension because at the end of the day I'm glad I got the audition and the job.

Do you think that your ethnicity has heightened your political awareness of those types of structures?

Yes, especially when I found myself missing out, or when I've experienced prejudice. It's just one of those things that you can't get away from, any more than you can get away from one's gender or anything else, but it's very hard to be on the winning side.

How do you prepare for auditions?

I try to work with some material that is going to give me something to explore: perhaps a piece of text from a play I've always wanted to do, or something that's going to give me a particular challenge, or a particular angle, something I can work on with a bit of craft, usually in movement or voice. I always approach them as if this is a two or three minute performance, as if the people auditioning me are punters. I try to make it feel like an event in itself so that I feel like I'm still an artist, still a performer in that moment, even though I'm going for a job – that two minutes is a tiny event. It usually falls flat on its face because you try to do it at performance level and that's when the lines go for me. At one particular audition, the lines just went, I couldn't hold it, I couldn't contain it all; in a rehearsal room you can call 'line' but I couldn't do that, but I think I got the job because of the spirit really.

Do you do any preparation prior to rehearsals?

I don't do a great deal, apart from studying the text, if there is a text. I like to have a pretty good handle on the lines beforehand, although not necessarily in that 'ready to go' kind of memory, but they are inside simmering. Sometimes I'll learn something completely, but usually they're in there, somewhere.

Some actors are reluctant to do that because they don't want to get stuck in a rut, or a rhythm, or a meaning, which could disbar them from fully participating in rehearsal, in discovering the meaning through rehearsal.

I respect that; it's very easy to get stuck in a rhythm, or to go with your very first reading of something and for that to be the same music for the rest of the performance. I feel easier if I'm familiar with the words because then I can start to play with them. The more familiar I am with the words the more fun I can have with them. I don't feel I get particularly stuck in a way of doing it, I find that frees me up, like learning a piece of music, I don't feel it fixes me.

Do you focus on rhythms and music, rather than the meaning of something when you're learning lines?

It depends on the text, but often it's about the patterns, more than rhythm. So for instance, for the sheer learning of it, it might be that one word ends in a certain letter, the next word starts with same letter, so it's lots

ACTORS' VOICES

of different shapes, whether they be the aural or physical shapes of the letters in the text itself, or the rhythmical shape if it's poetry. I think more about patterns, than about learning the emotional drive, or the desire of the character. Perhaps that helps with not getting too stuck because that's not what I'm interested in learning, that's to be explored.

What do you like to do in rehearsals?

I like to play with other performers, I like to improvise, sometimes with the script, sometimes without it. I like to find as many different alternatives to a scene as possible. I like throwing on a piece of costume, using props, I like the hands on materials and the space, lots of stuff to play with. I love having the opportunity to go out of a rehearsal room and play something somewhere else; so it's really about a sense of playing and experimenting. I don't like rehearsals where it's about mapping out a floor plan, blocking, etc. I find the character-based, or emotional technique route, into things – the walking and talking and standing and intellectualising – difficult because I don't have a particular approach to that and it doesn't stimulate me.

When you're in that situation, how do you deal with that?

A lot of it is about listening to and watching what other people are doing and trying to find an internal play through that. Responding in a moment reveals the nuts and bolts of developing a character. For me, a rehearsal room is about what's in the space, what are the raw materials, the other people as well as the text, so even if it is standing with script in hand and the director's saying move here, move there, then there's always something to play with – the other person usually – even if they don't know that you're doing that. There's a beautiful improvisation exercise that Emilyn Claid uses, where you stand opposite another performer and you respond to something they've given you. So for example, right now you've got your hands across your mouth so it's not necessary that I mirror that gesture, but it might be there's something about that, I don't know why but I feel like blowing kisses when you put your hand on your lips there, so that might start me blowing kisses, which will take me off into another improvisational space: I don't have to stand opposite you, I can go around the room and at any time I can come back to you and by then my blowing kisses may have started you off

78

with something, but I can always come back to you and start something else. This returning is important for it contains a duality of listening: It demands that you listen both to the other person and to your internal impulses and provides the space for you to do both things. I also like to play with the vocal musicality but I have to be careful because there is a danger of overindulgence in that kind of vocal play. It can become contrived; it has to be about telling the story and not just about finding as many ways of saying a line as possible. It's always about the story and the relationship with the listener to the story, even if it's a story that isn't explicit. If it isn't about storytelling you need to shed it.

Do you use external stimuli, like going to galleries or research?

Sometimes I go to a gallery or I might read other plays by the same playwright or around a specific subject. For instance, I needed to find out more about memory loss for *The Almond and The Seahorse*, so I read about that and it was helpful. However, I've never been entirely convinced about external research, which may be down to laziness, but more importantly, it's that a play's been written and there are other performers and there's me, so that's the precise thing we're doing. Research won't necessarily help you play the specific moment of any given scene in any given play – the other people in the room with you will. I do indulge in music to aid character-building. If I have time and it's useful I do a compilation CD or tape of the character's journey, so that music is almost like a soundtrack for that character – not a soundtrack to the play, but to that particular character I'm playing. When I'm a little lost or I can't find the right emotional connection, or I'm bored or I need to reignite the performance, I listen to that piece of music again.

Might that not lead you to doing something non-specific? For example, if you listen to musical lyrics, they have their own narrative, separate from the narrative of the text.

The music might have lyrics but I'm more concerned with the mood and the rhythms and the tone. I often learn lines on tape, so on the other side, there might be something that'll give me a bit of relief from learning those lines and that will also help me remain in the thinking space. I'm very interested in approaching the performance in terms of task – 'what is the task that I'm doing in this scene or at this moment?' Emilyn Claid advocates this type of exercise; I don't know if that's inspired by the dance world and creating work largely out of improvisation, but I find it a useful method of achieving and maintaining specificity.

Do you find it useful to have a sense of function, as an actor and as a character?

Function is hugely important to me because I find it very easy to get lost; you know, why the hell am I doing this absurd job, what is my purpose, what am I doing here, what is my function? In terms of the character, thinking about the function is a good hook to stop you getting lost and indulging an emotional moment.

Do you mean a physical action, which is parallel to the emotional or intellectual objective of the character?

Or something that contradicts it.

What, for you, is a good rehearsal?

A good rehearsal is where there are surprises, birth, creativity; an environment where surprises are allowed to happen, where the unexpected is welcomed and we don't know exactly what's going to happen. If you're surprised by something then you've learned something. It's where there's the opportunity to play and experiment with something, where there's a good level of dialogue between everyone in the room, where people are listening to each other. When the director, actor and writer share a dialogue, there is a shared sense of play, a shared sense of experimentation, there's a collective purpose where everyone in the room feels they are respected, as an artist, as a creative person.

Who is chiefly responsible for creating that environment?

I don't know whether the director should be chiefly responsible for that but invariably that's the responsibility they take upon themselves, or that they're given by the actors.

What is the director/actor dynamic and what do you think it should be?

My experience of directors has varied, from being perceived totally as a tool, as an extension of the set in the worst-case scenario, to being considered an artist in a collective experience in which we all have different roles and responsibilities. The director is the 'super audience', the ultimate audience member. That's not their only role, but the most important role is to be our one and only guaranteed audience. We all progress together through their reactions and responses, what they wanted to see more of, what they wanted less of, what excited them and what bored them. Ultimately they are the filter for us to find out what will help to tell the story in the clearest, most passionate, yet most entertaining way. Thinking about it that way it's a very privileged position for all of us: as actors to have an audience and for the director to enable the crafting of that story, to ensure those elements are working together to tell this story in the best way possible.

Do you think the timeline of the employment process and of production works against that ideal of a fully collaborative experience?

Yes and obviously funding goes hand in hand with that timeline of making a show. The earlier actors are brought into a process, the more it will enable a genuine collaboration to happen. If there's a sense of ownership over the work, the more detail there will be. When I'm making shows I think about them in terms of who is going to perform them. It's not that I will only write for a specific actor, but I need to consider who is going to be creating this show with me. I never understand why actors get a phone call a week before rehearsals start; didn't you think about who you wanted to work with and who excites you? This applies equally to the production side of things because it will be the actors who are going to be hulking round these bits of set, or using these props that you're making. Why does an actor very rarely get to speak to a production manager other than a polite nod? Isn't that the ultimate, pragmatic, working relationship? The practice of calling the actors two weeks before, four weeks of rehearsal, bish, bash, bosh doesn't facilitate actors as artists at all.

Why is it important to you, to have a sense of ownership?

As soon as I hear you say it back to me I'm partly resisting it because the ownership applies to the audience and artist, alike, to everybody who takes part in this storytelling or story hearing. If you don't feel it belongs to you, that it's part of you, that it's come from you, then what value do you put on it? You're part of the making of this work, it's from you and it would be different if it was someone else; otherwise it would be a science and not an art. It's inevitable that there is self-expression, that there is ownership.

So the text only comes to life when the actors give it voice and human form?

Yes, when they breathe into it. It doesn't mean it doesn't have a value as a piece of writing, but it's not theatre, theatre is a living thing.

In your preferred view actors would be able to conduct a dialogue with production managers and designers, to have an input into those aspects of a production: doesn't that encroach on their area of expertise in the same way that you might feel a director doesn't give you space to play?

Everybody's role needs to be respected and everybody's expertise needs to be respected. However, any designer, composer, writer needs to know that these things aren't fixed, that it's an interactive experience. The design isn't complete, the work is just not finished until it sits correctly; a set doesn't mean anything – it's just a piece of architecture or piece of fashion design – until it's embodied. Equally what the actor does means nothing until it's performed, until it's shared. All of those things are interrelated and the hierarchies in most of the theatres that I've known are frightening and reveal why so much theatre is not particularly moving, or interesting, or relevant and why it's so heavily subsidised because people don't come. The hierarchies don't really identify what theatre is.

Can you give me an example of a dysfunctional hierarchy that works against the successful delivery of art?

Ultimately, the only element you can't do without is the actors. During the discrimination court case that I mentioned, I worked with the Commission for Racial Equality, who didn't know anything about the theatre world in particular and I had to describe how this particular theatre worked and how this was reflected in the wider theatre industry. One of my examples was the hierarchy; I got a copy of the company structure and at the top is the board of directors, the artistic director, the executive director, all the middle management – publicity, marketing, education, etc. and another layer, production management and another, stage management, the technicians, all the way down to the actors, and below actors, cleaners, and that's the way most theatre companies run. I gave this information to the Commission for Racial Equality, and I said the only black people we've got working here are the cleaners and the actors and look at the structure, this isn't just a mental structure, it's a pay structure, it's a power structure, everything is reflected in this particular structure. We take that for granted in the business but the Commission for Racial Equality thought this was horrifying because as complete outsiders, their position was hang on a second, you can't do a play without those people, you can do plays without everybody else except those but they're at the bottom and many of them are black. I know that's a very specific example around race but it's reflective of the wider business. How many actors are members of boards of directors? Why not? And why don't we see ourselves in those kind of positions? Why don't we even imagine?

Why do you think that is?

Well I think it's systemic, institutionalised prejudice against actors which may have its roots in the relationship, the connections between actors and the worlds of the sex industry and prostitution and that perception of actors as rogues and scallywags. We trade in role and pretend to be something for somebody else's pleasure. As recently as the 1960s in Brazil, for example, actresses had prostitutes stamped in their passports. I know that's an extreme example and I know that's not exactly the same here, now, but the roots of that perception reach back to the 18th century and beyond, when actors were regarded as people of disrepute. I think that might be partly something to do with it. Within the industry, to apply a feminist analysis, in terms of how we're perceived, actors play a feminised role and we're subjugated in the business. In a capitalist analysis, we're exploited: the ones who produce the material – the artists, technicians and crew, etc. – are the ones who do worst out of it. This, for me, pervades the drama schools, the acting agencies, every area of the theatre business.

In what way?

For example, so many of us have a relationship with our agents where the idea that the agent works for you isn't reflected in the dynamic of the actor/ agent transactions. The begging bowl conversations: 'have you got me anything this week,' 'would you let so and so casting director know that I'm doing a show in so and so,' 'oh my agent hasn't called me,' reduce the actor to the role of a forlorn girlfriend waiting for their boyfriend to call and take them out on a date every now and again. Most of us exist in a state of intimidation, inhibition and passivity. Is it just me?

So why do you still do it?

Ah, because I'm a slag! *(Laughing.)* Yes you can put it in the book.

What's on your passport!? So the urge to act must be enormous?

Yes, yes that impulse to perform, to tell stories really, despite one's better intentions. You wrestle with the why, why, why, but there's nothing like it.

Given the recent McMaster report's focus on excellence and the measure of excellence, what, for you, is excellent acting or the best acting? How would you define it and how do you strive to achieve it?

The first word that comes to mind is discipline, in the way that a musician or a dancer might approach their work. It's harder for actors because we don't work in a group of techniques that are specifically defined, such as ballet or classical music. When I recognise or I employ discipline, I think that's excellent and that's about being specific in the delivery of the story, by refining its delivery, through movement, voice, emotion, etc. Team work is crucial; a sense of ensemble, of responsibility for the story, for each other and for holding the night for the audience.

What's bad acting, for you?

When I'm being bad it's a lack of care for how the story is told, for what people are getting from it, for the other actors or artists; a selfishness. It might be an indulgence in how I can reach as many different notes in a speech as possible, a kind of I'm going to do this for me, because I want it for me. The seeds for good or bad acting are sown in the rehearsal room:

when the rehearsal room has been a playful, creative, passionate, discursive place to be, hopefully, in performance, people will keep that, but when the rehearsal room has been a place where you're only a tool, sometimes you just plonk yourself on stage and go blah, blah, blah.

How do you cope with rejection, which is a fairly substantial part of an actor's life?

It almost always leads me to the question, am I good enough? Have I fooled myself all this time? So the task then is to avoid that because you can't consider it: unless you are willing to give it up, you might as well get on with the business of being better rather than stewing over whether you're good enough. What do I do? I usually become obsessed about what my next thing is and because I make my own work, I throw myself even deeper into that.

Do you think it feels like we're in an environment that is always judgemental? If we get a job it feels like we're being judged by the director or the theatres' full-time staff and then by the critics and audiences; if we don't get a job there's a sense of judgement as well. Is that a culture that is useful to the creation of art, or do we just have to accept that that's the way it is and get on with it?

I think that is the way it is and we do need to get on with it. That level of judgement can help, when striving for excellence. Sometimes it's fear of failure that will keep me working at my voice or reading around a subject. I would rather not have to audition: I'd much rather people approached me who had seen my work and we'd try something out together and we could decide whether we're going to take it any further. That is probably very idealistic but is it, really, idealistic? It's the way I'm working at the moment, making my own work, bringing people together who I'd like to work with or people I've worked with before, or I've seen or I'm interested in and we create something together and we share the glory or failure together. When I get rejected from auditions, I don't want to have this way in because it's hard to know why you get rejected, or what's gone wrong. It rarely helps you create the next thing and it very rarely leads you anywhere, unless you're able to have a dialogue with the people you're auditioning for. That kind of judgement, doesn't enhance the creative work. It seems our purpose is to get jobs, be seen, be liked by this director, have had that phone call, to be invited to something! Somehow it becomes about getting jobs as opposed to what the thing is in the first place that drove you to do it. Is that the point? We all do it, I do it, but was that why I wanted to do this thing, just to reel off who I met, who did this and who got what? We get really lost in it and it doesn't help creativity, it doesn't expand your intelligence, it doesn't expand your knowledge base, it doesn't do anything apart from make us more obsessed with this cult of individualism and personality.

How do you cope with unemployment, I know you're a writer, so you may not feel unemployed much of the time but how do you maintain your skills and your motivation when you're out of work?

I know what it's like not to have an income and I feel its pain and stress like anybody does. When I don't have any income in a particular week from doing what I want to do that knocks my confidence, so it's not that I'm blasé about not earning an income, but I try not to think of myself as unemployed. I'm either in a contract or out of a contract, but if I'm out of a contract then my role as an actor doesn't stop, my role as an artist doesn't stop. Dancers get that – they keep going to class, they're still a dancer whether they're in a contract or not, otherwise they just can't do it; for musicians it's the same. It is harder for actors, but I think it's good to have a dancer's attitude and I try to have that. It doesn't necessarily mean I'm always reading a play; I might be going to a gallery, as you say, or a movie or reading a book, or reading a newspaper or meeting with friends. In this way, I'm keeping my creative impulse going and I'm feeding myself and keeping the machine oiled, the physical machine, the body and the mind as well, or I'm writing something, or I'm speculating for a project. I try really not to have 'unemployed' or 'unemployment' in my vocabulary.

What do you most love about being an actor/performer?

I love to tell a story, with passion. I love being in a space where everyone is engaged in the telling and hearing of that story. Where everybody is striving to find meaning. I love the debate, the possibility that lives may be changed, including mine. I love collective pleasure, I believe it can be revolutionary. I love the fact that each new story and subject in a play, each new role enables me to have a new education. Being an actor has given me the opportunity to study such wide-ranging subjects, which I may have never looked into otherwise – from brain injury to Islam, veterinary science to learning magic tricks. I love to be able to see the world, be in the world, from another person's, the character's, point of view. From the work practice side of things, I really love the rituals in theatre and even in television. I love the conventions, the rules, the discipline, the language, the 'business', the tech, the half, the warm up, clearance, beginners, the stage managers, the notes, speed, rolling up to record, turn over, the 3,2,1 – I love it! It's sexy and somehow comforting at the same time. I love playing about with other performers in a rehearsal room. I love making people laugh. I love being an entertainer!

What do you most hate about being an actor/performer?

The dominant theatre and television industry and training systems. The exclusivity, racism, sexism, classism, anti-'actor as artist' fascism and how horribly uncreative and disempowering it can be. I hate the lack of access for people of all kinds of bodies and backgrounds to be makers and punters. I find it boring which is the definition of death in our industry. But I think it is changing, slowly.

How do you define success for yourself as an actor?

When I am chatting with audience members in the bar maybe after a show, I feel happy if they heard the words, if they understood me, if they felt I worked well with the other performers, if they believed our relationships, if they believed me, if they enjoyed the physicality, if my performance got them thinking, if they recognised that person on stage but in an un-stereotypical way, if they felt an impulse to talk back to my character, if the performance moved them, not necessarily emotionally, but that it moved them in their life somehow. Success is doing it.

What does it mean to you to be an actor?

To be an actor is to be an artist and an activist; to act and react; to be human.

TIM CROUCH

Tim read Drama at Bristol University and has a postgraduate acting diploma from Central School in London. He was an actor for many years before starting to write – and still performs in much of his work. His plays include *My Arm, ENGLAND – A Play for Galleries*, the OBIE-winning *An Oak Tree* and *The Author*, joint winner of the 2010 John Whiting Award. He has also written for younger audiences, including a series of plays inspired by Shakespeare's lesser characters, collected together in a volume entitled *I, Shakespeare* (Oberon Books, 2011). For the RSC Tim has directed *The Taming of the Shrew* and in 2012 he will direct *King Lear and I, Cinna (The Poet)* – all for young audiences. Oberon Books publishes all of Tim Crouch's work, most recently *Tim Crouch: Plays One* (2011), a collection of his plays for grown-ups. www.timcrouchtheatre.co.uk

POK   *Tim, how long have you been an actor?*

TC   Twenty-three years, a long time.

What would you do now if you weren't an actor or a theatre maker?

Teach probably, I nearly got to that about six years ago; I hit a brick wall in terms of enjoyment of the business and the craft and I thought of teaching. I found that to be a far more creative experience than the acting I was doing at the time. My parents were both teachers and it's kind of in my blood. I know how to control a space and how to control a group of people and those are really important skills in the role of a teacher – acting skills.

What people or events were most influential for you as an actor?

A drama teacher called Dorothy Wilson came to my secondary school; she blew my mind. She had very free and liberal ideas and allowed us to do what we wanted. So from the age of about 14 I've wanted to be an actor. She died the year after my A levels but she has, even now, been a huge influence. Her daughters, who both live in Edinburgh, are friends. Her son, who was my age, died about six years ago and his death was another impetus for me to start creating work.

Was it something specific that she said or did?

She just opened the rulebook: she liberated it. In drama we could express ourselves in a way that we were not able to do in any other lesson and I suppose I was good at it, which is always the thing isn't it? That's why your antenna is trained: you put yourself out and, if people respond, you think I'm doing OK, I'll do some more and you keep doing that all through your career. She thought I was great and encouraged me. My parents are another huge influence; they were both English teachers. My Dad, a Shakespeare scholar, taught me A' level Theatre Studies, because my school wouldn't give me any timetabled lessons. At university, in the performance side of things, I became quite politicised through being taught Marxist literary theory. I also got involved in the physical theatre movement, through Nicolas Yanni, who taught at Middlesex. He'd worked with people who had worked with Grotowski. I was seduced by the spiritual side of those things, so I had two strands at university: one was spiritual, rehearsing all night, moving physically and one was political, which led to the formation of a community company with Julia, my wife. That company was called Public Parts and was run as a cooperative. Big influences at that time were those small-scale companies touring the country – Red Ladder, Women's Theatre Group, Impact, Major Road, Joint Stock, Spare Tyre. They were more influential on me as a creator, a maker of theatre, than as an actor. When my involvement with Public Parts came to an end I went to drama school (I was 29), to Central, where I met David Bridel who had taught with Philippe Gaulier. He introduced me to clowning; I'd had no idea that there was a body of thought and practice around clowning. Bridel was illuminating for me about the discipline of that. I had missed out on the Complicité movement in the 80s because I was busy doing my own work in Bristol. After I left drama school, we did a production together in London and then he moved to the States. I've worked a lot with him in the States, so he continues to be a big influence. He informed my understanding of 'authorial actors'; an actor is not only an interpretative or a translatative being but is also in control of what they say – even if you're speaking other people's words you can recognise a responsibility to the bigger picture.

Do you think there's a tension between that creative environment and the literary, text-based work of mainstream theatre here in Britain?

Yes and yet I've ended up finding myself between those two places. In my work, I write, I sit down, I script, but I also come from that other background and that's quite unusual. A lot of people from the 'BAC background' have a healthy scepticism about the importance or dominance of text. That scepticism is a good thing. But there are very clear divisions in performers. Performers who work collaboratively, collectively, authorially, take responsibility for what they produce and the material they make. The other actors – and I was one of those, I became that passive thing blown about by the winds – participate in a creative hierarchy with the author and director at the top and the actors very much serving someone else's artistic vision. We're all capable of creating theatre, we're all capable of creating text and performance, but there are movements in British theatre that seem to discourage actors from recognising they have an authority in relation to those processes.

Essentially you feel that the writer and director have assumed the roles of the 'ideas people' and actors, in mainstream theatre, are not 'ideas people'?

They're not generative ideas people they are reactive, responsive, or interpretive, but in terms of the primacy of the idea, that's not necessarily the actor's role; I encountered that quite regularly and acutely because of having been to university, having created work with a company and having thought about those things. I found myself in rehearsal rooms where I felt any relationship I might have to the ideas of the play was not encouraged and, sometimes, actively discouraged.

Can you give an example of that?

Working on a new play, in the process of being written, I was subjected to the experience of the actioning world. I never felt that I was anything other than a three-dimensional being who was needed to flesh out the stage space. We'd action pieces of text that would then be thrown away by the writer the next day. The writer and director would then have their meetings and their discussions – discussions that I was desperate to be involved in, that I had lots of thoughts and ideas about – and at no point did I ever feel my input would have been welcome. In the structuring of the play, in the ideas of the play, that was the director and the writer's job, they handed us a set of *fait accompli* that we then actioned. It was our job to physically manifest the ideas that had been tussled over by the director and the writer and the designer as well, actually, in that particular production. That was the creative team and it's interesting how that phraseology is used; the creative team does not include the actor. Who is the creative team on this piece? Well, it's the choreographer, the writer, the director, the musical director and where are we in relation to the creative team?

Do you feel that the status of actors is reflected in the chronology of the employment process?

There are actors for whom writers write plays but that's very rare. By and large, in the employment market place of actors, everything is in place by the time the actor is employed. I can understand it, I'm not saying...

But should that lessen your artistic status within the creative process?

No it shouldn't lessen your status in the process; it probably lessens your access to the ideas, your ability to articulate or to be involved in the ideas at the level at which those other members of the creative team might be. I am tussling with the notion of the authorship of plays, that whole process of handing over the idea to the actor, so that it's no longer my idea, it's a shared idea; I'm interested to know what's lost in that process and what's gained. I'm intrigued because I write and perform my own plays. As a performer, I don't want to be pulled in at the last minute, I want to be involved from the beginning. I'm writing a play at the moment[1] where I think I know the actor who I'm writing for and the subject of the play is that divorce between the author taking full responsibility for what they write. I don't want the author to be hiding backstage or somewhere in the audience, or hiding with a cigarette out on the street – I want to have the author on stage, to demonstrate their responsibility. What happens is a shifting away – who is then responsible for the finished product? There's a hand washing, it's not me, it's not them, something went wrong in the process

---

1 This play became *The Author* and opened at the Royal Court in 2009.

or something didn't quite happen in the communication and so no one is ultimately held responsible for what is then presented on stage. I have no answers for that and I'm not suggesting that every playwright from now on should bring actors in at the very beginning when they engage with an idea, but somehow we need to find a practice that enables an actor to feel that they are not purely interpreting other peoples' ideas, that they are also owning ideas that they might have themselves or that they are entitled to have themselves.

In your experience of mainstream, literary theatre – even given that individual directors apply different processes – what is the relationship between director and actor? What do directors do?

A director should imbue in their actors a shared responsibility for the piece. That travels both ways – the actors then have to step up to the mark; we are our own worst enemies in not doing and not wanting to do that and being disempowered from feeling able to do that. So I think the director should empower the actor so that the actor can then have ownership over the project.

How can they do that?

It's about thinking of the project as a whole, thinking of the play as a whole, thinking about what is happening in the world of the play, what's happening in its relationship with its audience, the bigger scale of things, rather than what is often narrowly focused on, which is the actor's relationship with their character and the character's relationship with the other characters. I asked an actor in a production I saw recently at the National, why certain decisions had been made and he could not answer. He said 'I don't know, we were told to do this, we were told to do that, I don't really understand what's happening at that moment in the play'. When the actor is not able to own what it is they're doing in the bigger context of the play, that is a bad director/actor relationship; it becomes about disempowerment in that respect. It's empowering in terms of the purity of the actor's craft, but I'm not particularly interested in that; it's an antiquated notion to isolate the actor and their craft from the bigger cultural idea of what this play is saying about the world we live in, about how we talk to each other, how we relate to each other. Often actors are not encouraged by their directors to really take responsibility for these ideas. Then we just become mouthpieces for other people's ideas rather than finding ourselves in relation to those ideas. I wrote an article, 'Darling You Were Marvellous', about being in a post-show discussion and being unable to talk about what the play that I was in was about because we spent the whole of the rehearsal process finding transitive verbs and what our characters were doing to each other.

That process of actioning – finding a transitive verb for each and every thought – as I understand it, is to make each thought live, connected, separate but connected and therefore present; it's a device to help the detailed telling of the story. But in order for that actioning to work the question must arise – what is the story? If you ask that surely you have to ask…

What is the play?

Yes, why the story, why the story now and is the idea of the play not contained within the story? Therefore, if you serve the story as an actor by telling each point in as detailed a way as you can then you are in fact transmitting the idea and therefore you should be aware of the idea. So was your experience not just a case of poor practice on the director's part?

On that director's part it certainly was because I didn't get the sense that we were engaged in a microcosmic rendering of the macrocosmic idea of the play. We were just exploring relationships. I absolutely agree with what you say about the liveness of the transaction between two people on stage. The biggest theme for me is about the connections between what's happening on stage and what's happening with the audience. I'm not denying the efficacy and the potency of a process like actioning, I'm just questioning when it becomes a slavish process, applied willy nilly at any possible given circumstance, as the only way to rehearse the play, when it could be that the play doesn't require that. There's something in the truth of the story or the truth of the telling that doesn't require that detailed absorption in the small world. I'm using all this in a refraction through my own writing and the performance work that I do now because the process of actioning is just a hundred miles away from where I need to be now as a performer. What I have found is that by removing this slavish focus on the world of the stage, by opening it out and recognising that there is a third character in the space – the audience – who are operating as frantically as I am, as an actor, to make sense, to make connection, to keep the live contact, to interpret, to understand, to create story, to create their own story, my work now is about giving an audience authority to go where they like in relationship with that story, not to control it. My biggest frustration in the actioning process was that everything became incredibly controlled; what was often neglected was the arbitrary, the random, which is about – and I use this phrase by Marcel Duchamp – the unexpressed but intended and the unintentionally expressed. These are really important things to me about recognition, that we cannot control this very febrile process between the stage and the audience. There are things that we'll do that will provoke and spark something in the audience, over which we have no control whatsoever; I think trying to bring that into the process of a performance is really important. I felt with those actioning experiences there was a misguided belief that every moment of the play has an almost scientific exactitude in relation to the theme and the idea of the play, and the telling of the story, so there was an almost hermetically sealed, correct way this play is done. The director was famous within the company of actors because we would beat our heads about trying to find the right transitive verb and he would say 'I think the word you're looking for is this'. It was like 'oh, OK that's where we are'; I wasn't really free to find my own relationship to the live interaction, there was an agenda being set, an agenda not set by the actors, but by the director.

So the director wasn't enabling you he was essentially positioning you?

Yes, positioning, that's good.

So bad directing is positioning, which is different to staging?

Yes.

And good directing is enabling?

It's also recognising it is an art form and in every art form there is a randomness, an arbitrariness, to how you perceive what you are at that moment on stage and to how that is received by the audience. In *An Oak Tree*, I am also the director of that play, on stage, in the action of performance, so my job is to take an actor who doesn't know the play and to facilitate a sense of openness in them, that's my job. When I place them in the circumstances of the play they are open to each given moment when it comes and they are encouraged, through my process of direction, to be free to respond however they want in relation to the given circumstances in which they find themselves. They do so in the knowledge that how they respond will not be wrong. It's really important for me. I spend an hour with each actor before the show, maybe 50 minutes and the most important thing I say to them is there is no right way and there is no wrong way to do this play, there is just the way that you and I will do the play this evening and it will be different to how it's been done before and how it will be done again. So my vocabulary as a director in that play is all about opening and freeing, being positive and giving the actor a sense of their own authority in relation to the story because they are at the same place of discovery that the audience are, in relation to the story. They become the audience representative really for the play. The audience know that a thousand different choices are being made in this play, they see the choices being made by the actor because they know the actor doesn't know the play. They might sometimes be dissatisfied with the choices being made by that actor but, for me, that's almost a more successful performance, because it's about imbuing within an audience an understanding that what they're seeing is only one configuration of decisions, of choices. If you came to see the play another time you would see a completely different performance. It's important for me to contest that notion of perfection, there is that 'right' transitive verb for this moment, and there is the 'right' way of doing this play.

Is it not that there is a right or wrong way but that you search for the most effective way of telling the story, which, inevitably, by analysing it, you come to a consensus about? So the search for those transitive verbs is not about the right and wrong but the most useful or effective way of telling the story and therefore you must know what the story is.

OK, yes, but you also have to be aware that when you find that verb that works best for you and the other actor, or your company of actors, that the work you've put in might be completely misinterpreted by your audience. I'm not saying that's a bad thing but there is a process in the transaction of theatre, which is not between actor and actor but between actor and audience that is outside our control. We shouldn't be afraid of that, or spend rehearsal processes trying to minimise that, but see that as something that can be celebrated, or encouraged, because that allows an audience into the process, it allows their reaction to what they're seeing on stage to be validated. I feel, as an audience member, my presence needs to be acknowledged. The crux of it is that we, the actors, were never in those rehearsals brought into the discussion about how what we were doing was being received. To return to that question what does a director do: I think the director needs to be the representative of the audience, more than the writer, I think the writer is very well placed to work the idea of the play, to find the metaphors, the story, that will express the idea of the play and I think the director's job is to be the mediator between the performers and the audience so that what's presented is a true and honest act of communication with the audience. If that requires you to be detailed and minute in the transitive verbs that you find, that's great; if it requires you to be broad and chaotic then that's great, but I think there's often a reluctance amongst directors to recognise the breadth of their palate, what colours are available to them, in terms of how they enter into the dramatic or stage moment. Not allowing the actors into that dialogue about the breadth of the palate, keeps the actor contained within the psychology of the moment of the play and disempowers the actor from being able to talk about the bigger thing that is happening in the theatre, at that moment. I feel sometimes, as an audience member, that I have been very badly imagined, that there has been an act of imagination on the part of the production to make a play for an audience that aren't actually there because no one has genuinely acknowledged who we are and I find that deeply frustrating.

Can you give an example of that?

I worked with a writer/director who said 'I think we've really shocked them', after the performance, but I had no handle on what he thought the audience were, the audience he felt he had shocked. I felt he had an entirely fabricated notion of the audience that he'd written a play for, rather than acknowledging the complexity, the profundity of a group of people sitting in a space wanting to be together. So often theatre operates through division, divisiveness, so that there isn't that opportunity to be together. Often the force coming off the stage can repel an audience; I don't necessarily mean a physical energy, I mean a force of focus, of concentration, of technique that actually repels an audience and forces them back into a position of passivity in their relationship with the play. Some people find that great; I don't and, in the work that I'm doing now, I'm trying to explore ways of bringing the audience to an understanding of their own responsibility to what they're seeing.

What is the role of the audience, what are their rights and responsibilities and what should that actor/audience relationship be?

There is a shared responsibility – we as an audience are responsible for what we see in the theatre. We make theatre in relation to the audience, so the audience makes the theatre that it sees ultimately. An audience needs to be aware of its responsibility in terms of what it sees – the act of seeing is an active act, seeing is doing. On simple, sloganizing levels, the audience need to be able to leave if they're not happy and to challenge if they're really not happy. They need to understand that they are co-authoring what they are seeing. Furthermore they are very important in that they make the art of theatre unique amongst art forms. The mortality of theatre is its strength, it dies the moment it's finished, so it has to be shared in its generation; it's not like watching a film or television, which will continue to exist. So if that's its unique point – the USP of theatre – that is where we should be exploring. It's a frustration for me that a lot of theatre attempts to replicate those forms of film and television in terms of presenting a notion of realism, trying to be accurate in the rendition of another reality; audiences don't need that. Theatre audiences are much quicker and cleverer than we give them credit for. To return to my play *An Oak Tree*: it was inspired by a work of art which is a glass of water, made in 1973; it's just a glass of water and it's called *An Oak Tree*. The artist explains in a piece of text by that glass of water how he's transformed the properties of a glass of water into an oak tree without changing its physical appearance. Similarly, you could be Hamlet but you will still look like you – your Hamlet will always look like you, my Hamlet will always look like me – there is no definitive vision of a Hamlet, so in that respect, why do we make attempts to physically transform ourselves

97

or transform the space we have into another space, when an audience are all the time aware that we are both here and somewhere else, that you are you as well as Hamlet. An audience can accept those two ideas contained in one thing, and I think there is a paucity in the way that we look at theatre in this respect.

What about the suspension of disbelief?

We need virtually nothing at all to invest into the notion of the suspension of disbelief, we need the breath of a suggestion to be catapulted away from here and into somewhere else.

Do you not think the sooner you can get an audience to forget that Tim Crouch is playing Hamlet tonight and just to encourage them to think that's Hamlet each time you come on, the better?

It takes more time for the audience to suspend their disbelief, if you have put in place in your production all the visual signifiers of an alternative reality. With the costume, the wig, the backdrop, the set, the scenery, the lights, the darkness, you're setting yourself up for a lot of work there. If, however, I came in and said, in effect, 'I'm the Prince of Denmark' and I said it honestly, clearly and truthfully, I think the audience would suspend their disbelief almost instantaneously.

Are you saying that costume, make-up, wigs, setting, etc. are to do with fakery, lack of truth, lack of honesty?

That's not what I'm saying. It's not about fakery.

It's just that you said, if I came on and said honestly and with truth, 'I am the Prince of Denmark'; but does that not get to the kernel of all good acting, that at its core it has to be honest and truthful?

OK so what is truth? My last play, called *ENGLAND*, takes place in an art gallery – is only ever performed in actual art galleries, in exhibitions of art in those galleries. We don't materially transform those gallery spaces into anywhere else but different locations are manifested through the simplest of means. We say, 'we're here, in this gallery', and then we say 'this is Southwark Cathedral', and we're in Southwark cathedral, or 'this is Guy's hospital' and we're in Guy's Hospital, etc. There is no attempt to alter the physical reality because art doesn't operate on that physical plane, it operates on a conceptual plane. It's not that putting on a wig and make-up and a costume is a fake, I'm just saying it's not necessary. I would say it's a tautology: it's showing as well as saying, it's doing two things when the audience only needs one of them to be sprung into suspending their disbelief. Equally, there are always two audiences: there's always the audience who are in row G seat 15 and there is also the audience who are in Elsinore. The human brain can encompass both of those locations in one moment without having to have the otherness of Elsinore physically represented for us in a quasi-realistic way.

Do those things make you ask questions which are not to do with the storytelling, the idea?

In another play of mine, *My Arm*, an autobiographical persona piece about me living with one arm above my head for 30 years, I never raise my arm above my head, I don't need to be tautological with it. If I did show them the image of me with my arm above my head there would only be that image. As we co-author it then each member of the audience has their own image of me with my arm above my head. If you show them the thing it reduces the experience because it limits it to what is there physically in front of them. Inevitably, because I haven't got my arm above my head, there is no empirical evidence in this play and yet I think it is an acutely theatrical experience seeing it. I don't have to show it, I can tell you about it and you will make up your own mind about what the tragedy is. If I were to tell you that and also to show it to you, I would reduce your experience as an audience. With the traditional processes of theatre creation we are peddling an idea around an intricately rendered alternative reality and that can be fantastic, but ultimately, for an audience, it's not the most important thing.

What is important is that the audience believe that the actor is Hamlet for example, not one or the other, but that the actor believes he's Hamlet.

OK, is that important? They need to believe I suppose that the character of Hamlet exists in the relationship between…

…In that human form.

Yes.

Therefore anything that gets between that relationship is unuseful?

I think so, but theatre is a conceptual art form, in that respect; it's not about needing to have the visual props to support that contract because that contract can be established and supported in a split second.

Which is very Shakespearian, ironically.

Yes, Shakespeare didn't ever feel the need to rebuild the Globe Theatre every time he wanted to do a new play.

But, whether he wears a wig or a cape or not, the actor's primary responsibility is to release the audience's imagination, through the release of his own imagination.

Yes, I would say so. So for example, that whole issue of emotion in theatre has become a fetishised thing about true emotion; watching an actor cry on stage etc. It contributes to a distorted frame of ideology of what makes an actor a good actor because it completely destroys what the fundamental relationship of a theatre is: it's not about generating true feeling on stage within the actor, it's about generating true feeling in the audience. If the actor can do that while reciting that evening's lottery numbers, that's OK and if what's needed is the wig and cape etc, that's OK too, but what mustn't be ignored is that half the authoring process of that evening's performance will be done by the audience.

Therefore whenever your attention as an audience member is drawn to the actor rather than the character, you're taken out of the story and that's not useful?

Unless you want it to be that way, a dual presence of actor and character. The character of Hamlet through the eight weeks of rehearsal doesn't have an existence of its own, it only exists in Patrick O'Kane, or Tim Crouch.

Or the other people in that room…

That's right.

Then when you move to the theatre, with both the cast and the audience?

Who implicitly make the contract that this is no longer Patrick, it *is* but it's also this other person who embodies another idea and narrative and I will place these ideas and this narrative inside Patrick. Now in production I might want to remove those ideas and that narrative or see the relationship between the narrative of Patrick O'Kane in the play of *Hamlet* and the character of Hamlet in the play of *Hamlet*, that's a possibility.

But that's a different story, creating your own story.

It is.

What I'm trying to get towards is what is good acting, so...

That's impossible.

No it's not so impossible, you're starting to identify that, you're saying those things that are tautological are not useful, whatever the story you choose to tell. So for example, in any given moment – this goes back to the actioning thing – if that moment it is absolutely true and pure and honest it leads to another true and pure and honest moment, so whether there is to be no gap between...

Patrick O'Kane and Hamlet

or a huge gap, look here's Hamlet and here's Tim Crouch playing Hamlet, so long as that is true…

Yes, so with *An Oak Tree* I have written a play that profits many, many times by the two things being visible in one. So narratively it's a story about a man whose daughter has been killed and a stage hypnotist. The man, the father, volunteers for the stage hypnotist's act, the actor volunteers for Tim Crouch's play and there are scenes where the hypnotist discusses the experience the father is having in the stage hypnotist's show that can be read at the same time as Tim Crouch discussing with the actor the experience they're having being in Tim Crouch's play. I've made a positive benefit by having those two ideas contained in one person.

But that is the point.

Yes.

So because that's the point, that duality is crucial...

Yep.

...so therefore anything that would deter from that duality at that point would effectively ruin the play. So in an ordinary narrative play, anything that creates a gap between the actor and character, in the context of the story that they are telling, is not useful.

I would say that that gap exists all the time in the architecture of the theatre, in the scene changes, in the lighting changes, those traditional things. I'm not arguing for a theatre that doesn't ever have a set or beautiful lights, but if you have those things your performance must be concomitant, sympathetic, reactive to the thing that it's happening within. Going back to that notion of tautology, you can have anything you like in theatre but you need to be aware, fundamentally, that to repeat yourself is not satisfying for an audience. To return to the question of the responsibility of an audience, I think the audience need to feel they are completing the circle.

How can an actor enable an audience to do that?

Maybe this is good acting and bad acting. Well we talked a little bit about an actor taking on so much absorption, there is a real place for that but an absorption to the exclusion of everything else, into the world of the play, into the fallacious, pseudo drive to show as well as tell, so to feel, to generate emotion for themselves. I don't want to question those Stanislavskian things because they can be very useful, but, when taken to an extreme, they bring the shutter down between the stage and the audience.

That's masturbation: doing it to yourself for your own satisfaction.

That can be interpreted as great acting though.

How can it be great acting if acting is about telling a story through character? OK in the mainstream, literary theatre it's about telling a story, isn't it? So an audience comes in to form a social communion which has storytelling at its heart. The storytellers are the writers with their words and the actors with their voices, their bodies, their humanity in other words, so the actors give humanity to the words and the director and the designer create an environmental context, hopefully to enable both the writer and the actors to tell that story. But the prerequisite to all that is the understanding that we're all there to tell, hear and see a story, there is an interaction; if it's not going beyond the stage it's not good acting, which doesn't mean you can't emote in a certain moment to impress an audience but if it's only to impress yourself, that's not good is it?

My fear is that's not commonly held as such necessarily, amongst certain kinds of actors, it's not commonly held amongst audiences. There is a danger that that kind of stuff can mesmerise, can hypnotise an audience and render them unconscious, uncritical. They become no longer conscious of what they are and their responsibility for what they are experiencing. That can in certain areas be perceived as incredible, technical, virtuoso performing that blasts the audience down into their seats. It is lauded as good acting where the actor has believed the act of suggestion that has been placed on them and so has stopped being truthful and is performing their own mythology, their own act of suggestion; then the direct connection is broken, is lost, between the audience and the stage.

It's interesting that you think that is more difficult to achieve in mainstream theatre: effectively yours is a consciously interactive process isn't it? An Oak Tree, My Arm, it's like an interactive transmission of ideas rather than a sharing of a storytelling process.

In every one of the plays there is a story and that's the first thing that starts a project: a story that needs to be told. I then take the forms that are required to tell the story better. The device that we used in *An Oak Tree* wasn't the first thing, the first thing was the story and we only hit upon that device as a way of deepening an understanding of the story. The fact that the form and the content play with each other all the time is the most important thing. If it were just an experiment in theatre form I wouldn't do it because it would be deadly, we wouldn't enjoy it. University drama departments might enjoy it and that would be it.

How do you prepare for performances?

In the last five years, I've stopped completely doing warm-ups before shows and I've now become quite militant against it. With *My Arm* and probably with all the other shows I do now, I do a worse job if I've done a warm-up, physical or vocal. In that process of warm-up, I place myself onto a performance level and that performance level is different to the level that the audience are at. My dream preparation for *My Arm*, is just to be with the audience, to be talking about something else, to just be and not to focus internally, not to prepare my body for a set of extraordinary demands because the demands I will meet in each performance will be no different to the demands met by a member of the audience in everyday life. If I do set myself into this hyper place then I get a sense that the audience would recognise that I'm no longer, crassly, with them. Furthermore we think at the speed of light; in terms of preparation, I'm 44 years old, I've had 44 years of preparation to be in the moment on stage and how will standing and breathing, or stretching actually release a greater access to that moment? I often think now that it does the opposite.

Are you talking about an act of will as opposed to a reactive state?

I don't want to be different from anyone else when I walk on stage because I will become different, but how that process of becoming different will happen has got nothing to do with me, it has to do with walking into an aesthetic space, an important, enhancing space. It comes with walking in front of an audience who are architecturally configured in such a way to give me that difference. It's another tautology.

But is that the function of a warm-up?

In my experience it was about heightening oneself, heightening one's senses, one's receptivity, one's physicality, so that when one walks onto that stage, into that relationship, one is in some way coiled, sprung, different.

Or is it simply about enabling as opposed to heightening?

That implies that you are not constantly enabled.

You may have had a hard day crouched over a table with your shoulders hunched up and a warm-up may simply be about lifting your shoulders up and letting them drop down again, freeing up your voice technically. What you seem to be suggesting is we concentrate really hard, we furrow our brows a bit, that we get into some self-made zone in order to deliver the play.

No, it's not as simple as that. What I'm suggesting is that the performance of Hamlet begins with one line, OK, the first line. That's a line that opens the relationship, invites the audience and you don't know where that line is going to take you, to the next line, to the next line, and then a performance of a Hamlet is a thousand moments like that, played in the moment of each moment. There is no preparation for that first line because that line will be a reaction to something that has happened in that moment. What I'm saying is a reaction against the 'memememememe' and I'm being glib in that respect. However, I've been backstage getting ready for a performance and watched an actor go through – this is their process – all the physical moves that they're going to do in the scene that I'm going to be in and I'm thinking, 'well what am I going to do now – you are going to be doing that, so where am I going to be?'

That is just bad acting, nothing to do with the warm-up.

I am now in the honeymoon period of being totally relaxed, not better or worse, but just not recognising that I will have to be something different than what I am when I walk out on stage. So every play of mine begins with the moment I walk on stage and I'm just in connection with an audience – that can last 30 seconds sometimes, or it can last two seconds, but it's about making sure that everyone is in the same space at the same time and then we will start. I'm the one in this performance who's been authorised to do the speaking. I want to remove the sense of the performer as 'expert' in the proceedings and engender a sense of shared responsibility for what the audience is about to see. Not doing warm-ups is an attempt to root work inside the world. I'm not disrespectful of anybody else's process but for me and how it impacts on me ideologically now, I don't do warm-ups, I don't get ready, I don't put myself into any sort of heightened situation. Ideally, I want to be having a structured conversation and for that conversation to end when the play ends. That formal structured conversation is still part of the same dialogue that I'm having now with you or with my family; the same forces are at play, the same levels of suggestion exist in my family as in my world, the school, the office, as they do on stage. I'm not having to do all the work, half the work of making me will be done by someone else, more than half the work of making me will be done by the people who spectate me – in every walk of my life and in a very particular way when

I'm on stage. I understand the aesthetic nature of the stage; I understand how we accrue extra significance when we walk on stage. You put a pair of empty shoes onstage and – this is what *Shopping for Shoes* is all about – they suddenly become huge, but they are just a pair of shoes. The shoes aren't doing any acting but we are putting acting into those shoes and the shoes have done no warm-up, the shoes are just you and me and if I've got a stiff neck, that's OK, because we understand that Hamlet isn't Tim Crouch, Tim Crouch has a stiff neck, it's fine, Hamlet can have a stiff neck. That's a very pure and extreme extension of that argument.

The shoes aren't doing any acting because they're inanimate objects; however they are placed, positioned in a heightened environment, so an audience's eye is drawn to them. How the actors and characters they are playing relate to the shoes is what makes them big, that's what crucial.

Yes, completely and that's about context; it's about where we place them, how we place and frame them.

OK. Preparation/rehearsal time is about creating the context for the performance?

Yes and that can be everything; the sound, the music, and it can be the empty space, no costumes, the black box, the audience lit, it can be all those things. Every time you approach a new piece of work, you must understand its demands, understand how little is required to spring that piece of work into life, so that the audience can feel they are completing and co-authoring it – that is about context, it's about framing, architecture, it's about how the theatre has been set up. The experience of going to the theatre starts for an audience when they park the car, there's all that stuff happening. Some actors get placed in a narrow confine, where they're not encouraged to consider any of these things. I think this is true having acted for quite a long time, never necessarily feeling that I've really been expressed. I have a friend who recently stopped being an actor and he's a genius; I've seen him act for twenty years and not at any point in his acting career did I ever see the genius that is my friend. That always depressed me because I felt there was some repression taking place on that actor and that was never my idea about going into acting; it was about finding myself and expressing myself. We are such translators in the process; there is a language being spoken that is not ours and our job is to translate that language for the people in the audience, but we're not actually speaking our words.

Do you not think it's possible to sublimate yourself and simultaneously find self-expression?

Yes.

Is that not the real challenge and purpose even of acting?

What is the purpose of acting? To sublimate yourself and to find self-expression, God help us, is that the real purpose of acting?

OK, is what you're talking about, the difference between acting and performing?

That's been a dangerous divide between acting and performing and that's created a hierarchy, a class system in acting and performing with acting being the upper class and performing being the working class to a degree. Crassly, there is the classical acting model and then there is the belt and braces small-scale performing model.

No I don't mean that, because all acting, be it in a piece of agitprop or Othello or a Brechtian piece or a contemporary play, has a true line and that's acting as opposed to performing, which is about the persona of the performer. To be crass, in terms of these distinctions between the two, the performer is about his persona, his personality and how he relates to the audience, whereas the actor is sublimating the self.

I don't know if that's sophistry. To suggest that the actor is not working through their personality or is not visible in their performance, as themselves, is another bit of wool we're trying to pull over the audiences' eyes. That distinction between performer and actor might be spurious or problematic because it suggests that only the performer is going 'now it's me'; I think the actor is always going 'it's me but I'm also playing someone else'. It's not about not making the performer themselves visible, it's about an actor containing two things – the idea of themselves and the idea of someone else. Maybe that's the distinction between actor and performer. I find it odd when actors try to convince me that they are somebody else because they're on a hiding to nothing because it's like 'alright mate, you're working really hard there but we know, so just relax'. I suppose that's been the big thing for me, that notion of relaxation in my work. I always had a problem with it when I was doing someone else's. It is important for me that two thirds of my job is being done by the other people in the space and isn't that a release? What's a good actor? It's whatever the context allows it. Marcel Duchamp said, 'good, bad, or indifferent it's all art. It's not we, who are the artists, who will say we are geniuses it is the audience who will make those decisions for us'. To allow that to be a release for us, rather than an anxiety, is liberating.

Where do you think actors currently fit into the creative hierarchy?

In *An Oak Tree*, actors I thought would really fly with it, actors who are great improvisers, have found great difficulties with it. I'm trying to think about the authorial actors verus the classically trained, 'given circumstances' actors. If anything, with *An Oak Tree*, the actors who work best in that play are those classically trained actors who play the given circumstances and will do it and do it and do it. That's really exciting when I work with an actor like that because that's where they are from moment to moment. In fact, the authorial actors are spending a lot of time in the performance of that play conceiving it, structuring it and analysing it. There's something about that acting that isn't necessarily helpful. I've just shot myself in the foot by saying that! I'm now saying actors should be instinctive beings, shouldn't have ideas above their station, should just come in and respond to the moment!

No, you can still be aware of things like purpose, function, structure, architecture of a piece and still be committed to the idea of being in the moment.

In terms of knowing actors who are reliant upon other agencies – an 'agent' is used advisedly – to realise themselves, the actors who, I know through my experience, are the most satisfied in their work are actors who have relationships with particular directors or practitioners, and have been allowed to get a handle on what this whole thing is about. The actors who I have found to be most frustrated by that have not had that opportunity and are like pin balls who have bounced around from one thing to the next. They have no control, no authorship over their career because they don't know when the next thing is coming. I don't know what percentage of actors is like that and what percentage of actors is lucky enough to have a choice or to play the lead as opposed to play the person who isn't. It's like a hall of mirrors, you think you've got a handle on it and then you realise there's a whole new chamber of insecurities to travel down that won't ever take you to anything substantial or solid – that was the frustration for me as an actor. I talked earlier about wanting to move into teaching – that was because at the age of 38 I was chronically depressed about where I was with my life as an actor.

Because you had no control?

Yes, I had three kids, I was earning small amounts of money and I hadn't expressed myself – no, I didn't ever feel I had been recognised, that's what it is. That seems true for me, that notion of recognition, it's what we want in life; you can get it from your partner, or your kids, you just need to be recognised. It can happen just once in your life maybe, it's great if it happens more than once and some people go through life knowing that no one has ever really recognised who they are. I felt with my acting career that I was heading that way. I was doing a terrible TV job, having shockingly bad experiences and thinking I'm a clever guy and no one knows, no one's ever going to let me have my chance. Listening to Liz Smith on *Desert Island Discs*, that amazing old actress, she said, 'all I wanted was to get the chance and even if I failed that would be fine'. I could really understand that. Depression was quite acute at that time and so I decided to try to complete a project of my own before I was 40. That was the mission that led to the creation of *My Arm*, which felt like an outpouring. I had a story, I needed to tell it and all the ideas I'd been worrying about for the last 20 years fell into that story, not consciously, never in an articulate way. A lot of actors I've worked with haven't had the chance to do that. I feel incredibly privileged and lucky that, in last five years, things have fallen into place for me.

You have opted out of the mainstream experience and created your own work, you've had the combination of talent and good fortune to make that successful, but what changes do you feel could be made to the current way of making mainstream theatre, which would improve the theatre making process?

Well it's beginning to happen, there are little eruptions happening around form as much as around content. I think there's a huge issue around actor training: actors are still being trained for a classical model that doesn't really exist anymore and are not being encouraged to be authorial beings, to recognise your own responsibility to your destiny, your own responsibility to your art. One of your questions is do you see actors as artists – that's been the death of it in a way, actors not recognising themselves as artists and not recognising what they do as art practice. Because of supply and demand, because of market forces, because in the past actors have historically had to have other outside agencies to realise themselves and to make them an actor – I can say I'm an actor but if I'm not acting what am I? So if actors would understand that the processes they go through are art processes that are about recognising, representing and finding shape and form to the world – these are all art processes – and that they are doing them all the time. If they could understand their authority in relation to those processes rather than relying on other people to give them their sense of authority, then perhaps actors might begin to have a louder voice in the programming of theatre because that never happens; actors very rarely get asked to contribute suggestions to programming and so the programming of theatres stays within the creative team clique.

The next phase of that is for the public to be doing the programming.

That's interesting. Give the actors a chance first, anything that can give an actor a greater understanding of their authorial voice, which enables them to realize they are creative artists as well as interpretive artists; anything that can chip away at that Oxbridge elite who can make actors feel very stupid, make them feel that they really shouldn't have an idea or an opinion, because that's not their job, can only be a good thing. Years ago I was called a typical university actor by a director; he shouted at me in anger because I was questioning something. That was a very loud, clarion call to shut up, 'shut the fuck up you university fucking actor'. That's endemic in certain parts of the business; I'm not saying that every actor should be on the programming board of theatres, but as a slow, teasing open of this world, to start to bring that in would be a very good thing.

What is your rehearsal process?

My Arm never rehearsed; it's a storytelling piece – we went back to storytelling. I would never ask a storyteller to rehearse the story he or she's going to tell and I felt the same about *My Arm*: I will walk out and I will tell a story to the audience. I have some structural concepts that will be in place around that story but, fundamentally, how I speak, how I connect…

So the story isn't scripted?

Every word is scripted.

So you learnt the script.

I learnt the script, every word is scripted but my job is to tell that scripted story to the audience.

But you didn't practice the telling of it?

Not in front of a director, no and that felt like setting a benchmark. We did rehearse *An Oak Tree*, but mostly in terms of how to bring another actor into it. With *ENGLAND*, rehearsals were about 'stripping away'. For example, in the second act of *ENGLAND*, the audience are moved from one room in the gallery to another. They find out as they enter that room that they're entering as the wife of a man whose heart has been transplanted into the protagonist's body, that they are veiled, and that they are in a Western hotel in the Islamic East. It is never said explicitly, but they are the character. There are two actors, one of them is the protagonist and one of them now is the interpreter who 'interprets' everything the audience says to the protagonist and then everything the protagonist says to the audience. So there are whole issues around editorship, around what's interpreted and what's not, what's translated and what's not. When I started to write that scene I had the translator speaking Punjabi, when he was talking to the audience. I got a friend who speaks Punjabi to start working on the translation for that and then I realised that that was not necessary: the audience would get it immediately – when I spoke to the audience I was speaking their language and when I spoke to the protagonist I was speaking the protagonist's language. There was no need to do the reality thing because the idea, the truth of the idea was so much stronger – that simple.

So it was about stripping away all those traditional quasi-naturalistic props that we think we need to make a believable act of theatre. There's a belief, there's a truth that exists in the second act of ENGLAND that is so loud, so strong and so true, yet nowhere in that act is it physically present and, for me, that's the real excitement about where you can be in the processes of theatre. It's a conceptual art form and we will make it together and that's how that rehearsal process took place.

What is a good performance and what is a bad performance?

With *An Oak Tree* sometimes I have what could be termed a very 'bad' performance. I would argue vociferously and have done with angry audience members, that when the play is not successful it *is* successful because the idea of the play is proven every time. They are not successful, from the audience's point of view, when the actor isn't sympathetic to the cadence, to the emotion, to the tone, doesn't do the 'acting', might be a bit blank, might not emote but that's absolutely fine for me. It's taken a long time to get to that point, where anything that the actor does in that play is the right thing. That's what the play is about, it is not about, 'I need you to make an accurate impression of somebody else'. I need you to make an accurate physical impression of *yourself* in this set of given circumstances and if you, as yourself, fluff, fail, are too quiet, too loud, misunderstand the line, misread the line, don't play the certain given circumstance, that's still the idea coming through loud and strong. I think there has to be an honesty, that's really crucial. Honesty is not a concept you can accurately describe. I don't know what it means, but you sense it the moment that it exists in the room and what frightens me sometimes is that audiences are not being trained to understand that.

But surely if you can't be heard then effectively you're acting badly because you're not transmitting the idea, are you? Or if you can't be seen it makes it harder for the audience to hear you. Surely what might be thought of as old-fashioned stage craft is important: the fact that you fluff your lines makes it harder for the audience to receive the idea or the story, so therefore that is not good.

If they fluff their lines a whole new story starts. The most exciting moments for me are when an actor's dried, something's gone wrong, or a prop has fallen down. They're the most exciting moments in the theatre because suddenly, right up in my face, is an understanding of the reality of what I am in, which is some people pretending to be other people, in a place pretending to be somewhere else. I had a Mexican performer in Edinburgh who was extraordinary because she couldn't read English and I'd been assured that she could. At one point I just had to say to the audience, 'Gabriella is Mexican' and we spent a little while, because she'd said the opposite to the meaning of the line, we sorted that out, she said the line and we went back and actually I think we connected into the reality of the story at a deeper level than if we'd kept the whole thing going nice and neatly. It's not an easy science to say what's a good performance and what's not. It's about a moment and what's required of that moment. The danger is when a good performance gets set in stone; it isn't alert to the moment of communion that's happening between the 150 people and the stage but becomes a kind of museum piece and an actor is pulling out the same thing every night – that's bad acting.

We've talked a lot, about truth, honesty and present tense transactions. How do you marry the quest for truth with telling lies for a living by pretending to be somebody else?

I don't think we do that in theatre. We are telling the stories and that context endorses that truth of the lies that we tell so they become something more than what they are. I've never felt that I've lied, I have lied on stage a lot but that's when I've been a shit actor, when I've attempted to trick an audience into thinking something that isn't true for me. It happens in *An Oak Tree*: I will see an actor who, if they don't understand what's going on, rather than being truthful about not understanding, has attempted to give the impression that they do understand and that's a lie.

So what's all that about, why is there that need?

It's about insecurity, all those human frailties about not wanting to be seen as a failure. We have created that in the theatre that we make, to keep the illusion, sustain the disbelief, blah, blah, so if we do fuck up, immediately it's a disaster. With *An Oak Tree* I am almost happiest when it fucks up because the audience know that this is real. Theatre is often organised to prevent that suggestion being given and I think that's a lie – that you stay in character until you have the curtain call and then you have the curtain call and somehow there's some magical release and the actors can become themselves again.

How do you feel about the curtain call? Some actors, for example, don't like the notion of doing a curtain call.

No I feel that's absolutely fine, that's a point of contractual obligation in a way, although I think it's possible not to do a curtain call. I saw a beautiful *Thérèse Raquin* Julia Bardsley directed at the Young Vic years ago; I went with a group of drama school students from Central, some of whom were furious because it ended with a tableau and we all had to trail out past the tableau and nobody clapped; we weren't allowed to clap. I also saw a play in NYC, a Brazilian solo piece where he's wired to electrical live points and if the audience made a noise, it gave a shock, it sent a shock to him – that's the best curtain call in the world because nobody could do anything. But I do take a curtain call because there's a sense that there's transference from one place to another at the end. I enjoy a post-show discussion very much. I don't need to be left alone; I still want to be in the room. It's really important for me to make the act of theatre an everyday act, that anyone can have access to, anyone can do.

What about the notion that the act of theatre should be something special?

Why is that exclusive, why cannot everyday things be utterly special?

Because special implies different, other than the norm.

Than everyday? Well then that's sad. I think it has become a real event, which is a shame. It costs a lot of money and requires a lot of preparation and is not seen as part of our lives, like the storyteller is part of our lives. There's a pre-historic Irish storytelling tradition; the storyteller would stand behind the audience and the audience would face a wall or face an empty space, so they would then envisage their own version of it and wouldn't need the actor to contain the physical idea of the story. That's a really exciting idea for me; it's an egoless idea of the actor. So yes, it can be really special but it should also be seen as something we have in us, culturally, as an everyday thing.

OLWEN FOUÉRÉ

Olwen, born in Ireland of Breton parents, is an actor/performer whose extensive practice navigates the contexts of mainstream theatre, the visual arts, music and literature. A former artistic director of Operating Theatre, she established a new artistic entity called *TheEmergencyRoom*. Among her many artistic collaborations, she has formed longstanding associations with the visual artist James Coleman and the composer Roger Doyle. She appeared in two films at Cannes Film Festival 2011: *This Must be the Place* directed by Paolo Sorrentino – official selection in Palme D'Or competition – and *The Other Side of Sleep* directed by Rebecca Daly – selected for the Cannes Film Festival Directors' Fortnight.

POK   *What was your first contact with theatre?*

OF   When I was 3 or 4 years old I saw a picture of a contortionist and my first ambition was to be a contortionist in a circus. That desire to go to a place where you turn yourself inside out, where you can do something which is apparently beyond the bounds of possibility, and where people will say, 'Oh my god', is still there. As regards my first contact with theatre, I remember performing in school and a recognition, in the doing of it, of an alternative reality. When I was still at school I saw *Uncle Vanya* at the Focus Theatre in Dublin. I remember the unconventional staging: the actors were on stage throughout, under a little lamp, then they'd emerge out of the shadows, play the scene and melt back again; there was a very intimate connection between audience and performer. I also saw a production of *Oedipus Rex*, directed by Jim Sheridan when he was still a student, in a massive hall on Stephen's Green. The audience's foreheads were daubed with ashes as they came in, it was perhaps similar to something The Living Theatre might have done. There was no stage, just huge scaffolding, which we sat on. The theatrical frame was completely broken and we were all participants in an experiential situation. There was a real buzz about it, an anarchic energy at play. I started thinking theatre was really interesting. I was studying visual arts at the time very informally. I remember visiting a friend who was studying Theatre Design in London, seeing his sets and being fascinated. I thought I'd be a theatre designer but when I did become actively involved, the performance aspect won over automatically.

I was working on an archeological dig at the time, on Wood Quay, and I saw that Christopher Casson was giving classes in *The Gate Theatre*, so I started going to these elocution-based classes and then someone in that class said you should go up to the Focus Theatre because they do Stanislavski sessions at weekends. I remember approaching the door, my hand went to knock and I thought, Oh I don't know and I walked away. Then I turned back and I said, 'ah might as well…'. Life turns on those points. Deirdre O'Connell answered the door and said she was busy, come back later for a chat, so I did. I said I just wanted to watch and she said, 'Well you can't come and watch, but you can participate!' A few months later, Jim Sheridan set up a company at the Project Arts Centre and I then worked with Jim and Peter at the Project almost continually for the following two years.

You didn't undertake any formal training?

No, and I still feel the lack of it. I came across a career guidance leaflet on acting amongst all my old school stuff, and it basically told you don't be an actor. I've always had a great hunger for study and exploration but there was no school. Had there been a drama school in Ireland I probably would have gone to it and made a decision about being an actor much earlier. It was as though I didn't really make the decision because there was no option there. I didn't know that you got paid, or that you could make your life as an actor. It sounds strange but that's how it was, in the Ireland of the 50s, I never really knew that people were actors as a profession.

'Is this what you do all the time?' is still a fairly common question; the idea that actors make a living out of it is still alien to a lot of people.

Occasionally my hairdresser says 'are you still at the acting?' She went on a world tour and she said 'when I get back you'll be really big' – it's a funny view of what we are; the idea that you can't just be an actor, you're only trying it out until you're famous.

What was it about acting rather than design or visual arts that was so compelling?

Its liveness, but before I could identify that, it was something to do with 'core being': being inside the work or the work being inside the being. The actor is the site of his work – that was really where the exploration was endless and where it was connected to a practice. I was very pulled by the discipline, the practice, of being an actor: it's easy to say it's like a spiritual practice but it's not just that. It's like being a runner, training every day to a level where you can run a marathon.

Who or what have been the greatest influences on your career, so far?

When I was working in the Project with Jim and Peter Sheridan, there was a lot of performance art happening; artists like Nigel Rolfe for instance. I didn't know performance art existed as an art form and probably had I known, I would have ended up as a performance artist as opposed to an actor/performer.

Why was that particularly appealing to you?

Because performance is a live manifestation of something, which is not contained within the framework of theatre and is not necessarily in a safe space. The performance artist creates a particular set of circumstances into which the body enters. There is the physical risk of it too; to place yourself in physical danger, because to decide that says something in itself as well. When I was working with Jim and Peter it was in pretty rough conditions, with a very mixed bag of people. What was really exciting about it was the sense of community within a very fluid group; it was like living in another country, in an alternative state. In the Project company of that time, because it was Jim and Peter and because they worked with other community groups, the theatre was packed every night with people who had never been to the theatre before. It was a really vibrant, chaotic place; it felt revolutionary – it didn't subscribe to the conventional needs of the Abbey or the Gate.

So it felt like an agent for social change?

Absolutely, social change, cultural change. I was asked a couple of times by Tomas MacAnna if I would be interested in working at the Abbey and I said no, I was committed to the Project. I would have felt that I was selling out because the Abbey seemed to be a far more packaged cultural experience for both performers and audiences. For instance, when you're in another country you go to an interpretive centre and/or to the real site; well the Abbey was like the interpretive centre and the Project was like the original site. The Abbey felt mediated by history, expectation; it felt like it was fixed in a conventional idea of what theatre was. Another influence was Robert Wilson. I've never seen him perform but I saw him speak at a theatre conference; it was otherly, electric. It was a dissolution of the boundaries between life and art. He gave a presentation but it was a performance and he deconstructed his speech; while talking to us he started jigging round the words and it was just the most extraordinary experience to hear him and watch him.

In terms of people in Ireland, I met the composer Roger Doyle in the late 70s and we're still working together. There was certainly a key moment when we first met professionally; he was looking for a dancer who wasn't like a trained dancer, he played a piece of music he wanted to work with and I improvised – we still talk about that moment. When I heard the music I had that weird feeling of recognition again, thinking I know this and that's the connection we have. In 1980 I met the visual artist James Coleman, with whom I've done seven or eight different pieces: he's a big influence on my work. Visual art has a little more license to be inaccessible but there's a compelling nature to his work; it's not a seduction, it compels you. His work is like an enormous ship that's got about seven different decks, all moving together; there's a multiplicity of meanings moving inexorably, truthfully across the time-span of the piece of work. The complexity of those multiple meanings may make it inaccessible but avoiding the presentational, the didactic, makes it compelling. It's beautifully made, with high production values, and in terms of what it's saying, it is there as an invitation, nothing else.

Is that idea of not being explained true of the rehearsal and the creation of it as well?

Yes, up to a point, but I understood the connection that I made with James intuitively. If there were things I didn't know, I would ask questions around it until he gave me an answer I could work with. We collaborated quite closely eventually. He was completely the author of the work and I was a collaborator. It was very different to the actor/director situation.

In mainstream theatre many different elements are introduced in stages; the writing is one part of it, the direction another part, performance is another, design another. Working with James was like feeding in and out of the primary creation, which was his own, and which I utterly respected and believed in. So the development/rehearsal process wasn't about explaining, it was about intuitively interpreting a very complex idea. He wouldn't necessarily be able to explain, or he wouldn't even know himself. For instance one piece I worked on with him began with a text, which was vitually illegible; I remember going through it and saying to him, this is unreadable let alone unperformable, so we started editing it together. I would look at about ten lines and I'd say, 'what is that?' and he'd sort of tell me and I'd say, 'but you've got this here and you need it there', and he'd say, 'no I do need it here, I can't explain but I do need it here', or he'd say, 'no you're right we don't need it'.

Would you say that those rehearsals were less about preparation of a product and more a journey towards articulation?

Completely.

Were they good, creative experiences?

Yes, extraordinary. Although, almost every time I worked with him I'd have my moments of frustration and say I'm never going to work with you again. Then I'd look back and see how really valuable it had been; he gave me – I saw that more in retrospect – courage to go that far.

So effectively he created an environment for you to take risks.

We were creating it together; he didn't exactly create the environment for me to take risks but my experience of his work made me more courageous in the other work that I did, whether in mainstream theatre or my own work. Crucially, he taught me the value of form: form is a far more important aspect of what we do than is fully acknowledged. Form is the most developed 'text' that we have where it's not about narrative, story or words, although words may be part of it. I think as actors, what we're working towards is a language, a highly developed and highly refined performance language, a distillation of all the elements that we're given to work with.

Is it important for a performer or an actor to have a sense of purpose, to have an awareness of what their function is, of where they're going?

In the work with James, my function was to understand what it was I had to do in order to embody or fulfil what on the surface may have seemed very amorphous. I had an intuitive grasp of it; trying to refine that was my function. I also think one can work in a situation for maybe two weeks or longer where you're constantly in chaos, where you don't really know what's going to come out of it: it might be useless but it might be valuable. As an artist, I have to be open to that situation; it may be very frustrating and difficult to identify why you're there at times, but I think it's important to do that too, to be able to go into a situation where you have apparently no function and not even look for one, just be there, even if it's just to observe or experience.

What were key events in your own work?

When I did *Diamond Body*, which was the first big show that Roger Doyle and I did, there was a stage in rehearsals where I thought, 'nobody's going to get it, they're going to think this is a big self-indulgence, but I really believe in it, there's something here that is really important'. It's as though you're down at the bottom of a hole, muck all round you and you see a seam – they see muck, I know there's a seam.

So that required great self-belief or self-confidence?

I believed in it. I've never had much self-confidence, partly because of not having training, not having reference points for the things that I started to feel happening, and which seemed to be so separate. But I believed in this thing that I saw and felt and knew it was important.

And that enabled you to commit to it?

I didn't really have any question about committing to it but if somebody had said to me this is a load of crap and why are you doing it, I would have said, 'because it's important'.

That performance varied in length significantly, didn't it?

Not on different nights but in different productions; that was really about the staging. Every time I remount something I need to revisit it in a different way. I don't always trust that because sometimes I think I'm doing it for the sake of it but it can be a step further in the exploration.

How do you guard against changing something just for the sake of it?

It's really difficult to play a role again that you've played before. I can remember when I was playing Ariel in *The Tempest*; I'd already done it with the ESC and I thought well I can't do *that* again, I've got to do it differently, so I incorporated some aspects of what I'd done but it was a very different performance. Maybe we shouldn't guard against it, maybe we should just accept that we should do it differently for the sake of it. What do you think?

I think it is different anyway because theatre must always be a present tense transaction and therefore one must be responsive to the different environments in which the work is placed. For example, the first time I did Cold Comfort with Owen McCafferty, it felt really live and dark and brutal; when we revisited it, one year later, we were slightly afraid of returning to the darkness, so we dithered for a few days. We also felt, 'oh well we know how to do this'. Then something really significant happened, on the Thursday of our one-week re-rehearsal, we realised we had to completely transform it, but not for its own sake: because of the one-year gap and because we were doing it in an entirely different type of theatre, in an entirely different city, with its own, different cultural reference points, we were in a different place, in ourselves, so therefore we couldn't just replicate it: in order to make it present again, we had to do it differently.

Maybe *that's* the real question: not how do we avoid changing things for the sake of it, but how do we discover the things we need to change when we do it again?

In our case, it became a distillation process. What had already seemed spartan became even more so. Furthermore things seem to percolate away in an unconscious way; the knowledge that you are going to be returning to it means you shut down a conscious part of your brain but it's still working away subconsciously.

I'm a massive believer in the work that goes on when you put it away. I think breaking up a rehearsal period, even when you're doing something new, is ideal. So for instance, maybe you rehearse three days one week and then you don't revisit it for two weeks but in those two weeks in between, something starts happening within you, so when you come back to it again there's a different connection. Every time, there's a completely different connection because of the duration of time, the percolation. People say 'we need more rehearsal time', which of course we all do, 'we need two months rehearsals', but I think if you spread that two months over six months, it would be an even more effective way of working; that you trust and allow this other, unconscious side to do the work in between, instead of constantly barraging it.

OK, any other key events?

I was very interested in the work of Steven Berkoff – form again. His use of language, his writing, the delivery of an idea, rooted in an extraordinary truth and delivered in a heightened form. Having come from a Stanislavski background I began to realise that the distillation of all those impulses into a heightened presentation or delivery is like seeing what you're seeing from very far away being brought up close; it's a revelatory way of delivering something. He was working in a form and language which I wasn't seeing anywhere else.

And then you worked with him, didn't you, on Salomé?

I don't think he wanted to cast me really and he was terrible to work with but because I liked his work so much I put up with it.

Why was he terrible to work with?

He's hopeless at communicating, in creating the environment for you to work in: he can't tell you what he'd like you to do without doing it in front of you and he can be a real bully. That said, the two streams that had been informing my work – the mainstream and the 'other' work – came together in *Salome.*

Have there been other instances since then?

Fair Ladies at a Game of Poem Cards directed by John Crowley, which was Peter Oswald's adaptation of a Chikamatsu Monzaemon play, married a lot of stuff for me as well. There was a brilliant movement director, Jonathan Buttrell, working on the staging and performance style, which demanded a condensing of energy – there was a key element of absolute stillness and compression – I really enjoyed working with that both physically and vocally. It was a very sculptural approach to the performance; almost every single moment was chosen and incredibly sparse.

That was a physical/formalist aesthetic as opposed to a psychological one?

Yes, although the psychological was always in there; I was playing the part of the Empress, it was clear what my psychological drive was and the rest of it was simply choosing how this can be most effectively and powerfully delivered without 'telling' it. I had also been working on a devised piece with John Crowley, again that was a convergence, because of how you are accepted into a process as a fellow artist who is there to construct entirely your performance from words to persona.

Tell me about working with Selina Cartmell and what made that instinctive.

She was the assistant director on a production I was in and I sensed that she was special. The first piece of work of hers I saw was just before we worked together; I remember going into the theatre and looking at what she had already placed there before the show started. Taking my seat, I felt the hairs going up at the back of my neck – I knew it was going to be an extraordinary piece of work and it was.

Can you identify what she does that makes you aware of a special energy?

I can only identify it as an artistic gift, she was probably born with it. That is combined with excellent, extensive training so her gift is combined with great craft. She also has a very 'other' sense of aesthetic, not a conventional aesthetic at all; it's very quirky, funny – which isn't necessarily what I am, I'd like to be quirky and funny but I'm not. She has a very powerful visual imagination. I would say all of her thinking is through visuals, seeing rhythms of movement, rhythms of light. I had a sense of recognition with her – this planet is very close to the one I was born on, or possibly even the other side of it! She went to Bali and, by chance, ended up training in Balinese dance for six months and dancing in the temple. I think that gave her a hugely spiritual grasp of theatre. Balinese dance influences her work: there's an otherness to the rhythms and the images, which tapped into me as well.

Marina Carr has been significant in your career. Could you describe what the significance of her influence has been and how that manifests itself?

The relationship opened up quite a lot for both of us. I think the real, big connection happened for me when I was given the script of *The Mai*; Marina said 'I wrote it with you in mind'. I didn't particularly like the character of The Mai, but I could see there was a journey. There was a crucial scene in the middle of it, which was so authentic and one that I recognised very clearly. I decided to take the leap, take on *The Mai*. Marina gave me one brilliant note, she said, 'she's more of a tinker' and it opened a particular part of me as a person, my sensibilities, my psyche, all of those things, it's like I connected to everything in a completely new place; the interface between myself and the work became very charged. I experienced it as an alchemical relationship between the writer and the actor.

Can you give an example of that interface getting charged?

In my daily life everything had become suffused with a new light, a new energy, and that came out of the work. Art and sexuality are very combined and it was very connected to a sexual energy, it was a similar energy. Marina has also said I'm sitting on her desk as she writes and similarly, when I perform her work it's as though I'm going further into something and she's giving me the material. It is like a symbiotic relationship, although there's no obligation one way or the other.

When she said she'd written By The Bog of Cats with you 'sitting on her desk' did you understand that, or did you need any further explanation?

There'll always be questions, but when your essential energy is being accessed in such a positive way, it's a two-way thing and that is an important part of any creative relationship. It's not just the work you do on the floor, there is also the relationship in memory between people and then it becomes more like influence. I can think about how I worked with James Coleman or how he interrogates stuff, and that will inform my own thinking or open up certain areas of questioning for me which then informs something that I'm doing, completely unrelated to it; that's the combination of artistic relationship and artistic influence.

So the art and the life are integrated?

God I think they have to be; it's not even as if they have to be, they are. How do you get to that level of integrity and profundity, when you don't have some kind of personal relationship with the author? Maybe with a writer you've no relationship with, you can still go deep, if not deeper – who knows? It's not necessarily as symbiotic a journey; but you're not necessarily going to be travelling on the road together. If the writer is in the room I think you've every chance of having a symbiotic relationship.

In the case of Marina, or in a similar situation where you and the writer have that personalised level of communication, what role does the director have?

What should happen is that the director facilitates that communication. With *The Mai*, for example, the director, who was not very experienced at the time, had the good sense to not interfere and to let it all happen; only at the last week or so, did he start to tweak, structure, pull in the production around it.

So when you say 'he let it all happen', what happened?

He allowed all the energy in the room to be engaged and for people to play and did not come in with any overriding vision.

Did you set up Operating Theatre because you were dissatisfied with mainstream theatre or your role in that?

No it wasn't a dissatisfaction, it was a pull into unexplored territory.

Was it about expression of yourself or formal experimentation?

The important work we do has nothing to do with self-expression, it's to do with knowing there's something out there that needs our attention, that needs to be uncovered. It's like being in a desert; you know that next to that bush there's something that has to be uncovered and you start digging and if nobody is digging there you think, 'am I the only one who really wants to go and dig there?', but it's important to take that object out and place it out there for everybody. So it's different from self-expression, which comes from inside you. The recognition of the object comes from inside you but the thing itself, if it's of value, is outside of you.

And what does it offer you that mainstream theatre doesn't or can't?

The courage to dig, the courage to create. Mainstream will offer me the craft, or the opportunity to practice the craft, but there are whole areas that I can't practice in mainstream theatre that I can in this other work.

What are the restrictions that mainstream theatre imposes on you as an artist?

We still understand the text to be the play. For me, the performance text – nothing to do with what you're saying – is a far more powerful text. 75% of perception is through the body and only a tiny percentage of it is through words and then another percentage is through the sound that you make around the words. There are many other 'texts'. Mainstream theatre is largely dominated by the idea that the written text is the centre of all the drama; I don't believe that.

Do you not feel the performance text – body language, the stage picture etc.
– starts from text, so yes, the text is only the text of the play but that it is the
starting point?

That, for me, is what's restricting about it; the starting point is always the written text. I am interested in forms of theatre where the written text is not the centre from which everything springs. There's a hierarchy, at the moment, and the text is at the top of that hierarchy, the director's usually the next on the pyramid of hierarchies and so on. I find that a very limited way of making theatre. A lot of the time we're not really talking about theatre we're talking about plays, we're not even thinking about all the other elements, so a whole season will be programmed by plays and then the director's chosen, and so on and so forth. What might happen if no plays are programmed: this group here are working on…and that group over there will be doing something else?

How would that invigorate it?

It might kill it, but what's restricting about mainstream theatre is the hierarchy and that the main site of the art is written plays, things that are written on paper. With Operating Theatre, certainly in our more recent work, we stopped thinking about plays, about written texts. We were working from an idea, an impulse, like some kind of archaeological exploration.

You said that mainstream theatre offers craft and that Operating Theatre and performance offers you the courage?

Ultimately, craft is being able to work truthfully with the most refined instruments you have at your disposal and the more you refine the instruments, the higher your craft becomes; you can never lose sight of the truth of the impulse. That's constantly demanded of me in mainstream theatre because you're always having to adapt to certain situations; it's about bringing that integrity to a situation which may even be alien to how you work most efficiently. Say you develop a very elaborate kind of knife that can cut through stone as well as it can cut through butter – that's the craft for me. My work with Operating Theatre gives me the courage to discard all that and go after something else, to find a new knife or even having to find new instruments through which I can articulate certain things. It is a more naked exploration.

You've recently done Macbeth: *how did you bring to bear your experiences as a performance artist and working with Operating Theatre on working within the discipline of that classical text?*

Selina proposed the idea of playing all three witches as one. She had an image of a woman with two prams and that image completely landed and inspired many more images for me. I went through the script in order to make it clear that we are in both worlds and I constructed a silent score throughout the piece with her: we did it together. Without my other experience, I wouldn't have trusted the continuity and the juxtaposition of the classical, traditional three witches, with the composite character I became, which had its own development through the play and which I threaded through Shakespeare's text. I hardly spoke, I used very little of the language, I cut all the witches speeches to ribbons of my own volition; I said we can do without that because we've got the action and the action is more powerful than the words; the words are part of the inspiration but they're not the alpha and the omega.

Do you still regard theatre as an agent for change?

I see it as an agent for alternative ways of thinking, of breaking down our perceptual patterns. The big issue is how many people will be around to hear you ask those questions? It's so contained now, people say 'you've got to put the ticket prices up because we know it's only middle-class people who go to the theatre; if they're going to pay 200 Euros to see Electric Picnic [music festival] why can't they pay 100 Euros for a night's theatre?': I think it should be free, however much it costs.

What is it that the arts offer?

Resistance – we are handed a reality, ways of thinking, by other people, by a very dominant, mostly invisible, group who control pretty much everything about our lives and art is probably one of the only forms of resistance left.

What does theatre offer specifically within that?

Similar, except that we are bound, as a lot of the arts are; theatre has also now become part of that whole controlling view, we've become part of the commercial world, we've started to adopt all the vernacular of the world that owns us. If you go inside a system how much can you affect by being inside it? Much of Art and, specifically theatre, is becoming part of a system that it really needs to be resisting.

How could and should theatre resist ?

To return to the idea of art as a practice – as something that informs every aspect of your life – hence there is a responsibility on every level of our lives, to push the boundaries even further. We do that ultimately by taking responsibility for everything, even the bad work, which we might end up doing – we take personal responsibility for having agreed to do that. Other artists might feel differently but, for me, the space I have entered into is that space of resistance. I may resist very badly, or ineffectually, but I still see this as my primary function, to do so with as much integrity as I can. As a single actor in a production, it is about working for all the right reasons, I am doing this because it's important for this/that reason; what you put into it is what you'll get out of it. The rewards are not immediate ones and maybe you never see the rewards. I see it as part of the job.

Is it a job or is it a vocation?

Most artists are called in some way, similar to a vocation, but I resist that word because it allows us too easily to be put into a little vocational corner. That does not work to our advantage: 'They don't need looking after, they've chosen this and that's their lot'. Art is really crucial for any kind of life.

Is a personal sense of satisfaction the primary reward?

It always seems relatively impersonal to me; you have a job, you do it, you've done it well and it's not all down to you that it's been well done. Once a job is done, it's almost like it's forgotten; maybe you look back in time and see the body of work and think, 'that was a great piece of work and nobody saw it'. You won't always get personal satisfaction because maybe the best thing you did was hardly seen; that's why, to me, it's more like a practice of some kind, it's like doing yoga every day or running every day, maybe the best run you ever did was on your practice.

The idea that you do your best run in a training run and not in a race is frustrating for a runner, just as it would be frustrating to think that the best run of a play or a production took place in the rehearsal room. The rehearsals are for preparing yourself for the performance, which is the raison d'etre; it's about the transmission of the idea through the performance, which is also an act of social communion – that sharing of experience – telling the story with an audience bearing witness; the silent, but nonetheless active, interaction between stage and auditorium. The idea that that wasn't as successful as it had been in another environment without the audience would be very, very frustrating.

It would be very frustrating but I think some piece of work that you did, either alone or collectively, which you know is of very high value, yet only 30 people a night saw it, for reasons beyond your control – how do you feel about that? There is really no reward other than the doing of it.

Do you think that need for a sense of satisfaction is brought further into focus by the fact that jobs are scarce, pay is poor, and the demands made of the actor in the enacting of the story or performance are so personal? The Arts Council of Ireland commissioned a report, which found that 73% of performers had third level qualifications and yet the average time spent working in their specialist profession was 22 weeks a year; 75% of actors had been required, when they were unemployed, to retrain; the average pay for actors in Ireland is 456 Euros; across the sector the average pay is 513 Euros, so therefore actors are getting paid less than other sectors. Do you think that all contributes to a need for personal fulfilment?

Yes and often negatively: the work can become over-personalised, less of an artistic path and more of a therapeutic path. It can be a problem, in terms of the distance that's needed; it's really important for artists to have an aesthetic distance from their work to be able to look at it dispassionately. The acting profession, which has so few obvious monetary and other rewards, attracts obsessive people. I'm one – I'm long enough in the business to know that I'm not in it for therapy but I think that can happen. Because there's an element of sacrifice involved, it can pull in people who feel they are justified in a therapeutic search. Now there's a really grey area in all this, between the artist and the self-therapist and it's probably dangerous to draw a line down the middle of it, but it's definitely a danger zone.

I think it's crucial to draw a line. That's where the discipline of the form comes in, so that it doesn't become a personal voyage, which happens to use Chekhov's Three Sisters, *for example, as a ground plan.*

I do think so and I would personally love to draw a line, ferociously, down the middle of it, but consider the history of art and artistic movements; when the boundaries are rigid and when something starts to push up against that boundary, it is often the beginning of a new movement. Maybe it's good to have that boundary there to push against, but there's always a worry of excluding something that doesn't look right at the moment but might still be valuable.

There is a further tension between having a distance in order to look in or at something and being actively involved. The idea of the artist being outside society doesn't work for me, and yet implicit in looking at something is that you're outside it.

You've got to be outside and inside at the same time. When I'm talking about a space of resistance, I think that space is inside. Theatre captures non-fixed essences and acknowledges the importance of non-fixed essence in life, society and history. That space is inside – inside society – and perhaps our role is to push from inside but to be able to look from the outside at what we are pushing against.

Do you feel that the artists are facilitated by the industry to do that?

No, because it's all casual labour, so it's not facilitating that at all, in fact it's constantly encroaching. Even the fact that it's called an industry is constantly encroaching: to make this space into something that is there to be controlled and consumed, as opposed to something that is active and changing all the time.

As an artist, what is your experience with the theatre institutions, funding bodies?

I've always pushed the importance of individual support for individual artists with the Arts Council; within theatre, the idea of an actor as an individual artist wasn't really recognised, although now it is. The Arts Council don't actually control all of the arts money – they are the channel for it. I would generally say my relationship with the Arts Council has been good.

Is that because of the nature of your work with Operating Theatre? If you hadn't had that strand of work, would you be as aware of what the Arts Council could and would do to support you?

No, I probably wouldn't be as aware, although I did push for another shift in policy that has happened since. There has always been a training fund, but it didn't apply to professionals and, of all professionals, we need to keep training: we need to have access to different ways of working, we need to experience them, to learn what they're about. Now we have what is called mid-professional training in place: you can apply to work abroad, to experience other countries and other work.

Do you think enough actors are aware of those things?

It is our responsibility to find out, there's only so much people can do to tell you about them. Many actors are very mixed about independent, representative bodies such as Theatre Forum, but if something is called 'the Voice of the Performing Arts', I see it as my responsibility to find out about it and be part of it.

You also helped set up Associated Theatre Artists.

It was unsustainable for three or four people to keep that thing going. There was a huge amount of work involved, a huge amount of responsibility; the last thing we wanted to do was set up an office, because once I am performing I can't really think of anything else. I currently serve on two boards – Theatre Forum and the Abbey Theatre – which demand a significant commitment and carry a considerable responsibility, which I am happy to undertake, but I feel that unless I can be really effective, why be on them?

Do you feel your status is affected by, or reflected in, the timeline of the employment process in mainstream theatre?

People are hugely affected by that – it's another hierarchical stream in the mainstream. The written text is one, the other is the hierarchy of constructing a production.

I understand the chronology of it on a pragmatic level but I don't see why that should necessarily affect the creative hierarchy. Because you were hired last in the process shouldn't affect your status within the creative environment but I feel it does.

It's massively problematic that a hierarchy exists because of that chronology. There are times when you can shift it, for instance, if you have a very strong relationship with the director, or the writer. However, what I find happening, more and more, is that within the production body which hires the director or the writer, there's often a desire to break down that relationship and say 'Oh no, you've been working with so and so for so long, I think it's better if you work with somebody else,' 'I'm going to put so and so together with so and so, won't that be interesting? That'll be my contribution to the arts'. That is an incredibly hierarchical way of working. The whole point is to facilitate, rather than suppress, the development of those creative relationships.

What reasons are you given for this?

The reason might be given to a director, 'This writer needs a higher profile so we want a star director to direct stars in it' – I can understand that, especially if the writer *needs* to be more widely known, but, worryingly, it's also happening on a small scale. When it's on a smaller scale it's very much this paternalistic idea of development – now this can apply to a writer in their 40s or a director in their 50s – 'we develop you onwards from here; you're not a big star so we'll develop you, but we don't think you should work with this person you normally work with'. In another case, a director known for a very particular style of work, was more or less pushed away from that style by the organization who were hiring him – why? Where does that come from? It's a power thing, for sure, but it's coming from something else as well, what is it?

Where do you feel, from your experience both in alternative performance theatre and in mainstream theatre, the actor fits in to the creative hierarchy?

In mainstream theatre, they are at the very bottom; they should be primary creators, they should be on the same level as the director, the writer and the designer.

Why would that be a healthier state of affairs?

Because it's a collective art form, and while the director should be the leader of sorts, that doesn't mean he has to be the boss, there's a difference. A leader discerns what is important to do with this group of people by dint of what is coming from them; a boss decides to tell them what to do. A leader is someone who is travelling through the mountains with you and there's a point where the whole group are going 'where do we go next' and the leader has a map and he says how about going this way and they look at the map and they say, yeah, that would be good but look at this, why don't we go there and the leader says, 'OK I think I can get you down there'.

In your experience what should be the director/actor dynamic or relationship?

Honesty, listening and mutual respect are very important; you're not pussy footing around each other. You can't control how creative somebody will be, or how artistically gifted they are, but certainly the conditions for that exchange are honesty, respect, listening, space and time for one another.

What's the best direction you've ever had?

I worked with Garry Hynes once, I had a ten-day rehearsal period with her, I was taking over in *The Playboy of the Western World* in New York, 1986. In between I had to go to Avignon for a solo show, for three weeks – so I had a ten-day rehearsal period, then two or three weeks away, then fly to New York and open to 2000 people – quite a tall order. I learnt my part before we started rehearsals and I wasn't rehearsing with the whole company! I managed to go back to New York and we did a rehearsal that day, a technical rehearsal and then Garry said to me, 'That's all great Olwen, any questions, problems?' I said, 'Because of the way we had to rehearse I don't feel a sense of power when I'm up there, I don't feel I'm accessing my power and she just said, 'don't concentrate on anything else except that, find your own power, use your own power, find your power.' That was a great piece of direction because it made me think OK all those little details, they're all important but they're there, go back to the basic now, with your power, feel that powerful, umbilical connection you have with an audience. And Marina's direction, which I've mentioned, 'She's more of a tinker', was a brilliant one; they're very often the general ones, funnily enough, you can ask for lots of little specific things but the general ones are often the most useful – they switch something, they unlock something.

What's the worst piece of direction you've ever received?

Things like, 'That's funny you need to get a laugh on that line'. Bad direction assumes an audience's reaction; it's insulting to audience and actor alike. It assumes that audiences are stupid and respond to formulaic things and that actors are just there to perform a formulaic function.

Is the director not a kind of super spectator?

Yes he is, although it's very hard for he or she to remain objective once they've been immersed in the process for so long; they are more like one of us at that point. They're more like a painter who's looking at his own painting. The director is also there as an artist not just as a super spectator or a facilitator. I think the director has to have an artist's courage as well as an artist's eye.

What does an audience have a right to expect of you?

They've got a right to expect that you know your lines, that's fundamental, that you are absolutely taking responsibility for your presence, that you're acknowledging your own presence, acknowledging theirs. I think they have a right to expect that and so we should be giving them everything.

What about keeping a little bit back?

Yes but that's a craft choice; keeping something back because you've chosen to is very different to, 'I can't be bothered and anyway it'll make me look stupid if I do this'.

What can and should you expect from an audience?

An audience is entitled to heckle, to throw things, to tell me to get off the stage, I'm a bad actor, etc. Audiences have been beaten into submission and obedience and politeness. The whole thing about a live experience is yes I expect them to be there because they want to be there, because they want to hear and see; I don't expect them to be forced to sit through something they feel passionately against.

Do you think that theatre has become cursed by politeness?

There's nothing wrong with good manners; politeness and good manners may mean different things and even good manners is a slightly cursed phrase for me because it implies politeness. The manners that are important are about listening, exchange and honesty. Overall, there's a lack of real exchange, which has caused, maybe created, a culture of politeness or is maybe caused by politeness.

The McMaster Report for the Arts Council England sets out its stall to measure and achieve excellence; what for you is excellent acting? Is it possible to define?

It's so subjective, but I guess commitment is probably the biggest prerequisite; commitment, discipline, rigour, courage, danger, craft. Commitment is important because you have to have a good reason for doing what you're doing. If you are committed the stakes are high and you are giving it everything. With courage, we don't fall into formulaic ways of doing things. Personal courage and artistic courage are related. Craft comes and goes; in our theatre world there seem to be years where there's great craft and other years where craft all falls apart.

What do you understand by craft?

Physical awareness and control, being able to speak with clarity, articulation, timbre etc. Craft is not only learnt, it's accumulated over the years, so experience is nearly always a component of craft. I remember seeing Schofield in *John Gabriel Borkman*; it was extraordinary and it wasn't fashionable to act in that way, but by god that was craft if I ever saw it and I don't care what era it falls or doesn't fall into. Discipline and rigour are ways of maintaining and developing your craft and they're also very essential to the ensemble relationship; a company has to have discipline and rigour in order to be able to really function as an ensemble.

What about truth and honesty?

To me they're all tied up with commitment and courage. Everybody has a different version of what truth means, honesty of course is important but truth…what is truth? I have seen productions where I could say the performances were really truthful but I didn't like them because they didn't have depth, any kind of primal energy to them, they were sentimental but truthful.

I don't think you can have a truthful performance that lacks those qualities and that's not to do with the style of a piece; if it doesn't tap into those primal human energies then it doesn't have truth, because it's a huge aspect of our humanity you're not including.

That's a definition of truth that I would agree with but I've seen truth used as a description for stuff we talked about before, where it's somebody exorcising their own problems; that's truthful but it means damn all to me because it isn't tapping into something more fundamental, and collective.

Is fear always an enemy to creativity?

Not at all. I don't remember who said 'fear is poetry' but I remember a friend of mine was playing Lear, it was the opening night and he was terrified: I sent him a card which had a man in a big coat flying off into the air with black winged birds all around him with 'fear is poetry' written on it. It did the trick, he remembered that you can use it, so he went on with all that fear and was able to give a fantastic performance. Fear is part of our material; often it raises the stakes and works as a creative energy. I have seen actors with that cold white fear where everything gets paralysed; if it does become your enemy you have to crack it, either by fighting it or by accepting it. You also have to get beyond what anyone else in the room is thinking about what you're doing.

Does negative fear make you self-conscious?

It can make you confused – the arrow gets diverted because it's not going where it should go.

What about confidence, how important is that?

I don't know really, confidence can be an enemy too; at its worst can make people cocky and that's just as closed a state as terror.

Is that not arrogance rather than confidence? With arrogance, as with fear, it becomes about yourself rather than the job in hand, but surely you have to have a confidence in order to be creative?

Unconfident people can be extremely creative in the right environment. Often, in the case with great artists that can be the way. Confidence isn't a prerequisite, it helps you progress with your work and stand behind it but it doesn't necessarily mean that if you're very confident your work is great.

*I understand unconfident people produce really great work but I would suggest
that when they are working they get into a zone where they can be confident
and I would suggest, therefore, that one of the jobs of a director is to make
actors feel confident about being creative, about exchanging, being generous.*

Confidence is a massive part of my ability to progress but sometimes
when I've felt very confident I've missed things, which maybe slightly less
confident, I might have seen. So large amounts of humility are necessary.

*What about the impact of the loss of confidence? Have you ever experienced
that?*

Yes I have: I played a lead role with the RSC and I was clear and confident
about what I had to do, but the director progressively undermined my
confidence. He never accepted anything I offered and consequently never
allowed himself to be surprised by anything I did and, if he was surprised,
it was discarded. As a result, what I was offering became less and less
good. He succeeded in blocking me completely; because I took on all of
his objections, they became embedded in my body, so there was constant
self-doubt every time I did something. There's only so much you can fight;
I kept fighting, but my instinct was getting interfered with to the point
where it was pushing against his instruction, which was building up like an
armour, imprisoning me.

*Have you ever experienced those internal blockages – 'I don't know what I'm
doing' or 'who I am at this moment'?*

They are often little messages to start looking and thinking about why is this
happening, is it because of me, is there something wrong with the direction
we're going, or where's it coming from? It can be helpful sometimes; for
instance, I said about feeling that the sound I choose is very important
before I started rehearsals for something, but once, in rehearsals, I realised
it was bringing my energy to the wrong place. I solved it by trying to wipe
it away and keep going back: centre, back, centre, back: go back to base. If
a block is well established it's quite hard to break; maybe you're better off
trying to find ways around it instead of trying to break it.

What is presence to you?

It's a heightened state of being. Being present, your whole body's there but there's an extra vibration around it.

How do you achieve that?

Readiness; an awareness that you've entered a heightened environment, because theatre is a very heightened environment. Openness, as though all your pores are open to it. Being centred, voice centred, so that your whole body is talking, the body and being. If you are in that state, you hear and see more clearly, so you are capable of having an intense conversation – if we were doing this on stage we could be talking like this and I could be completely aware of every single ear out there and they're all part of that presence, there's an effect of Being.

How do you distinguish that which is being truly present from upstaging?

Someone with presence can just be there and your eye is drawn to them but they're not doing anything that is taking you away from what's going on, so your eye is drawn to them but it's usually automatically drawn back if what's going on there is good enough. An upstager is more of a fiddler, overusing, overexploiting moments. They often have a pathological need to be watched and usually it's very obvious when that's happening.

Do you think that the public perception of what great acting is, of what great presence is, is different from the actors' perception?

It's not always easy to distinguish those things, especially when it comes down to opinion/taste. I think overall the great stand out as great, but there are a lot of greys in between. What do you think?

I do wonder if truly great acting is quite often missed. Showy acting is celebrated and that cheapens the experience for everybody. That type of acting is ungenerous and for me acting is a fundamentally generous act, both within the internal story on stage and in the transmission of that story to the audience. It requires a selflessness, which can mean that your work is not necessarily appreciated – art that conceals art – and anything that draws attention to itself, for itself, is not a good thing.

I've often felt that the best actors are the invisible ones, the ones you don't actually see. Everything they're doing is so much part of the fabric that they don't stand out as an individual, yet if they weren't there you might notice it hugely.

For me specificity is a really crucial part of good acting; it's something always to strive for. What is it you do to try and be specific?

If I'm vague about what I'm doing or saying I will use 'actioning'; whatever you are doing is an action that is going to change the person you're doing it to. Then I can discard the actions once the specificity is embedded. Physical specificity is important as well and quite often that's overlooked, even by physically and visually orientated directors. In performance, I'll often try to hone down to one turn of the head at the right moment or on that word which somebody else is saying. Developing specificity is something I strive for all the time; it's a continuous process of refinement.

Therefore generalisation is the enemy to good acting? What do you do to avoid that?

Questioning I suppose. I'm in rehearsals at the moment, it's a solo – it's easy in a solo to get generalised. But usually, with a solo, I will say OK, if I'm speaking to an audience, why am I speaking to them, who are they, where have I come from, are we in a theatre, are we somewhere else? Establishing specifics of time, place, relationships and detail for each moment and the action of each moment.

It's always asserted that failure is a learning process: do you hold that view?

Well one hopes one does otherwise it's a terrible waste of time but I don't know if you always do. When you're doing something that is a failure, you know it, and maybe the lesson is when you have that little feeling – the voice at the back of your head – you need to really listen to it to see if you can avert the disaster. Alternatively, what is a failure? Some things are seen as failures and you know very well they're not; it was a great piece of work, but it bombed at the box office and the critics hated it, but you know yourself it was a great piece of work – that's just part of the journey.

Sports people say they learn more about themselves in defeat than in victory and similarly artists supposedly learn more about themselves through failure than success but, for me, if you've failed in something, and I don't necessarily mean whether the public accepts the production or not, but if you've failed to reach your artistic goals or whatever, it seems to have a demoralising effect on me which inhibits my ability to be creative for quite a long time afterwards. I'm not sure if you do learn constructive lessons – a string of failures can actually kill you off.

Well yeah it makes you think, I had it once, I don't anymore, perhaps I should do something else.

So what do you do to overcome that?

What I would regard as failures were the result of decisions I shouldn't have made. I could have averted that, if I'd really listened to myself. I've got a great stubbornness and I suppose I have a great deal of self-belief, which probably serves me well. I'm trying to be honest – I can't quite think of a circumstance to back this up – but if I really believed that I had done my work well and fulfilled all my own criteria, I will think, 'well sod them, that was a good piece of work and I'll carry on'. Even if I carried on feeling that way and they carried on failing it, sod them again! But if I felt I was not delivering, either at an acceptable standard for an audience or at a high enough standard for myself, which would be the main thing – who else can judge you but yourself, at the end of the day? – I would take time out, do something else for a while and come back to it if I felt I should. My attitude to my work from the start has always been, 'I will stay with this work until it comes to an end, if it comes to an end.' It hasn't come to an end yet! I don't *have* to do this; I do this for as long as it has meaning for me and for as long as I feel I'm serving something important. I hope it doesn't happen because I have great affection for this way of life and work. I would hope that, if it happened, I would be able to face it and say that really is finished now and do something else.

What does it mean for you to be an actor?

Being an actor means being an artist and accepting the challenges and the responsibilities of being on the margins of society. It's very easy to be told by the vast majority of the world that they're indulging us.

That we're a luxury item?

I even heard an actor saying he was in a luxury profession and if I really felt that I don't know if I would want to stay in it. I don't see it as a luxury profession and it's really important, for me anyway, to reassert that it's not and also to constantly be resisting and challenging the systems that we, by default, are part of, in order to do the work. Therefore we have to have the courage to risk being impolite, to risk so and so not employing us because they don't like what we said in the papers; it's about having courage and not being afraid to carve out that space. The great luxury of getting older is that you give less and less a fuck about whom you're going to offend.

GERRARD MCARTHUR

Gerrard is an associate, as director and actor, of the Wrestling School, the company with an international reputation for being dedicated to producing the work of a living author, Howard Barker. His directing work for that company includes Barker's *The Dying of Today* (Arcola) and *Hurts Given and Received* (Riverside). Other direction includes a site-specific production of Heiner Muller's *Quartet* (Queen's, Adelaide), and with Stewart Laing, Copi's *The Difficulty of SExpressing Oneself* (Glasgow Tramway and King's X Depot). As a Wrestling School actor he played the protagonist Priest in Howard Barker's 8 hour epic, *The Ecstatic Bible* (Adelaide Festival), Vanya in *(Uncle) Vanya* (Hebbel Theatre, Berlin), Toonelhuis in Barker's most formally experimental work *Found in the Ground* (Riverside), and Blok in *Blok/Eko* (Exeter Northcott/Vanbrugh, London). As an actor he had a 10 year association with the Glasgow Citizens. He also played Prospero for Romanian director Silviu Purcurete in Europe and Japan and has worked with film-makers Derek Jarman and John Maybury.

What was your first experience of the theatre?

We never went to the theatre, but I knew I was an actor, I felt it in me. I could see other people doing it, on the telly and I knew that I could do that. I felt what they were doing, imaginatively, in me, so I knew I was associated with those people.

So when did you first go to the theatre?

I honestly can't remember. It must have been when I was in something. My comprehensive school put on plays; one year the teacher asked people to put up their hands if they were interested in being in his next production. So I put up my hand. That is really how it started: I was in a school production.

And the reason you put up your hand was because you had seen the TV and you thought you could do that?

I put up my hand because I felt that I could do it. But it is more than that: I felt that that is what I was. I would have been about 13.

And what did you think it was?

I knew what it felt like – a feeling or sensation, not connected to the idea of being an actor, or what an actor was or anything grounded; it was just a sensation, a feeling, but I knew in my head that it wasn't merely an imaginative fantasy, that I was emotionally, chemically and even technically able to do it. It was a very strong deep visceral idea of myself, or a sensation of recognition of the possibilities in me, in response to the idea of putting my psyche into other characters. That is how I started – and that was in Berlin's comedy musical, *Call Me Madam!* It was an all boys' school, and I played Sally Adams! I really enjoyed it, and I just knew what to do. I knew where I should be in relation to other people, I knew how the scene was going to work somehow, where we were going to be – basic things, stage procedure – I didn't need to be told. I don't know how I knew that, but I did, and I enjoyed it. I was also the quietest boy in the school. I was incredibly shy, I had a couple of very close friends, but I was very bookish, very quiet really, embarrassed at talking to any adults.

So was performing a release from that?

Yes, absolutely, they go hand in hand don't they? You know there is a huge thing going on in you and that is obviously a key point.

Did you start going to the theatre after that?

The school took us to see *The Misanthrope*, at the Old Vic, with Diana Rigg and Alec McCowan, in what was quite a famous production. I have a vivid memory of the set and colossal amounts of talking; very high levels of speech-making, people talking for a very long time when they have a thought. For someone like me who didn't say anything, to have these people building a whole plethora of ideas and drawing them to a precise concluding statement, was amazing. More than that, however, was the physical thrill of being in a theatre; the sense of ceremony, the physical fabric of it, the instinctive excitement of bodies in space on stage and the visceral excitement of the spoken word – physically thrilling for me and still is, to this day. A person in space, making movement, making a sound, is a really beautiful thing. It's beyond words, actually, why that has such a powerful, primal, effect. I still have that, and walking onto an empty stage in a theatre, it holds some instilled beauty and powerful energy for me.

So you went to university and you studied Classics. Did you not want to be a professional actor, at that point?

No, I didn't and that was probably the right move. I should have stuck to it. And so I went to University, I didn't do any plays, I didn't go anywhere near the theatre department. I didn't complete the course at University. I left and came back to London. I thought, 'what shall I do?' I thought I should do the thing I enjoyed doing. A friend called John Maybury, who now makes cinema films, was making super 8 art movies, in the way that Derek Jarman made his before that. I acted in those early films of John's and I enjoyed it and so I thought I will apply to RADA. I never had a realistic conversation with myself; I thought I will apply, it is the only place I have heard of and if they want me, great, if they don't, then I will do something else. I applied and I got in and so I went there. If they had said no to me I might not have continued.

What were your expectations of the training at RADA? What was its point of focus?

I had no expectations about the training at all. I was very glad to be there very quickly, it was full of interesting minded eccentrics on the staff and everything seemed to be focused, but lateral, which perhaps is how I think. Nothing was over-explained. You were allowed to experience things rather than being told what you were going to experience and why you were doing so. There is a real intelligence about people, who just let you discover it, and see you discovering it and lead that line with you; that is very high quality teaching and they had the confidence to do that. I was there at a spectacularly interesting time; there were a lot of good people there training and it was the last period of Hugh Cruttwell, who was extraordinarily gifted at running a drama school.

In what way?

He chose and cast people extremely well. Everybody was able to get a sense of themselves through the way he cast them and he could spot things. He would put them in places where that had a possibility of finding its expression. When you are performing that function for a group of 24 people and they are all getting that from you, then that is a pretty big accomplishment. I know we all felt that. We had a reunion a couple of months ago; we had 24 in our year and 21 people turned up.

Were you all still actors?

Not all, a couple had become casting directors, but most people were acting, which is extraordinary.

What was the impact of your training on your career?

I am in two minds about that, because it was both esoteric and practical at the same time, which is a fantastic combination, as was the Citizens, very esoteric and practical. In a way I was unprepared for the dull, ordinary, everydayness of the business of being an actor, meeting people, getting jobs, servicing those requirements; in a way, RADA had been too special.

Is there anything about your training that you would do differently, that you think was lacking, or needed more attention?

I would have liked to have been drenched more in areas of process and the history of process and to have been introduced more to Continental models of acting, in a systematised fashion.

In your experience what would improve the theatre training process?

Well, there needs to be a more somatic training.

What do you mean by somatic?

Just to do with the body, to do with sound-making, and treating writing as a musical notation; writing is a notation of a psyche on the page and it invites you to make sound and that sound has an implication for what is happening in your body, and so the somatic. You need to find a way in which the physical training is integrated into voice classes, so they are one and the same thing and you are not doing things separately. As students come into rehearsal-type structures, as they begin to put plays together, you have to take the somatic, the sound-making, the body sensitisation and the intellectual understanding through in a cumulative way. One of the most difficult things for a drama school is that they have all this different expertise, but they are all separately thrown at the young actor, so the learning gets segregated. So an Alexander teacher for example will come and say, 'good performance, but I think you have a neck thing here, which is just holding the expression of that voice'; then you get vocal teachers telling them different stuff in a different vocabulary. None of these things are incorrect technically, but if you are sending them, like mechanics, with a toolbox walking around their own psyche, walking around bits of their body, thinking, 'I have just got to hold my neck this way', or 'I just have to release my larynx this way, and I have to rethink that kind of structure in my head this way' – the nuts and bolts of fixing it – like a mechanic in a garage working on bits of a car, you will be endlessly working on bits of that car, without a picture of the whole car. It is about having a sense of focused wholeness, bringing all of these things into the actor, under the bonnet, so the whole thing has a connected tissue. I have worked with a whole variety of different people at all different ages and they say that they haven't properly had that experience.

What impact has your training had on your career?

I don't know. In a way, I think my training was up at the Citizens.

What was your first job?

I played Romeo at The Watermill, Newbury, with Kathryn Hunter as Juliet. I was amazed that, on the first Friday, somebody gave me an envelope with money in it. I don't know what my expectation of it was, it was immediately after RADA – it followed straight through. I was completely exhausted and what I should have done was rest. I do find institutions, no matter how good, are very institution-like inevitably; the wrong kind of energy had been going on in me for a while before I got let out of RADA. I needed a rest. It is easy to make so many mistakes with Romeo, it is really a very difficult part and looking back, I did find it difficult.

What did you find difficult?

Partly because Romeo is reactive, which, in a way, ought to be a gift. It is an easy mistake to play Romeo like Hamlet, but Hamlet is a thinker and Romeo is not. I wasn't reactive enough. Furthermore, it is quite hard playing Romeo when you had this idea of what Romeo is, symbolically, and I never thought for a second that I was Romeo or that I could be, I didn't have the requisite ego to think, 'oh yeah, of course I can be Romeo'.

Tell me about those people or events which have helped to form your artistic sensibilities. You left RADA, you had done Romeo and Juliet, *is that when you went to the Citizens in Glasgow?*

Funnily enough it wasn't. I left RADA in 1983, played in *Romeo and Juliet* almost immediately and then didn't work on stage for six years, when I did Büchner's *Leonce and Lena*, in 1989. It's an amazing piece; it almost invents about three different strands of theatre, which are absolutely central to the history and development of European theatre. It uses the structure of a fairy story to hide a satire that is both expressionistic and stunningly naturalistic. Doing that play was a plunge-pool experience.

Did that whet your appetite for theatre work again?

Yes, it really did. It's a communicative piece, but it's also tremendously mysterious. One thing I remember about *Leonce and Lena*, was that the local paper sent their football correspondent to review it. And he had a really good time. He said, 'I don't know what this was about, at all, but I thought it was bloody great'. It goes to the core of what I feel. Theatre shouldn't feel the need to explain itself. That man came, he frankly hadn't followed it, but he saw what it did, he felt what it did and he said so. It was honest and wise to say so; I wish some of our professional critics could be so wise. They think that they have to understand something for it to have merit; I simply don't know where that idea comes from. It is a completely false basis for reviewing, or looking at anything. If we fully understand the art piece, then it probably has limited value. It was then that the Citizens asked me to work there, in the early part of 1990 and that was the beginning of a ten-year attachment, which was extraordinarily influential, working for Philip Prowse, Robert David MacDonald and Giles Havergal.

You said previously that was where you received your training as an actor, could you explain that?

Well, the training was one of sensitisation to the experience of being in a thought structure, a picture structure and a directing structure – all the one thing – that the Citizens provided, because their design of everything was fundamentally responsive to the thought structures of the play and their own artistic response to it. That is basic for all design, but up there the level of accomplishment, as is well recognised, was quite considerable. I think Michael Coveney once described the style at the Citizens and the style of Philip Prowse as one of 'lush austerity'. They were very elastic and flexible, there was not just one look, but every look was informed by a visceral, direct and modern response to the thought structures of the plays. They did amazing translations of scenes exploding one into another. The first thing I ever saw there was Schiller's *Mary Stuart*: the first two thirds of the play were in near-pitch black, with just faces picked out, emphasizing the enclosed, the secretive, the politicking and subterfuge. At the moment of the big meeting between the two Queens, suddenly the faces disappeared and you heard this dull thumping sound: the stage had been surrounded by a black curtain, that fell away, thump by thump, revealing a complete white box behind. Everything which had been entirely black was now entirely white and leaves floated down to indicate you were in the open area in the forest and then the two Queens came on. Blazingly simple, extraordinarily effective; when your eyes have been used to an hour of utter blackness, to get this absolute blaze of white, exaggerated by light: you had to blink, literally blink, which, of course, was the feeling that Mary herself was feeling, having been incarcerated for so long. So everything is tactile, everything is essential to the passage of the plays and the experiences the characters are going through and they make you feel that in the audience too. That is just one very simple example of something that was characteristically and consistently rich and complex, at The Citz.

How was that applied to the actors in that framework?

Being directed by Philip was like finding yourself in exactly the right emotional position at any given point on the stage, and you either know that is what is happening and accept that, or you muddy it and you will find you are failing. The people they liked were actors who had a sense, a realisation, that they were being given an opportunity to be in the right space, at the right time, at the right rhythm – the emotional rhythm of the play. Prowse was a tremendously incisive, emotional and visceral director. It always felt that you were never in the wrong place emotionally, and that is a pretty difficult trick to pull off.

One of the charges laid at the Citizens, is that everything looked very pretty but the acting was poor.

The people who were at the Citizens constitute a long list of extremely famous people: so either they were just shockingly bad then and have come good, in some mysterious way, or the myth of The Citz not living up to the image in terms of the acting, is simply rubbish.

So what is the legacy of the Citizens on your personal development as an actor?

Well, everything. If I ever achieve a compression and authority about being the person I am portraying, about having a sense of emotional space and being aware of the rhythms of that space in relation to the language I am speaking, and the conflicts that are being enacted with the other bodies in space, all of that is entirely implied by every piece of direction that Philip gave. It's a compression of focus and a sense of the structure of things.

What was going on in the rehearsal room in The Citz masked a very great degree of sophistication. If you really fully gave yourself over to the sense of the emotional and picture space he was creating, then you would be all right.

Were there any other significant events or people at The Citz?

Yes, they then opened two new studios during the redesign of the building. At the same time, the ENO were really pushing forward the design of opera and shaping up the way opera was done and causing a lot of controversy (and also pleasure), so it was very active, at the edge there, artistically. Being an opera director and designer himself, Philip invited radical opera designers who wanted to direct in the theatre for the first time and gave them the new studios. So you had these really amazing designers directing plays for the first time and designing extraordinary things in the two new theatre spaces. I was very lucky to be in the first directions of some fantastic designer-directors, such as Stewart Laing, Antony McDonald, David Fielding and Nigel Lowry. Because it was a compressed example of it in those studios, that experience reminded me just how much design is an expression of a fabric of thought. When you are in a design you are in thinking, in a space where you have to plug into its thinking in order to execute that space to its best advantage: that sense is the single greatest thing that I got from my experience at The Citz.

When did you start working with Howard Barker?

I started working with Howard Barker in 1996, on the European tour of *(Uncle) Vanya*. It was a real baptism – every time things have lurched forward for me, it has tended to be like being cast into a plunge-pool. So *(Uncle) Vanya* was a fantastic shock by virtue of Howard's theatrical sensitivity to language, his sense of the flesh of language, its sinew, bite, what felt like its disciplined electricity. I'd only ever felt that with such force in the Jacobeans, and yet this was decidedly modern. I've just been talking about the thought fabric of a theatre design; his language is a theatre design, it seems to explode with a sense of space, and like all great language you will find that it will tell you where to go, by speaking it. I think with Pinter, you find the same effect – you will find yourself in the right place. Very different writers, but these are poetic texts, raised texts, that possess great, rigorous, practical force.

So the pattern developing in your work is about giving yourself permission, as an actor, to embrace both the physical and oral world in which you find yourself because, when you give yourself that permission, discoveries become apparent?

Completely.

Does that underpin your philosophy of acting?

Entirely. Maybe I am wrong about this, actors sometimes can think it has got to be a fight, that there is going to be a struggle, that it is going to be really difficult. And of course you can *predict* that difficulty into your thinking and cause yourself a lot of trouble that you need not have. It's a confusion about what serious work is; it's the wrong kind of hard time to be giving yourself. You have to nurture a facility for allowing yourself to be told something by the language itself; psyche is implicit in language, and that's the information that it will tell you, if you let it.

How do you prepare for an audition?

I've just been casting a production I'm about to direct. A stream of actors came in who were very impressive and I thought to myself, these guys really know what they are doing, I'm absolutely hopeless!

What were they doing that gave you that impression?

They just knew how to deliver the best of themselves in a frank way. They were allowing me to see what sort of actor they were; I suppose they were playing themselves very well, and that's a very useful talent in itself.

So, your agent phones up and says 'Gerrard, I've got you a meeting, for the National Theatre, they are doing a Strauss play, and you are up for part X'. How would you prepare yourself for that?

The basics: I read the play. I've always loved reading, and reading plays, and I tend to absorb them as much as read them, and I tend to be able to do this very quickly. Then I'll concentrate on the pages which they have suggested I take a look at.'

Do you learn it?

No, I don't think it is necessary and I think it is better to read off the page; often you are called into meet someone very quickly, and I don't think to have shallow-learnt it, is a good basis for delivering the best of yourself. So I don't ever learn it. Maybe that is where I am completely going wrong: in America, people turn up so prepared, so learnt, so ready to give every single possible reading and then they are told after thirty seconds to get out; that is what they do and that is what is expected... What is your experience, do people expect you to know something?

For television auditions, I have been finding myself learning things, because I think there is more pressure to be the product, in that medium. I think that is less true of theatre. However, the more familiar one is with both the play as a whole and any particular sections that you want to discuss, the better you are: the more you can equip yourself to talk about it, the better. Sometimes, because I am a very fast study and rarely have to sit down and learn lines, come the audition, I semi know it, in sections.

I read it, but I can't learn as you learn, I can't absorb it. In terms of learning, I just have to learn.

If you were auditioning for a play and you were going to play a fireman would you research firemen, fire-fighting and fires?

Well, I have always thought that the world of the play will give me what I need to know. But I am not sure if I am entirely right about that. I worked with Kathryn Hunter who does an enormous amount of work to do with the experience that goes on in a play and she will investigate everywhere outside it: if she is supposed to be a painter, she'll spend days with a painter and paint. Because I have never done that, I am not able to judge its value. The question is open as to whether someone with extraordinary imagination, such as Kathryn, actually needs to do that. But that's what she does and she obviously does it for very serious artistic reasons and so I can only respect them. You are in a play about horses at the moment. Have you gone and seen horses? Would you find a need to do so?

I am playing a character that is expert in his handling of horses, so I did go to a horse-training centre, The Kelly Marks Centre in Oxfordshire, where people send horses which are regarded as difficult or problematic. Kelly and her team train them to be calm and responsive and actually, what they are really doing is training the owners, not just the horses, in a new vocabulary of communication. As I have to interact with the horses, in the action of the play, I learnt physical gestures and psychological insights.

And those physical gestures, I imagine, must have informed other things.

They certainly directly informed the staging. It is probably hard to say whether an audience member would have known that I had done that. I don't think so. Whether it helped me in my creation of the character, I can't tell, but it raised as many questions as it answered. For example, Kelly's progressive training methods are based upon a late 20th-, early 21st-century view on how you should train horses (developed, articulated and taught by the horse-whisperer, Monty Roberts), but I am playing an early 20th-century character, somebody who was born at the end of the 19th century who, although he clearly has a good relationship with horses is nevertheless, from that world. The question arises as to whether adopting the 'new' received behavioural practices of Kelly's training is a period anachronism and therefore hindrance to the storytelling. On the other hand, what does that phrase, 'from that world', actually mean? Is an adherence to so-called period behaviour a useful, specific detail or simply more generalization, in disguise? I was quite often confused during that rehearsal period, in respect of wanting to be faithful to period detail while telling the story effectively, to a 21st-century audience, of a specific man who is profoundly, joyously, at ease with horses. I am always wary of doing generalised research, because I am not sure how much it contributes to the specificity of the character. On the other hand there are things like knowing how to hold a paintbrush or, in a restoration comedy, knowing how to use your handkerchief – those are technical requirements, which one should learn. Whether I will learn about my character, who happens to be a painter, or enrich my characterisation, if I do an art course, or if I sit and talk with professional artists, is unquantifiable. There is a danger that it leads, not towards specificity, but to generalisation. So you can say let's see if this will happen, and an actor might say 'Well, no, painters don't do that.' But it's not any painter, so that is not a useful thing to say. I think that research has to be underpinned by the question, 'What is useful?' You should always retain that at the forefront of your mind's eye. Is this useful? How will it be useful?

Me too: I have always been dubious that it has been necessary, or that it might even, in a way, muddy and conflict, if I wasn't careful. But I really don't know the answer to it.

Let's talk about rehearsals. You have had your audition and you have got the job. In your ideal world, you have a couple of weeks, while you enjoy the fact that you have been given the job, unexpectedly – to this day, I am still shocked when I get a job – so you get that period of enjoyment, of elation…

In many ways, it's the best bit.

Why is that?

It's pressing the pleasure centre without any hangover, I guess.

How do you prepare for the start of rehearsals?

I tend to do very little overtly. I read the play and then I re-read it several times; an enormous amount of stuff will be happening in the back of my head while I do other things. I suppose this is a common experience. Ideas will come to the surface: ways of walking, ways of breathing, sensation of language, sensation of the character, will begin to enter me while I am doing something else.

And that happens as a result of multiple readings of the play?

Yes, a few.

Do you ever learn the lines before rehearsals?

Never. I find it really valuable walking around with a script. It allows me to sight-read and feel, at the same time. Once you have learnt it there is inevitably a tendency to dictate what you should be doing to yourself rather than allowing yourself to do something. I think it facilitates you: it allows you to be released into something, rather than to dictate it.

What do you like to do in rehearsals? If a director said to you, 'Here we are, you are playing Prospero, this is day one of rehearsals, what would you like to do?' What are the favourite things that you have done over your extensive career?

One of the reasons I, latterly, became interested in process is because I have never done any. I mean, the companies I'd worked for had not largely been interested in using unusual processes to arrive at an aesthetic. The Citizens, or The Wrestling School Howard Barker Company already had aesthetics that provided a clear landscape for you to respond to, and inhabit. When I worked with Improbable, I was absorbed by their processes and their flexibilities, their playing around with things and their sidelong looks at the doing in a rehearsal room, looking out of the corner of their eyes at things, as opposed to looking at it straight on. That has always been attractive to me, because I think that I think in a sideways way as well. Experiencing that in the rehearsal process with Improbable made that physically apparent: they take the assemblage of lateral thinking out of the body and put it on view. It was a fantastic experience, a good human experience. I liked the serious comedy of doing that, very much.

When you say 'put it on view', did you find an object to represent something and place it somewhere so that every time you talked about it, you went there?

It's not as explicit as that; it was a way of talking and thinking about it. When you do something in a space, you are really dropping into that space and, having done that, you represent a shape in that space and that is a very graceful thing. The Improbable sensitisation to that way of feeling about oneself, in terms of persona or character, is attractive and true. They were making explicit things that I have always done, in my jumbled assemblage of oddities. To have that made explicit in a rehearsal room and to allow yourself to make that a concrete experience, seemed true and sentient.

What in your experience is a bad rehearsal? Or a bad rehearsal period?

I worked for somebody once and I didn't enjoy the process at all: it seemed to be a process of constant interference rather than allowance and that is about judgment isn't it? This was a person, actually, who believed in process and I had always worked for people who had no knowledge of, or interest in, an actor's process. Because they didn't have knowledge of it, they weren't going to affect it. They wanted to see what you did. So it is ironic that the person who was most interested in process was the person I felt least free with, and most inhibited by.

Do you think the process director essentially didn't trust the actors and the people who are uninterested in actors' process trust you to do what you do?

Completely, of course he was simply not doing it well enough, in terms of allowing people to feel free. This is wildly discursive, but it relates to being dictated to and being free, and how some critics want to talk about theatre as if it's a social program. I read an article in the paper this week about anger in California. There is a whole industry spawning in California out of people getting angry with each other. The courts are sending more and more people to anger management courses as part of their sentence, whether it be as community service, or merely accepting that you have a problem with anger. For example, a woman, whose disabled child needed to go to hospital because he was hurt, was angry at the ambulance worker who didn't seem to be doing anything and so she shouted at him. The ambulance worker complained, she was taken to court and sent to anger management classes. The journalist who had written the article said she had the perfect right, in that stressful incident, to let off steam about the fact that nothing seemed to be happening about her disabled son who was in physical trouble. He expected her to say, 'it's ridiculous being sent here'. None of them did: they all said, 'they were right, I do have a problem with anger, it doesn't resolve anything, it doesn't make anything happen more quickly'. They accepted that the courts in California had been right to remonstrate with them and to force them to understand that they couldn't be angry people. These people are being reprogrammed because they are not allowed to be angry in California. Now this can relate to what is seen as the social purpose of theatre.

In what way?

It goes back to my complaint that theatre has to mean something, that it has to have a moral purpose, that you have to learn something social from it and that it will reprogram us in better ways of thinking and behaving. The Californian action is not so much about controlling aggression as being aggressively controlling. And neither can you control the experience of art, or of responses to art. Theatre is an experience; it is not about teaching stuff. Van Gogh isn't teaching you stuff, when you stand in front of a painting of his. He is not teaching you anything: he is communicating his experience of himself, in response to those cornfields or to that sunflower. That is what you should be allowing yourself to feel through that dry paint. Van Gogh does have moral force, if you like, but that isn't his purpose, in the utilitarian sense. He is not telling you about cornfields. It is not an agrarian subject, in the sense of a learning curve and my complaint about critics is that they seem to keep telling us that we have to draw conclusions of some kind from our experience of the theatre. I think Michael Billington, in particular, is very bad in this area; I am frustrated by it, because it stops people from seeing what is actually in front of them. If critics cannot see what is in front of them, because they are looking for the programmable, often humanitarian, morally improving 'meaning', they cannot report the experience. People talk about why Tynan was fantastic and why we don't have someone like that now, to the point of boredom, but I think that the essence of it is that Tynan wrote about experience and today's critics think they need to be writing about something else, that to report experience is not enough. That's wrong. It just is. To relate it to that talk about California, that phrase, 'what we learn' in this play is of agressive intent, because it dictates the, 'what' and the 'how' of how we, as an audience, receive a play: there is not one thing to learn from a great play. What one thing do you learn from *The Tempest*? I don't know what that is. But I'm constantly reading critical reports that tell me the thing that I learn from this or that new play. There aren't things to be learnt, there are just things to be felt and communicated. That is why theatre is theatre and not journalism.

Just to relate that back to the bad rehearsal: bad rehearsals prescribe the limits of potential investigation and therefore good rehearsals liberate and enable a breadth of exploration?

It's complicated isn't it? Because the most liberal of rehearsals and the most conducive for passages of creation have been by directors who very often tell you what to do.

They give you a structure or a framework?

Yes that is the key. And both a director who is interested in process and a director who isn't can do that. It is just that simple: you are given structure.

Is there any particular rehearsal technique that you find useful, in your experience as an actor or as a director? Something which liberates a script or the character you are playing?

I would say an entire disjuncture from what you are doing is sometimes the most informing thing: you learn a great deal by suddenly not doing the thing that you are supposed to be doing and doing the opposite. When I worked with Improbable, we were waiting for the boat to be unloaded at the dock in Sydney – we had no set and we were up on Thursday – so we had more rehearsal time than we otherwise would have. We did an 'exaggeration run', where you exaggerate everything to the nth degree, so that you really make manifest intention and feeling, physically and in your voice, and you are invited to express it in the most various ways possible, according to changing instructions. It is a complete dislocation, but it is extraordinary the level of information you get back – about what seems true and what seems false. It is a really effective and fun thing to do; a real liberation and test of your metal – but, again, as you say, in relaxation and without pressure. This goes back to the idea that when you are not looking for something you allow yourself to be sensitised to the information you need.

When you are not willing something to happen, things happen because you are in a state of readiness, or openness, to receive them?

Yes, that's right.

How do you deal with technical rehearsals? Does your own sense of rehearsal go into suspense, or does it actually develop, or even accelerate, during technical?

I enjoy techs: rehearsal doesn't get suspended during that period at all. Because you are fulfilling certain technical requirements, there is an interesting displacement: being on stage when people are still walking around and banging nails, or reaching to put lights on you, allows you to be in the space and feel things in a different way. And it is very enlightening.

It is also the first time that you will really begin to feel the sound of yourself in that particular space, which is also extremely instructive. So, I certainly don't switch off at all, I find it absorbing: it's like putting on a pair of shoes, in a way. Enormous things can and do happen when you set foot on a good set. It's a fusion process: things, which have been in your head and your body in the rehearsal room, suddenly find their place where they can settle and expand. One is always sensing how this might work, how to expand into that space, it's a gripping process – the things in your head being made physical and real.

I have recently come out of a technical rehearsal phase, which reminded me what a pragmatic art form it is. It is a time to find what worked – why and how it worked – and also, therefore, what didn't work. Certain things that you cherish in a rehearsal room have to be sacrificed, as a result of what you discover in the technical rehearsal, because the new environment is where the storytelling is going to happen and the auditorium is where you have to deliver that story.

I also find the technical romantic; there is some real romance about being in a technical and having the set finalised around you and everything coming together; all the practical business is very romantic still for me.

What about when you step onto a set, which just doesn't work for you, or if you step into a costume, which you don't find useful? Has that happened?

In the case of a set which you don't find particularly inspiring, you are working so practically at that stage, because performance is imminent, that you tend to dismiss things that don't work and you look for positives. You look for the thing that does work. It is a very practical, time-pressed period. Techs are all about time, in a way: the whole play slows down, because you are not doing it at proper speed. It is a fractured, slow process, but it also has this sense of impending doing, so you have a squashing feeling too, because you know this is just a little bubble before it pops and you are on the stage in real performance. It's a practical lacuna where you simply have got to make a lot of pretty fast and often very sensory decisions, to do with costume, lighting, with all of those things.

Do you find, in your experiences as an actor, that you are enabled to make those decisions? For example, if the costume isn't working for you, do you have to put up and shut up – particularly given that it is a time-pressed situation – or can you have a discussion where you reach a situation, which is to your satisfaction?

I can't recall a big problem of that kind. Anyway, I think, the great thing about theatre is that it is a team sport – it is not just your own ego. I love being a part of something, a part of a group, a part of the practice of putting something together, so one tends to be entirely co-operative and want to make something work as much as you possibly can, and if it doesn't, then hopefully you are with people who can see that it is not going to happen.

Does your work, as both a director and a workshop leader, positively inform your work as an actor?

Yes, undoubtedly it does. I think I understand how things are much more complex than I thought, which is always a useful sort of car crash experience.

Are there things that you see when you are in your director's seat, so to speak, which you can then apply to your next acting job?
I have always had a problem with trying to work too fast and when I see actors slowing themselves down, I am reminded that I should do that too. I really begin to see that value of things which, before, I had not found to be useful: ways of thinking or ways of allowing. I admire actors more and more; they are quite remarkable. I think human beings acting – at serious play through acting – is so deliciously fundamental to being alive. It resonates something out of the human, which is touching and brilliant, and it reminds you of the grace and ability that exists in the spirit of people, which puts you back in touch with why it is good to be alive.

Are there occasions when the move from directing back to acting work has been difficult, where it has not been useful to have a director's perspective?

It is a little difficult sometimes: you have to be sure you have your actor filter on and close off the directing filter.

How do you cope with rejection, and unemployment?

With somnambulism.

Have you developed that consciously, or is it part of your character?

I think you have to develop it. I remember auditioning for a play that I really, really wanted to be in and it was being directed by somebody who knew my work and had seen me in something that I had been very proud to be in. And it would have been a good career thing, not that I think in those terms at all, but it was important to me. I didn't get that job and I was genuinely upset, and I did think, 'I really, really just wish I didn't do this'. And someone said to me, 'yeah, but you choose to do it' and I said what I think is true about actors: 'I didn't choose to do it, it chose me'. I think that is a very common bond which actors have – they haven't chosen to do it, it has chosen them. Otherwise you would be mad to do this job, it is an appalling job – at least psychologically. That was one time, when my somnambulism didn't work.

So what did you do then to get over it?

I don't think I did anything, that's the thing, you just accept.

How do you maintain your motivation and your skills base if you are unemployed?

I don't go to acting classes, I don't do that sort of thing at all. I don't know if I do anything. Coming back to stage work, after that early six-year break, I could hardly walk and chew gum at the same time and I remember feeling completely discombobulated, as if I had just been dragged off the street and told to put a costume on and do something. The thing that works about acting, whether playing Sweeny Todd or Mother Theresa, is that it has grace and rhythm in it; I felt so graceless and so unrhythmical when I was trying to rehearse after my six-year break, and it was a really unpleasant experience. So you do have to find ways to maintain that sense of yourself; it can perish; it is not like riding a bike, it really isn't.

It is, slightly tricky though: you can attend classes, but unless the process is orientated towards a product it can feel like navel-gazing.

I was thinking that. I only work well when there is a product in view, without a product I feel in limbo. But then I was asked to lead a series of workshops in South Australia where there was no explicit objective, except for what I decided to pursue myself, and it made me consider my approach to the work that I am doing, because I had never thought it through, in any fuller way. I'd been struck by reading of the aspirations expressed by the Russian formalists at the beginning of the 20th century. Briefly, they sought to free poetics by stretching language beyond its ordinary range of meaning and posed the question of how does literary language function versus ordinary language? I became particularly interested in a Russian formalist called Shklovsky, who assigned all literary devices to one central use that he called ostranenie – making strange, to defamiliarise, to creatively deform the normal; and that seems to be going on in the searching, explorative theatre here. I was also thinking of Gertrude Stein's uses of language: she wrote a series of small plays in which the event of the play is the word itself, as much as any actual narrative. In fact the narrative is actually the use of and the cadence of the word, which she has plotted for you. So, as a result of the invitation to lead these workshops, I was actually going through a process of de-familiarising myself with what had become extremely familiar to me.

What was that?

I was trying to see fresh the things that I very quickly made decisions about. I always read readily and quickly off the page and I loved language and speech, the physical sense of one word spreading to another – how it jagged and exploded, one from another. From a very early age, I found a sense of excitement and play, a relish in the physical notation in the mouth, of what the tongue is doing, and a sensory pleasure in making language, and sound. I'd become interested in stripping language, on the page, down to physical sensitisation and re-sensitising yourself to what that actual pleasure is, by slowing everything down, so you could re-find that fundamental pleasure. and crucially, away from the tyranny of a customary conception of character. I wanted the focus to be trying to arrive at a feeling for the identity of a persona and its possibilities, through the cadences, the sound structure of the text. The speaking of words is a wholly visceral experience, and the sound is coming from your body, so of course the sound affects the body, in how it is producing it; naturally, it's all one thing, and that is what I was trying to get back to, and see what sense of identity arose by making almost no traditional character decisions. You can work backwards, can't you? If you don't know what something means you can investigate the pattern of its consequence and then work out what it means. So, if you are puzzled by your character – you don't know how he moves, how he sounds – any great writer will have instinctively been unable to do anything other than write in a way that will tell you, in the patterning of the language, all about that character, in the innermost beat of him, out of the texture and pulse of the language. I was interested in something Gore Vidal wrote. He said he stopped writing history because, 'I never cared *what* happened, I wanted to know *why* it happened. I couldn't find out, so I quit. Well, then I changed my mind. I started wanting to know *what* happened, and I don't care why it happened, because if you get *what* happened in the proper sequence and tell it as truthfully as you can, it is like stringing beads and you are going to end up with a pattern, which will be the answer to the question, "*Why?*"' In the same way there will be a pattern, information, in language, on the page, which will tell you the why because of the what; because of what is happening in your body, what you are allowing yourself to be sensitised to, because of the way in which the language is forming you, taking you and what it is doing to you. I very strongly believe that. It is beyond sense-meaning. It's allowing the language to enact itself on you.

How do you enable yourself to allow that to happen?

I think it is a question of predicting less. We can fail to recognise how highly predictive we can be when we read something and in the way it comes into us. These workshops focused on ways of slowing everything down so as to allow as much as possible. It wasn't about thinking about meaning, it was about thinking about sound. If you went with the sound, meaning would come and once we stopped thinking about meaning, and just concentrated on sound-making, instead of thinking about character, most particularly, which can actually be the biggest block of all to real discovery in the text; these assumptions about character. It was surprisingly interesting to find just how much meaning there was.

And how did you do that, did you first of all take the words away completely so that all you made was sound?

No, not that, but just to play with this idea of ostranenie – to creatively deform the normal – all the exercises aimed creatively to defamiliarize one's own way of working towards the sense of things. We are all caught up in meaning: 'what is the main meaning of a play? What does the character mean?' There was an interesting game Keith Johnstone spoke about, which is not even numbered as one of his exercises proper, but one of the first things he ever tried was to make people go around the room, point at objects and call them by a different name. It is an amazingly powerful and ridiculously simple game and fun, pointing at a clock and calling it a bin. By disentangling an object from its known name you release yourself into the sound of the language because it no longer has a connection to the object and so you just naturally get sensation. You are immediately put into an abstract sensitisation process and you feel a word on your tongue much more readily than just pointing at a piano and saying that is a piano, it is a completely different experience, re-sensitising yourself to the feel of making language in your mouth, and to its suggestive power. Then he asked, what is the room like now? It is a very unexpected question. And most people's replies were that a) the room was bigger and b) there was more colour in the room; so dealing with your tongue and disconnecting it from your brain had in fact sensitised them entirely, in spatial and in colour terms, and that was a very profound discovery of experience. It is remarkable because it is the simplest thing you could ever ask anyone to do, but incredibly effective.

Johnstone speculated that, according to Socratic principle, genius involves the unlearning of that which we have learned, shedding the skin of our culture and education. Once experienced, genius can be recaptured again and again by the person who learns. Anyway, whatever the truth of that, what we were trying to do was a little 'un-thinking' of accepted ways into text or conceptions of character, governed by the idea that any kind of poetic writing will have, inbuilt in it, cadences and sound structures, a shaping of the instinctive and in terms of a persona, a psyche.

Take, Macbeth's 'tomorrow and tomorrow and tomorrow…'. The 20th century philosopher Adorno said 'we don't understand music, music understands us', so the aurality of meaning is vital in how we receive and deliver language. From 'tomorrow' to 'heard no more', we have a symphony of the plosive *t*, *d*, *p* and sinuous, insinuating *s*, in conjunction with vowels, which are, by turns, either curtailed by the consonants (petty, pace), in order to give them bite, or opened out (day, to day), in order to give the thoughts momentum so that, in a way, you can't do anything but land on 'no more' because a) of its placement, and b) the plosives melt away to assist the landing on 'no more'. Then you are back: 'It is a tale told by an idiot,' *t*, *t*, and *d*, 'full of sound and fury signifying nothing'. So if you have a whole speech predicated on *t*, *d*, *p* and *s*, you have a speech which basically would seem to me to be about a man just spitting at life. This whole speech is one long spit, which seems absolutely right, for this character at this point. This whole speech is tomorrow...nothing; everything in between is a musical notation, which takes him from the thought of tomorrow to the thought of nothing and the compression of that. And furthermore, tomorrow and tomorrow and tomorrow creeps; that is a very ugly sound, the double *e*, creeps, the *s* into the *i*, creeps in this petty pace, so they expand into the last syllable of time. This speech is telling you how to say it, isn't it?

There are clues.

But it is more than that. If you allow yourself to lean into the language and let it take you from tomorrow through to nothing, you can hardly not get what is going on in every facet of Macbeth's head – if you have proper confidence that Shakespeare has written the whole psychology of this character at this point in his life, at this point in the play. The sound sense of his spitting weariness and utter decay of self is in the entire soundscape and rhythmic patterning of this speech and if you allow yourself to say it without thinking how you are going to play Macbeth, you are going to get an enormous amount of information from it because you will not be predicting the way you want to play Macbeth. Struts and frets is a platform that sinks into the opening of vowels in his hour upon the stage, the former embodying the sort of spitting structures that I was suggesting, and the hour and stage become certainly sardonic, deeply sarcastic, in whole withering, sinking tones; this is not a line or an idea that is going upwards, it is falling downwards.

In its inflection, as well?

Yes, it necessarily must, because of the structure and patterning of cadence: the language is a notation of a whole poetic sensibility and psychology and not just a series of psychological clues; it is much more than that, and if we could get back to some sense of that in the way people play these plays and speak them then I think we would be plugging into a better sense of the rhetorical.

Why do you think we are divorced from that currently?

Practice, custom, a misapplied Stanislavski, which can lead people to think that the play is all about them. The play is about Macbeth, it is not about them.

Them as actors?

Yes, their feelings. Their twists and knots and turns. Of course, to be fully inhabited, you need to be in Macbeth and Macbeth has to be in you and you cannot be anything other than what you are, but there is patterning and colour and music and flavour in 'tomorrow and tomorrow and tomorrow…': you need to let that come into you first, before you start bashing yourself about on it. You don't know what you are bashing yourself about on, until you have allowed yourself to soak that up, like blotting paper and have some sense and feel of it; if you don't do that, you will be blocking yourself, because you will be making decisions too quickly, or you will be making decisions that are based on you, not on the text. So before you make decisions on you, you need to not make any decisions and allow this to do something to you, through its sound and how it forms itself in your mouth and on your tongue. You will come to a sense of utter clarity of Macbeth's degraded situation and his degraded self, that he is this fool, he is this idiot, this spitting self-contempt: that is in every single wretched lengthening of vowel and spitting of plosive. It is an entire self-loathing, self-aware, degraded poetic self-examination and, naturally, of Man himself, hostile to the whole species, and the stretch, tug, compression and feel of this whole examination of self in nine and a half lines is incredible. 'Signifying nothing', and then four empty beats at the end of it. Those lost beats are the nothing, the 'petty pace' beating in a void. There are ways of responding to rhetoric and allowing it to come into yourself, and allowing yourself to bathe in it and it can tell you stuff that you need to do.

Before you apply an intellectual sense-meaning?

Yes. I think that order is crucial. I went to see Sarah Kane's *Blasted*, in a production by Thomas Ostermeier, for the brillliant Schaubühne Theatre, last year; well the stage set certainly got blasted, huge set resources, fantastic, the rhetoric of the design was so big, yet the way in which they all spoke to each other was so small and it seemed to me that that encapsulated what I feel is a flight from rhetoric, which exists in our theatre culture: the rhetoric, the actual speaking had been reduced in the flavoursomeness of its own sonic power: as an act of artistic expression, it had been deliberately reduced to a very null, nothing sound and instead the rhetoric had been pumped into the devices of staging. It did demonstrate for me that rhetoric is so embedded in theatre that it can't be squeezed out; it has to go somewhere. It's like squeezing a balloon in your hand, it just expands around it. I saw Martin Crimp's *The City* recently where there was such a strong attempt to completely disenfranchise the audience from any rhetorical experience, any emotional experience, that the whole thing really had become a kind of enigmatic art object; a cul de sac nullity.

Can you define what you understand to be a rhetorical experience?

An experience of sound, with all that that implies, because sound is emotional, sound is psyche and the Greek word psyche means soul and soul is in sound-making. The other word for character which we use is 'persona', which is thought to relate to 'personare', to sound through – a character is created and transmitted through sound. The house of theatre has a lot of rooms and, at the moment, the room where you hear sound, where actors can speak in that sensitised way, seems to have been annexed down a long corridor off to the side; it is partly a fear of being melodramatic or rhetorical in the wrong way, or of creating a wash of sound, an unfeeling sound, an un-thought sound, or a generalised expression of emotion. But I think the flight has been way too strong. People are running for cover from it, but what I am speaking about is repossessing the expression of psychologically-driven sound released from the body, and the skills and sensibility involved in finding it's resonance on the modern stage. This is emphatically removed from any 19th century idea of declamatory noise, if that, in fact, is what went on. But it IS rhetoric, and it is not just speaking on a stage, with variably successful attempts at projection, with emotion or truth, naturalism, or reality; it embodies those things, but it is a much larger thing, and more fundamental to a living, vivified, resonating theatre than any of them. That is why I enjoyed the discovery of working with Howard Barker. Sarah Kane called Howard the greatest playwright of her age. She was right, I think. Known internationally, played all over the world,

University departments and Drama schools absorbed in his work, and yet as far as the established theatre culture in England here is concerned, he's been sectioned. But I wonder who is in the prison? Theatre has been turned into an entertainment culture almost entirely, or into a programme of moral or journalistic enlightenment, as we've been talking about. In that culture you not only don't require rhetoric, you can't allow it. The first thing I ever did with Howard was (Uncle) Vanya and I went for an audition with him for the part of Vanya. The play opens with Uncle Vanya self-incriminatingly saying, 'Un-cle Van-ya, Un-cle Van-ya': he is investigating the sound of his own name, which is a diminutive – he is absolutely patted on the head when people call him Uncle Vanya – so the play starts with his renunciation of this. I started reading it in a kind of musing fashion, musing on the sound of 'Un-cle Van-ya', and there are separate strings of these, and Howard said, 'I think it is a bit more than that, these are really cries from the soul, and we meet him at the beginning of a crisis'; so I had to address the intensity of it, testing the sound of that diminutive and really you have to do that from the bottom of your self and that is really what Howard wanted and that was quite right for the character. I knew I was in the right place because someone had written a text in which I knew there was a huge diversity in the landscape of sound and it was written on that basis and I was unafraid of it: a lot of people seem to be afraid, in the writing of a play, of the fundamental potentialities of the voice.

Can you identify the cause of that?

Well as I say, it is a fear of all the wrong things, because if you do it truthfully, in response to the right moment, in the right text, nothing is ever going to seem melodramatic or wrong. I think there is an embarrassment factor, a cultural factor which says that an art object should be cool; it's fashionable to be that kind of cool, to be cool is apparently to be thinking and to be a cool object is culturally acceptable at the moment in the theatre, because coolness shows rationality and intelligence and a clarity of thinking and it is a fashion.

What about the idea that the emotion, the hot as opposed to cool, is expressed through the thought and therefore the clarity of thought is important for that reason?

Yes, but your question pre-supposes they are opposed to each other; but hot is not unthinking, passion is not lacking thought. Barker is 'cool', Barker objectifies, and his characters objectify themselves, under the severe scrutiny of event, and of their own consequent examination of their identity, and yet the temperature of their experience is hot, as it is for us all. Their depths exist on their surface, resonant, visceral, alert, alive, complex. They have an immediacy of self, and are consumed by thinking, re-thinking and then recreating themselves all the time, and they have to do this with the most fantastic resource, otherwise, if they stopped speaking they wouldn't exist anymore. They need to speak in order to define the situation they are in and to be hot does not mean to be incapable of rationality and thinking.

Is the retreat from rhetoric related to the influence of television and film?

Yes, inevitably, it must be.

What is it that theatre offers that other art forms don't offer, or can't?

Well, it offers itself doesn't it? The thing that it really offers is the breathing living psyche that is in the space in front of you, that makes psychological sound, that comes back to you and hits your body and you can't get that from other media. It is a visceral experience based on the breath of the human body. That is why it is great and that is why I am talking about breath and sound-making and allowing those things to infuse you. There was an interesting study that showed humans creating a neural representation in their brains of actions or emotions that were witnessed, that were indistinguishable from those that would be created by the actual experience itself. This would fit the contention that sight and sound in the theatre would have neural effects on the audience beyond surface comprehension. And this is the feeling I'm talking about. When we remember that the sounds on the stage that the actors are speaking are a notation on the page from the mind of a poetic writer, then there is a direct channel there from psyche to psyche that is happening at a neural level.

What do you think is the greatest threat to theatre currently? Or what is the greatest threat to theatre making?

I think there is a lot of diversity about and the testing is there and I think that is good, but I think that we, in the theatre, have got to fight in a certain form the same battle that the Saatchi generation, the YBAs, fought in their critical art culture in the early Eighties; fought and won. The only reason they won was because Mr Saatchi had enormous amounts of money and could put on shows, could utilise the money in the market, had key people at various points in the art world, whether it be Norman Rosenthal at The Royal Academy or Nicholas Serota at the Tate that were all agreed on that same agenda. As a result, they were able to defy critical culture and keep shows running, to create time and space for the public to come and say, 'well that's not just crazy sensationalist, thin, unfabricated work that doesn't in any way reflect skill.' So artists and public alike were given the structure in that art culture at the time, the space in which the critics could not just say 'oh that is horrible I don't understand it, it is just rubbish', but where the public could take time to get to know it, and that is what I think we need in the theatre and we don't have that space in the theatre.

What is art, and what is it for? You talked about the Damien Hirst generation having space to create shocking work; is that the point of art?

No, the point of art is not to shock. It may be one of its aspects. The point of art is to construct something, in some media, that is a way of fashioning who we are at any given point, whether it is a theatre piece or whatever, something of what we are.

Francis Bacon said the point of art is to deepen the mystery. Arthur Miller would say that there is a very strong moral purpose to art. Andrei Tarkovsky suggested that it is to bring man closer to God, so where do you stand in those things?

'A very strong moral purpose', I'm probably not going to go along with that one. I'd tend to think of that as an effect more than a purpose, as a definition. I like this definition of ostranenie by Shklovsky so much, which was to defamiliarize; to creatively deform the usual is a fantastic function for art. To refresh. To re-see. To define us and to experience us.

Does art necessarily have to have a transformative impact?

Because it has a transformative impulse it has got to have a transformative impact. I just don't see how one doesn't lead to the other.

Is that what distinguishes art from entertainment? What is the relationship between art and entertainment? For example, Tarkovsky would say there is none.

To be entertained by something I think is a very, very good thing. I am entertained by what Robert Wilson does. I don't see to be unentertained is a necessary condition of art.

Is there a difference between the public's need for art and the artist's need?

Yes.

What are they? What does the artist need?

The artist's need is that Van Gogh couldn't have been Van Gogh unless he painted. Barker cannot not write.

So it is a drive for self-expression?

Yes, it is a completely innate need. And people, who go to drama school, take that step because they need to do that. No one makes a career move in that direction, do they? Well, maybe some do, maybe some think, I've got good pecs and a washboard stomach, I'm good looking and I can make as much money as Brad Pitt and live with sexy Hollywood goddesses, I mean it is not a bad drive, is it? But, I don't know.

Is it entirely egotistical then?

Well, it should be egotistical with a purpose, and as long as the aesthetic purpose remains bigger than you, then the drive in you is being turned to a useful creative energy. That question is hinting that ego is regarded culturally with some suspicion here, it's not polite to be seen to have any, which is curious since nothing could be created without it, but it's a good drive, that should come from creative need. I get a sense that, at the very root of feeling about actors in this country, that underneath appreciation and even pride, that there is still something instinctive in the cultural bloodstream, in England, which is that somehow acting is still, really, only showing off. I mean Judi Dench is hugely admired and deservedly much loved– but are people really aware of what, technically, she is capable of and what she is doing? Not really.

Would you want them to be?

Yes, I would want them to. Theatre is a completely practical ordering, it is not some slumming around in some emotional wash and you need a big range of skill in order to achieve the highest effects possible and to resonate at requisite levels. That is the way Harold Hobson and Ken Tynan used implicitly to regard what they were watching and I don't believe that is in our critical culture today. I don't believe it is in the English bloodstream culturally, to recognise the skill sets that are on show. For example, sound-making and rhetoric are not being addressed, and I am not really seeing that skill level sought for in the product, because they are making 'cool' product, or because the dominant lingua franca is naturalism, and there can't be rhetoric in naturalism, can there? But naturalism IS a rhetoric, and you have to use rhetorical skills very skillfully indeed to make naturalism resonate in the theatre space. The range of skill to release that too often is not sought for, recognised, or wanted. This saddens me because I think one of the essential skill sets is the sound that comes out of our bodies and the psyche, which that feels and expresses, and the technical control of that. You can't control it if you are not doing it, you are not doing it if you are not showing off that skill set, and that skill set is the central skill that is at the core of the performer, who is a bigger performer and a greater one when they know that stuff in their bodies and in their heads. Mark Rylance in *Jerusalem* is an example of a performer treating naturalism as simply another theatre rhetoric, which is right.

When does an actor become an artist? Is an actor an artist?

I don't know and I don't care, but I would like there to be a greater cultural appreciation that you are certainly watching skill, not just ego.

I sometimes lament, when I go to the theatre, that that is all I see.

What, skill, professionalism?

Yes.

That is not what I am talking about though.

If I am aware of the skill all the time I lose that sense of magic that I first had when I first saw theatre. It was a visceral experience which affected me physically, I watched something and I wasn't aware of what they were doing but I was completely impressed by it. If you have a critical culture, which alerts an audience to the fact that so and so did a, b and c and that was brilliant, will they not always be looking for that? Will they not be looking for skills rather than receiving a story?

No, I don't think that is a consequence. I am not just talking dry sets when I am talking about skill sets, and when I am talking about sound-making I am talking about getting to the visceral projection of psyche, feeling and truth expressed outward to the audience, physically through sound when it hits you. This, of course, requires a skillset to be able to transmit it, to discover it to the audience as it were, but I'm really speaking about the actor first discovering what is really there in the notation of the text, which is a notation of psyche in sound, which is drenched in subtle and creative information for the actor, particularly when it is wrenched away from the traditionally perceived tools for making character. So I am completely at one with that earliest experience of yours. That is what the flight away from rhetoric is precisely missing: you are just getting a skill set in a dry way being presented to you.

GABRIEL GAWIN

Gabriel is a founding member, Principal Performer and Associate Director with Teatr Piezn Kozła in Wroclaw, Poland. He also holds a part-time post as Senior Lecturer in Theatre Practice at Manchester Metropolitan University in the UK where he teaches and directs across the Acting and MA programmes. His work as a Theatre Practitioner includes collaborations with Peter Brook and the Centre International de Création Théâtrale; *Macbeth* for the City Theatre in Addis Ababa, Ethiopia; 8 yrs as Principal Performer and work leader with Teatr Piesn Kozla in Wroclaw Poland; *La Tempestad* for Zecora Ura in UK, Spain and Brazil; *Twelfth Night* for OffdeBic in Sopot; 5 years as Artistic Director of New Breed Theatre, the ground breaking disabled Peoples Theatre in Manchester. He has directed and created work with many UK Theatre companies including: Communicado in Edinburgh; The Dukes Playhouse in Lancaster; York Theatre Royal; Contact Theatre Co in Manchester; Northumberland Theatre Co.

POK   *How long have you been an actor?*

GG   Twenty-four years.

What would you do if you weren't an actor?

I would probably go into some type of therapeutic practice. I'm interested in the notion of using the human skills that I have learned through working in theatre, to help people resolve issues, which affect their lives.

Do you believe that one of the fundamental properties of theatre is its capacity for healing?

It has become a strong part of my understanding, particularly through my experiences Poland. It's not why I first went into it, but I came to understand that working in the theatre is a humanizing practice. It demands a searching into oneself, a coming to terms with who and what we are. It is also primarily about listening to and understanding other people – an author's voice, a character's, a colleague's, a director's – reading who and where people are and seeking to work and create with that. So I see a wider virtue in the way that theatre practice can sensitize us to tune in to and engage with other human beings, honestly and directly.

What was your first contact with theatre?

Play-acting as a child: dressing up and playing fantasy games – imaginative play. I would root my interest in theatre in the imaginative life that I had as a child, although not a formal contact with theatre, for me as an actor this sense of play – of making stuff up and living it, is fundamental. My first experience of a more formal contact was a production in school – it was an extra-curricular activity in a private school I attended for a few years – I was about 8 years old. It was dark, serious, very formal, it could have been T.S. Eliot's Thomas Becket play. I was a standard bearer, a very minor role but we were beautifully robed, and everyone took the whole thing very seriously. It seemed almost ritualistic - strangely important.

What made you want to become an actor?

It never occurred to me to be an actor. I had returned to the state education system but I left school when I was 16, with no particular idea of where I was going to go; I worked in a steelworks, which is what everyone did where I grew up, then drifted from one experience into another – the steelworks, building oil pipelines, travelling with the country fairs, scaffolder, rat-catcher – all kinds of weird and wonderful stuff. I spent years moving from one job and experience to another – then I joined a punk band, I squatted, I went south to Manchester and then London, where I joined another band, was part of that whole music scene and lived a very underground lifestyle. Eventually I got ill and retired exhausted back to Manchester, to recuperate. At 23, I felt I was just about mature enough to go to college and applied for an arts foundation course at Manchester, but it was full. I asked what else was available and they suggested I try the Drama School. They invited me for an audition; I prepared 2 pieces –a piece from *Macbeth* and an excerpt from a D.H. Lawrence short story, which I really loved. I didn't have the faintest idea what I was doing. They offered me the place, there and then. It was bizarre; I was both shocked and a bit suspicious.

So you fell into it by accident, but did you have any expectations of it, at that point?

I don't think I did but somewhere deep inside me was a belief that acting and theatre were something. It was like walking into kindergarden: you get to play, to mess around, just like going to the sandpit! I didn't know what to expect but it was very exciting.

Were there any significant individuals or events during your training that fundamentally affected your artistic sensibilities?

To be honest, , I think that a lot of the teaching was rubbish.

Why was it rubbish?

The delivery of actor training in that school – I don't know whether this was true of other conservatoires at the time – didn't seem to be that serious: they tended to brush over things, it felt superficial and ad hoc. I felt I had more to give than was being asked of me. There was little true exploration of the potential of acting or theatre. No search or enquiry. I think the tutors weren't trained, dedicated teachers, but people who had drifted in from the profession. The training was almost at the level of the anecdotal; they would tell you some stories and then you would do a bit of 'telephone acting', or 'blind acting', a bit of movement…but it didn't feel dedicated or focused. It felt like they were teaching us bits and pieces that they had picked up along the way. There was no fundamental discipline, no principles enforced.

Was it not a systematic course?

It roughly followed Stanislavskian principles, so we were asked to read that material and it was a reference point for them – although not in a particularly rigorous way.

You teach at Manchester Metropolitan School of Theatre now. How do you feel about the Drama School training that is currently available?

It is more rigorous, there are professional teachers who are qualified in and dedicated to their particular areas of interest, who take the teaching of acting seriously. I have been exposed to different cultures and practices of teaching as well, which has very strongly driven the way I teach and my expectations of the work of the students that I engage with. However, there are still issues to deal with; not many people can agree on what they believe to be the right way to train actors: your way is your way and mine is mine, it's inevitable of course, but it's important that all teaching retains its rigour, vitality and integrity; and that students are encouraged to develop a sense of ownership, responsibility and respect for their own practice and craft.

Are the students invited to participate in that dialogue as well?

Not enough, for my liking. My feeling is that drama schools in our theatre-making culture have a tendency to function as institutions, with all the attendant downsides. Institutionalized training promotes institutionalization. In my view, the process of understanding what it is to really open up the potential power of theatre, as actors – it's an extraordinary gift and opportunity to have – is often very limited. A mentality dominates that prioritizes conformity and adherence to a particular way of organizing and understanding the world: and of living in that world. The timetable is organized to facilitate many complex needs: financial; spatial; workloads; student numbers; student hours; teaching hours; a particular cannon of dramatic literature; the list goes on. Somehow the drive for the work –for that which is extra-ordinary, alive, unexpected, and original – this drive towards the unknown is forgotten; deemed unrealistic or unachievable, perhaps undesirable. We fit our actor training around an already very complex set of needs, ideas, checks and definitions. We are of course training actors to meet the needs of 'the profession' and so tend to mirror and replicate a particular understanding of professionalism, but I think it can be counter-productive for particular individuals. I have chosen to continue my training in cultures that work outside mainstream definitions of what acting and theatre are, that exist in highly disciplined small groups of self-selected people who chose to define for themselves their own theatrical art and practice. I believe that we don't have to accept the dominant definitions of the culture we are born into, rather we should seek out the training and practice that truly speaks to us, individually. The reason I went to work in those cultures was that I didn't feel, personally, that I could get what I wanted and needed here in the UK.

Can you give an example of how that limits, rather than liberates, students' imaginations?

Any young adult, working or training within an institution, will quickly though often unconsciously, absorb the prevailing culture and expectations within that institution. These are mostly invisible, and often contrary to the mission statements or pronouncements made by any particular school. But people accept it very quickly, we learn the rules and we live by them – students and teachers alike. These rules can silently inhibit, even kill off the artistic and creative individuation of students. We are each individual, unique, sentient, living beings, but the insidious nature of conformity tends to celebrate the safe, the known, and maintain the status quo. For me theatre and acting are not agents to be deployed in support of prevailing social or cultural definitions.

Do you acknowledge the need for rigour and discipline within that?

Absolutely.

Has actor training in this country successfully addressed a tension between furnishing students with the skills for the professional theatre, as it currently exists and enabling actors to regard themselves as artists who question both the form and nature of their art?

It is interesting to consider what a school's contract with its students is. Often the expectation is set too low. There are probably too many schools in this country and often a uniformity to the provision of training provided. It can be difficult for individual students to feel an absolute dedication to their own personal development, within a system that errs towards cultural and artistic conformity. Different people develop in different ways, different students bring different abilities, but we tend to treat everyone the same or use a gold standard, to which we want everyone to aspire, but this can rule out individuality. There is a tension between the teacher and institution, student and teacher, if the institution is saying 'be a good student, conform to our knowledge and wisdom, our way' then the inspiration that is so essential to the life of an actor can be compromised. Institutions inevitably err towards uniformity.

So it doesn't encourage students to think the big thoughts?

Nor to believe in the contract they have entered into with their vocation. To justify your right to walk onto a stage you have to accept a certain responsibility in the way that you work with and on yourself, the way that you are willing to use yourself, the things that you are willing to reveal of yourself, because an audience has an expectation that perhaps goes beyond entertainment. An audience may have yearnings that go beyond the mirror; to see and witness that which goes beyond the easily or instantly recognizable – the currently un-lived life: in our everyday lives we live by rules that often contain us. The stage can be a special place where we can watch, experience, learn and engage with our own stories – not just of what is, but also what is possible beyond our personal boundaries. So the actor has to be prepared to give of himself in a strong, brave, sensitive and fearless way, with all the subtleties that are entailed. I don't think that vista of possibilities is held up to students: we don't encourage them to scrutinize their responsibility to their own artistic destinies and possibilities. It's a strange mix of bringing different energies and destinies into an active relationship with each other. The actor is someone who carries a special license.

In practical terms, how do you instil that philosophy and those values in your students?

There is a balance to be maintained between the known and the unknown; between the knowledge and ignorance; assumption and actuality; bios and logos; freedom and discipline. Teaching is in itself a living art. The level at which we as teachers live and work is directly communicated to our students. My work is part instilling a respect for technical discipline, part creating an environment in which the students can explore the joys and challenges of their chosen vocation and gift, and to encourage them to take responsibility for that. I try to encourage them to sense the possibility of mastery of their extraordinariness, of carving life and time through your own action and presence on a stage, of making art, of creating live within themselves and with others, because that is what we do.

What were the significant experiences of your early career, after drama school?

I left drama school half-way through my final year, I felt that I wasn't learning anything any more and I wanted to discover what I was capable of in a more exposing and demanding environment, so I auditioned for Northumberland Theatre Company, a touring company based in Alnwick. That was a shock after Drama School. They had a really wonderful director; he wouldn't cross the line between director and actor, but he demanded that I did the work – he wouldn't do it for me, he wouldn't give me the answers. In a way he was saying, 'That is your work, so you do it, you come up with the ideas'. At theatre school, I hadn't been given that responsibility, so this director used to get incredibly frustrated with me, in exasperation, he'd scream that he couldn't believe that I'd been to drama school. But I was doing what I'd been getting away with there, where it had appeared to be entirely satisfactory. So it was a great shock, very stressful for me and I got quite ill as a result. But I learned more during the first three months of that production than I had in two and a half years at drama school. I learned about rigour, to take responsibility for what I was doing, to hold my own on the rehearsal room floor, I learned to listen. He'd say, 'Stop acting!' and I'd think, 'Isn't that what I'm supposed to be doing?' I didn't understand it then, now it is completely clear to me, of course, that I'd been 'putting on' now it is completely clear to me, of course, that I'd been 'putting on'. I learned to shed that 'acting' skin and start to be more present, more transparent, which was very scary but a brilliant lesson. He worked in a 'method' style, so he'd want units and objectives, he'd expect you to come up with lots of playable ideas, specific to the line and to the relationships within the scenes and then to play it. That was my job; you could come up with whatever you wanted, as long as it worked! It was a great discipline; no one had really demanded that of me at drama school. I had not experienced that comprehensive, unitary precision, in which I would make decisions about everything that I was doing on stage. I was there for one year and I did three productions – it was like a probationary year for learner actors. I remember auditioning for them – my first audition – I did a couple of pieces, which weren't particularly great. However, I really wanted that job, so on impulse as I was leaving, I went back and said, 'Look, I know that what I just did was rubbish, but I am really much better than that, I just wanted you to know.' He looked at me and said, 'OK, thanks, I'm glad you said that' and they offered me the job. Good thing I walked back. Another way this particular director inspired me was that, by watching him work, I began to think, perhaps it was more interesting being a director than an actor. I realised that all I ever thought about was one aspect of it – my part and my relationships on stage – but I saw that he had an overarching idea of how it would work: the bigger picture. I found the scope of his involvement exciting.

Did he encourage you, in your function as an actor, to participate in that kind of thought?

He would talk about the concept of the productions and introduce that to you so that everybody understood it – that's just good practice. It was more that I used to enjoy watching him direct: I thought that it looked deeply satisfying, creatively and artistically, perhaps more that just being an actor. Now I work as a teacher, director, actor: it's all making theatre, it's just that sometimes you work from a different perspective.

Do those different roles that you play have a useful relationship to each other?

Personally and professionally I find it useful, each role informs the other; but for some directors that is not necessarily the case: they sometimes feel you are a little over-qualified as an actor, perhaps.

Why?

I suppose there is a feeling that you have too many of your own thoughts or ideas – I don't think I do – or that those ideas are a potential source of conflict. Such doubts can be easily negotiated, if there is a will to do so. The work is the thing. Like everyone else, I carry my experience with me.

How do you negotiate that situation, when you encounter it?

I give myself the space to act, but I resist the need to take on any directorial role, or an over-vision of things. It doesn't stop ideas coming through, but they come through me differently; I'm an actor on the floor, so, of course, I have a voice and I expect to be able to express that voice, but I know where the boundaries are within the work. As an actor you process ideas and information through your self, your own behavior, your physicality, your being, whereas a director is working into the bodies and minds of others.

Who or what have been the most significant influences on your career, as an actor?

I'd been acting, teaching and directing in England for a while and I was getting bored; it wasn't turning out to be what I had imagined. I found it pointless that such a lot of effort went into an event that really meant very little to anyone. Most of the work and people's (actors, directors and theatre managers) commitment to the work, was pedestrian – it was a job, people were bought only for what they could do, so therefore the possibility of exploration, of venturing into new territory and feeling a creative burn, that risk, simply wasn't there. I'm not making a judgement on anybody else, but for me, that work, on the northern rep circuit, felt pedestrian and often mundane. I was using virtually none of the human, artistic and creative skills that I had imagined acting and theatre to require; I thought it would be a bloody exciting and extraordinary business, but it turned out to be something milder, safe.

What was your view of the function of theatre, in that context?

That theatre was simply an entertainment; it was a night out for people, a pretty safe diversion. It was something that people did out of habit, but I found no outlet for the spirit of theatre, which I had instinctively and was alive inside me.

Is that true of the material that you were working with, as well?

Yes, I think so.

Were you able to articulate your need for theatre as a transformative, spiritual experience, at this point in your career?

No and I felt disillusioned because my own experiences seemed to be endemic. Peers and colleagues also reported that after the initial rush of getting jobs, which were initially very exciting, things started to get a bit quiet in terms of work that was inspiring, or even interesting. This cycle of disappointment was broken for me when I went to Derry, in Northern

Ireland, to do a workshop with a Polish company called Gardzienice; I had read a review of their performance in Edinburgh, which raved about them, so I went to Derry to join in with the workshop. I hadn't a clue what they were doing and it was amazing, just mind-blowing, the work: they were singing, doing gymnastics, there was extraordinary discipline. Nothing was explained, you hit the ground running and they took you on this journey; they would do night runs, they would sing amazing, beautiful songs, they had a relationship to nature – they would work inside, outside, through the night. It was like being exposed to a world that was like a Chagall painting or a Picasso and you were integrally involved in it. You didn't understand the rules – clearly there were rules. These were artists who profoundly understood their work and it was an entirely new experience for me.

Did they explain a context for the work, retrospectively?

No, the work is the thing, you find its meaning, or resonance, through the doing of it; that is an unspoken rule of that culture of work.

What is 'night-running'?

They said, 'we're going to meet at this place, at this time, bring loose clothes'. We were driven to an unknown place, the darkness was fast approaching, there was silence, no talking. The group formed a line, three abreast, with members of the company dotted around, guiding us. We linked arms, silently – it's all done in silence – no one explains anything and we set off into the night, running into the darkness. It's the most extraordinary experience of going into the unknown; you have no idea where you are going, or what's going on, but what you are doing is running – quite slowly – with linked arms. You have an amazing physical relationship with the other people that you are running with because you are holding each other up, in a way, so you can't fall because you are tightly packed together and a rhythm develops. They work with rhythm; a breathing rhythm starts to establish itself. What happens is you let go of things; your questions, you let go of 'why?', 'what is this?' and you surrender to it and connect with it. Along the way they stop and we do exercises that we have learned from the workshop – gymnastic and breathing exercises, which are sometimes physically very intimate, not sexual, intimate – in which you work very closely with colleagues. Songs are sung, at night, in the forest, music is played, or you'll sit in the silence, listening to the breathing, to your heart. It was the most amazing experience – and this was a theatre company! I thought, 'this is what my soul had imagined'. I hadn't found it in England and had started to believe it didn't exist. At one point in the workshop, I remember lying on the ground, doing a meditation exercise and I started to weep and weep and weep; it was the first time that I had really released something from inside me, I was 28 or 29 years old. I was embarrassed, I didn't know what was going on, whether I was having a breakdown; now I understand these things, but then it was a big breakthrough for me. Following the workshop, I went to see their performance work; I saw a play, which lasted 45 minutes, it was amazingly physical, condensed, full of images, sounds and texts in Polish. I had no idea what it was about, but I had an absolute experience of recognition: this was what I understood, this was my theatre, this is what I believed it could be, because it was strong, passionate, physical, sexual, erotic, crazy, touching, moving, all of those things. I had been introduced into a different world of theatre creation.

Were you able to apply what you'd learnt in the workshop to your text-based work?

No. My initial outlet was the teaching, but I knew it was too early for me to put those things into my own practice as an actor; it is a new way of training and working, which takes years to fully appreciate within oneself. My teaching provided an opportunity to try out some things; I started to teach much more through the body and started to understand or appreciate that acting was a physical activity, which I'd previously understood to be an intellectual activity. The workshop completely physicalized my approach to being an actor: I hadn't understood how you have to root yourself into your body when you work. So I started to invite some of those Polish practitioners, who had been in Gardzienice, to come to Manchester, to work at the School of Theatre and to develop a relationship, in order to understand more of what they were doing and to expose our students to what they were doing. They decided to create a new company, Piesn Kozła, to create a new way of working and they invited me to join them and to help develop that work.

How do you bring the Polish perspective to bear upon the literary theatre we make here?

I haven't been able to fully reconcile it yet, but I am interested in how I can apply what I have learned – not so much the form, but the underlying principles – to my work as an actor here. The Polish work, for me, has a spiritual dimension, achieved through the physical embodiment of the work; it develops its own rules and own way of being. It was very personal in that we were devising a way of working that was both interesting and powerful for us. The work came from us, we didn't define our practice from existing models. I had to let go of much of my understanding of what acting and theatre were. We were making ourselves into our own actors. We were a small group, maybe eight or ten, working together, in laboratory conditions, not really knowing what the endpoint was, but working rigorously until we found a practice, which was personally and passionately resonant.

How do you translate that process work to the performance? At drama school, there was a teacher/director who we all loved working with because the personal experience of working with him was profound, but when you watched another group that he had directed, it was dull for the audience; an enriching rehearsal didn't translate to an enriching performance. I also remember going to see a Gardzienice performance and I thought, 'I bet these performers are having a better time, doing it, than we are, watching it'. How do you guard against that?

I believe we always have to consider how the work is going to engage with an audience. For me it is very important to be open and mindful of the audience's experience and to be sensitive to that. It's an active partnership, like dancing with someone, you can't ignore your partner, and you can't dance for yourself. It's important to be in active relationship with the audience, moment by moment. In Poland I think the emphasis is different. There is a tradition of work that is self-contained, of work that exists with or without an audience. They have a tradition of rigorous and artistically driven experimentation, of work that thrives and grows behind closed doors, and training lies at the heart of that practice. Perhaps there is a tendency from our perspective for this work to be almost deliberately esoteric. But it's a living culture and it needs to maintain its integrity. Their practice brought life to me, and a way of understanding myself creatively, for which I am very grateful.

How do you bring that to bear on the delivery of a text?

Any text will have embedded human truths and our jobs as actors is to find what that truth is and make it manifest, within ourselves. For me, that is an exacting process, in terms of bringing our own humanity actively to bear on the task that we are undertaking. The Polish work has radicalized me and opened me up to the individual creative possibilities that I have as a performer and I resist compromising those. It has made me wary of directorial concepts, or of a prejudgement of a character, a text or a production, because what happens if the concept or prejudgement is not what you find as an actor? Surely the production can only be based upon an agreed truth, which has been arrived at through the work we do together, collectively. I don't want to conform to a concept, which denies me the possibility of arriving at a truth through the experience of action, because to do so compromises me as an actor and an artist.

Does the artist's/actor's need for self-expression have anything to do with the delivery of a text? Should we not merely be serving the text?

I acknowledge of course that acting is a discipline: characters are written and our job is to channel ourselves into that and to bring that to life; that's my job, as an actor in text-based theatre. In the search for the essential truth of the character, there will be self-exploration and the self-expression derives from my ability to bring that to life, by giving my life to the character's fictional life and relationships. I have to make myself into a conduit. Not all of my ideas for the character will be accepted, I am not arguing for an unchecked self-indulgence, but I am arguing for the right to apply myself to the craft and the vocation that I have dedicated my life to and to do that to the best of my ability. So it's not an expression of self in the sense that 'this is about me': it is about transforming myself into another's mindset and relationships and living that and believing that if I do that, I will release the truths within that fictional life that will be valuable to an audience. Sometimes this will meet, exceed or transgress what the playwright originally had in mind.

What is the actor's position within the creative hierarchy, in mainstream British theatre?

Although I regard myself as an actor, I have had no interest in working within the mainstream industry in Britain because it wasn't where or how I wanted to work; there seemed too many limitations and restrictions put upon actors, so I wasn't interested in pursuing that as a career path: I wanted to discover what I understood acting to be, within myself and therefore I kept aiming to choose the kind of theatre that I would be involved in. It happened to be the kind of theatre that was not based in a culture I was brought up in. In a way, each of us has to find the home, the culture, the practice, that we are best suited to and it doesn't necessarily mean that it will be our culture of birth; you have to search it out.

You are working on Macbeth *with Piesn Kozła in Poland: in Britain, as an actor you are quite often the last group of people to be hired – a chronological fact, which needn't necessarily, of itself, affect your status or contribution, creatively, although more often than not, you turn up on the first day of rehearsal and all the decisions on design etc., big and small, have been taken – so what is that chronology in Poland?*

It is very different, in the sense that a group of us gather together, people who have self-selected themselves to engage in that work; it is a small group to begin the project. That project is made through the work of the actor – all of the material, including elements of design, is made through the actor – it is the actors' bodies that create the cineography, the actors' voices that create the music. It's like those cultures in which you use every bit of the pig and then you eat it: you use every bit of the actor in this work, so it is extreme in that sense, it demands of you an absolute commitment. As an actor there, you sing, you speak, and move – it's not dance – but your body is an instrument that moves through and creates space. All of the performative disciplines manifest themselves within and through the body of the actor. We are not simply moving bodies that speak, the active inter-relationship of all those disciplines is at play in the actor's body. The work finishes when it is ready and that can take up to two years because you are searching for something that will ultimately stand the test of time. It is a particular piece of work created over a long period of time, which is specific to the particular group who are making it.

There is a visual brand to Piesn Kozła's work: how is that selected?

It's a mix of things with its own cultural back catalogue: Piesn Kozła arose out of Gardzienice, which itself arose from the tradition of Eastern European avant-garde theatre dating back to Grotowski and, indeed, to Stanislavski; a tradition of experimental theatre practice. Now, of course, and just as significantly, there are Western practitioners, who bring their expertise and knowledge to bear upon the substance and practice of the work, so it is a living theatre in that sense. It reflects both the experience, or expertise of the people involved in any given project – and also their ignorance.

What is it that you have brought to bear on their work?

Myself. It was a way of making theatre that I felt I was absolutely able to give myself to: I felt free and creative, I was able to work in ways that were intuitive and natural to me – though I had to search and open myself to activities and energies that made little sense to me at the beginning. I was given the opportunity to invent and propose things, to release myself into ways of being that were really taboo for me. I knew I'd never be given the opportunity to explore like that within our tradition of theatre making, so I grabbed it. The line between life and work is very blurred there, to a point where it is nigh on impossible to separate them. This way of working is a way of living, an ethos, it influences many aspects of my life. There is a spiritual and philosophical level to the practice about growth, healing and the human condition. It is also a practice that teaches, but it does so because you have to give of yourself. So I brought who I was and I didn't have any qualms about giving myself to it because all of my manifestations of myself – as a young man, older man, man who has just lost his mother, who is in love, who has just been divorced, who is a father, who is still at times a child – are actively allowed to flow into and influence the work: nobody says, 'leave that at the rehearsal door'.

By 'actively', do you mean subliminally, by virtue of the fact that you are who you are?

By actively I mean there is a going forward. When we are training, speaking, singing physical texts and there is no given way of doing that:

a song is a song but the relationship between song and singer is very personal and intimate. What animates a song are the living forces of loss, desire, aspiration, celebration, fear that live within the singer, and you have to make contact with those forces, which are real, they are what we live for and fight for. You have to find the reason the song needs to be sung. One has to listen to what the song is asking. The same is true of a text, it's not about literal understanding. So there is an active living relationship between the material and the performer. It's never settled or done. In our contemporary urban environments, these forces are generally suppressed because we have to agree to live at a certain level, but over there, the level of animation of those forces is more liberated and time is taken to discover the ways of expression from within yourself. If you are playing Macbeth you can, of course, perform it in four or five weeks, but in order to really catch it, within yourself, takes time: I'm not saying it should take you two years, but there you are given time to discover how you function as an actor, what works for you, which means there is no pressure on you to conform to a particular time-frame or a particular way of playing a character, dictated by external factors. It seems that, very often, we accept a way of acting here, which is fundamentally compromised. Maybe, if you are very lucky, talented, or powerful, in terms of status, you can transcend those compromising factors.

When you say two years, do you mean you are working for fifty weeks a year, for two years?

We tend to work in blocks of three or four months at a time, the work is percolating in between times, but it is not just that a particular performance is percolating, you as an artist and human being are percolating, a process is alive and developing inside oneself and that is perhaps more valuable than holding on to specific stages of the work. The work evolves. There are certainly elements that are useful to my work in this country. I have no qualms about working here now: whereas previously I hadn't been sure how I would fit in. I feel experienced enough to propose what I need to propose, which is a direct legacy of my work in Poland: to propose that what I bring into the working space is myself, my body, voice and imagination and instinct, for the director to work with, encourage, alter, reject, as is appropriate, but that my work comes from me.

Are you well funded for the two-year gestation periods, in Poland?

The funding is precarious and limited; we do it because we choose to do it and it is valuable to us. For me, it is what it teaches me back, it allows me to grow and to experiment with what acting is. I get as much from it as I give to it, but financial reward is not a factor – I come back to Britain to earn money to fund myself over there.

What do you think we, in Britain, can learn from the Polish, avant-garde practice, in terms of what happens within the rehearsal room and the timeframe for creating work and how you might create a season of work?

There is a spirit, a sense of adventure, a way of creating outside of the accepted definitions of acting and theatre – making that, whilst demanding absolute technical proficiency, also requires the actor to be alive and free to live precariously, moment by moment. There is a volatile relationship between performer and material, performer and partner, performer and space, performer and audience. In many ways this genre of theatre is closer in spirit to a gathering of a small group of artists or performers who belong to a particular cultural tradition like flamenco or perhaps troupe of Sufi performers. The event, the happening is the thing. Conditions need to be right, the instruments, energies tuned, a sense that the performance itself – be it *Macbeth*, the *Book of Lear*, or *Bulgakov's Table*, is a means, a vehicle through which other forces and energies can come into being. As in duende, a force is conjured through the action of the performer. Beauty is not something that is predetermined; it is something that occurs. The song, or action is not an end in itself, but a means through which a higher end can be touched. So it is a practice that is particular to its own culture, genealogy and circumstances and as such is inimitable. However there are elements of the practice that are applicable to creating work in this country. For example: the centrality of the actor's energy and being; the emphasis on action and doing rather than explanation or understanding; a rigour and sensitivity to maintaining active living relationships; a respect for creation; the drive to maintain a living theatre, active living relationships, an intolerance of passivity. I find a lot of theatre I see quite exclusive, in that respect, it casts me as a passive spectator who is anonymous within the live event – it's a bit like watching television: you watch it for the exposition of its narrative or style or how beautiful and interesting the actors are, but the medium is oblivious to the life of the spectator. But I do not want to be a passive spectator, I want to be a participant and I believe that I can be a participant, as a spectator; I believe that the theatre cares enough for me, if it acknowledges my humanity as a spectator, and places my experience as central to its existence – then the potential for a dialogue exists between us. This sense of acknowledging the audiences is a real strength of British theatre. For me it's important that we understand what our responsibilities are as theatre-makers and often we need to expose ourselves to different practices in order to redefine those for ourselves, as opposed to confirming and conforming to what we think we know works, because something essential disappears with compliance and formula. We need to keep fresh and sharp. Directors and artistic managers and producers have to keep thinking, 'what is the value of this?' You have to be careful where you take the money and other encouragement from, because they may be the forces of conformity and that is not what our role as artists is.

What is your role as an artist?

When we were children the world was a place full of the most extraordinary, magical and unexplained events we didn't understand. We experienced life with vivacity, and I believe that theatre should continue that process into adulthood: it should be an opportunity to declare that life still is extraordinary, wonderful, strange and elusive. It should invite us to experience and search for what it is to be alive, to be human, to continue to aspire and to touch beauty. Of course we do this in our everyday lives as well, but a theatre is a special place; it can remind us that all is not lost, the materialistic fantasy is not pervasive. Theatre can be an alternative fantasy, that challenges the moribund, the mundane, the unthinking, the acceptance of truths that belittle and compromise us, by calling us to look again upon the beautiful, simple things, so that we cease to fall to judgment, or that we remember how good we were, are, and can be.

What is the greatest threat to theatre at the moment?

The same as to life – cynicism, laziness, arrogance, it's exploitation for individual gain and ego, lack of inspiration, institutionalization, a lack of courage and imagination. We should be on our guard against the forces of atrophy that invite us to close down and prematurely accept our limitations. This is all too understandable: we will most likely be invited to participate in a project, based on the evidence of what we have done before and with the expectation of reproducing that for the next project, but within that we have to search for the extraordinary, the unusual, the new. There is something about keeping the creative drive alive; there is an extraordinary frisson of energy when something new comes into being and that energy creates a subliminal quality in the work that we do that an audience picks up – they sense something unusual and powerful. However you can only create that when you loosen your grip on what already exists, on what you think you already know. The power of creativity as a way of life is important to me, it creates value, something extra, intangible.

SELINA CADELL

Selina has worked extensively in theatre over three decades and hails from a family of actors and impresarios stretching back over four generations. She has applied this rich blend of experience and tradition as a highly regarded teacher and director at many of the leading drama schools in the UK, including RADA, Central School of Speech and Drama, the Royal College of Music, the Royal Opera House and the Coliseum. She has written for the *Guardian* newspaper on Comedy Acting and her many TV appearances include cult comedy *Lab Rats, The Catherine Tate Show, The Rory Bremner Show* and *Doc Martin*.

POK   *How long have you been an actor?*

SC   I finished my training at Central in 1975, so that's thirty-three years.

What would do if you weren't an actor?

My family comes from four generations of theatre. I couldn't think of anything else to do: I wish I could, but now I teach and have set up my own things, so I don't depend on the precarious nature of our business.

What was your first contact with theatre?

Through my parents, my grandparents, my uncle – we go back a very long way. My great grandfather ran a company in the 1880s called Squire Bancroft Gentlemen Players, so it's in my blood. I found that very embarrassing at first. People would expect me to follow the trend, as my brother Simon had done. I pretended I didn't want to do it for a long time. My parents thought that was hilarious but they went along with it. I went through six rigorous interviews for a fantastic job in a wine merchant, which would have been three years training in a French vineyard and then working for a very posh company in Park Lane: I was offered the job, but, as he made the offer, I suddenly realised I didn't want it. I said, 'I'm going to be an actress': he said 'get out of this office now'. I auditioned for drama school and then I came clean to my parents who knew all the time.

You went to Central: what were your expectations of the training?

I knew that I would be getting a rigorous voice, movement, and physical training. I didn't think that was very successful, as it happened. I don't think I was quite ready for it. We had voice and movement every day, the voice department was excellent, the movement department was terrible. I felt awkward and I didn't feel anyone was constructively helping me towards finding a neutral place from which I could depart. I found myself getting more self-conscious and confused. The plays and the work were great and I did have some great moments of teaching, but they were not formative enough though. There were a couple of teachers who made me realise that it was about me and that I could choose to make this better. My most formative training experience was at school, before I went to drama school: I had the most amazing drama teacher there, she was taught by Elsie Fogarty, the famous voice teacher. She picked on Daniel Day-Lewis and me. She gave us private lessons, which in itself was a mixed blessing because she was such a dragon, but she taught us to breathe in a way that I've always used – even at Central. To make our diaphragms strong, on a Monday, she made us lie on our back on a wooden bench, and she would put a Penguin book on our tummy and we had to raise it; by Friday we had to do five. She made us aware of having a voice down here and a voice up there. She taught me sonnets by Shakespeare. She also taught me to not pretend to be somebody else all the time – she taught me to be me and to believe in what I said. The teaching at Central frankly wasn't as good as I wanted it to be.

So Central didn't make a huge impact on or contribution to your career?

No, it did: the habit of flexing the muscles for three years is essential and it did its job in terms of relating to a company of people, having the nerve to get out there and do something on your own. In the third year we did play after play as part of the repertory company thing: that was fantastic and that is essential.

You have taught at various drama schools: in your experience, as student and teacher, what do you think could be changed to improve actor training?

This is crucial isn't it? The thing that would really change a drama school would be to have a real, constant relationship with the profession. The training should centre round the needs of the student and not the needs of the teachers. The people who timetable classes at drama school need to recognise the value of having professionals coming in is greater than the need to change the timetable to accommodate their work. So they would say, 'you've six weeks of this class on a Monday, we really hope you can do it; if you can't do it, you will deputise someone of your standing, who you respect and trust, to take over'. In that way, there will be a constant relationship with the profession and philosophical continuity for the students, which is absolutely essential. That's what happens in opera: experienced singers give master classes. If you're prepared to run a timetable by the week, you can get actors and directors in who are working all the time. Occasionally I have had students come and watch me in a television rehearsal. That was an unbelievably flexible thing to happen.

Flexibility is important, not just in training, but for the profession as a whole.

It's key. Flexibility within the profession is the macroclimate that should be the microclimate in the drama schools. We have to create space for emerging creativity, supported by rigorous technique. It should really be about approaching each student differently, about being creative in the room and saying, 'I've no idea let's find out together'; let's not constantly search for, 'I'm right and you're wrong': let's really look at something in a team way. What I perceive to happen, quite often, is that staff have an, 'area of expertise' – which never worked in the profession – like translating some Russian masterpiece. Suddenly students are doing said Russian masterpiece, which clearly isn't a masterpiece and is only being done because of the residual issues of a failed actor or a director – that's not right. Often there's a weird sense of ownership – 'you come out of here and you represent something' – I don't believe in that. I believe in the individual and, most of all, I believe that in the really creative space people simply say, 'I don't know let's find out together'. You can always learn from the pupils. In too many drama schools, it's about the power of the teacher rather than the creativity of the team. I'm not talking about a touchy feely area where the students have all the power; I'm talking about an understanding that creativity comes from trust – it doesn't come from people saying you're not good at that, or you've got this problem. It comes from people saying when you do that it doesn't work, so why don't we find another way, or, 'that's really interesting, I'd never thought of that before'. I can look at a piece from *Hamlet* and think I know what it means and a student at RADA says, 'well I thought it meant this' and you think, 'what an amazing thought, I never understood that line so well and you're right, I've slightly misinterpreted it'. That can be a fantastic gain for a teacher, but too often the teacher has to be right. There are exceptions, but not enough and one reason is that a lot of the people are not gainfully employed in the profession. I was taught Shakespeare by someone who had never been on stage and it's not good enough. You wouldn't get a football coach who didn't know how to kick a ball.

Are voice and movement satisfactorily integrated into the acting work in drama schools?

No, a lot of the drama schools are aware of this now, but the application of voice and movement to the work that you're doing on the text is still separated too much. If you don't actually act – if you only teach – you don't really know how to say, listen, you're not taking that breath there, that's not going to work on the Olivier. They're not going to understand the rigorous, scientific nature of the actor's body and the way in which you can really use your voice and body.

That creates a cerebral barrier. People get hung up on things, because they're approaching it intellectually; they don't realise the physiological nature of acting.

There's a neuroscientific dimension to acting, which is rooted in trusting the thought of how you feel. For instance if you hold your breath for long enough it'll make you feel like you want to cry, that's what happens when you cry. Everybody knows, or used to know, that it's just pretend, but in order to just pretend well, there are physiological things that you can trigger. Now, however, the search seems to be about some weird mystery. There's no mystery: there's talent and technique.

How do you define talent?

Talent is an innate quality, which you didn't know about and didn't nurture, it's a raw sense of passion and a need to express it. Some people have no idea of their talent and what's exciting about teaching is to try to help people develop their talent, to know it and learn to control it, or let it go out of control in a safe environment. They need knowledge of it, so that they can begin to make discerning choices about how to best employ it.

Do you need a talent for having talent? The two most talented actors in my year at drama school didn't last more than a year. That may have been down to their personalities but I wonder if they were adequately prepared for the industry.

You have to have a thick skin to survive this business. It's shot through with people who pay homage to commercialism. You can't take it too seriously: if you do you're lost. You have to try never to feel like a pawn in a chess game and as soon as you do feel that, you have to do something about it. It's an irony isn't it because most actors *are* pawns, without control and yet they manage to survive by getting parts, but they're not happy because they feel they have to sit at home waiting for the phone to ring. They're grown up, they've got kids, they've got to make a living and they're still waiting for the phone to ring. That's not a great place to be in one's life. You need to recognise that this business owes you nothing and you have to decide how you're going to deal with that. Some people, whose talent is precariously mixed up with their own emotional world, are never going to get enough distance to see that. They're not prepared to play a game in an interview: they know it's all nonsense, but instead of finding a way to make themselves feel rewarded or stimulated, instead of having the nerve to say, 'I know it's a terrible business but I still love doing it and I'd like to find a way of being in control of my life', they're just immersed in it.

It is frustrating to go for an interview for something that everyone knows is rubbish but having to pretend it's great: it takes us all away from the ideal of telling the best stories in the best way that we can, because, before we have even crossed the start line, we are contributing to a lie and that runs contrary to our pursuit of the 'truthfulness' of any and every given fictional moment in our work. Surely, it doesn't have to be that way?

We're getting at 'the game' – nowadays, in interviews, when they start telling me the plot, I've got the nerve to say, 'listen don't worry about the plot, I've read it, it's ridiculous but I'm still here: let's talk about something else' and then I feel I can deal with it. Some people appreciate that – they don't have to pretend it's brilliant. However, if the author's present, there's no point in saying I think your script is dreadful – that's stupid. In fact, that's the creative spirit I'm interested in. In a rehearsal room, we should be able to say, 'some of this works and some of this does not. Let's look and see if we can push the barriers further'. In the same way, an interview should be, 'we have the money to make this programme, you want the job, we want to make it, let's put our best behind it'.

Was it a shock to leave the structured environment of drama school?

Because I'd had so much experience of theatre in my life, before I went to drama school, it wasn't a shock. I knew I wasn't owed anything, I didn't expect anything, I still don't expect anything; that's my virtue, the reason I succeed. I have a cynical respect for the industry, what does it owe me? Nothing.

What was your first job?

When I left Central several of the teachers said I wouldn't work until I was 35 or 36. I got a job at the Birmingham Rep immediately.

What did they base that judgement on?

The way I looked: I 'wasn't good looking, pretty, juvenile', I'd be, 'very good as an older woman, later on'. It was completely untrue because I worked a lot. On another occasion, in my third year, I went for an interview at the BBC. I went to a tiny office and there was a man, there was that much smoke I could hardly see, but I could see his toupee had slightly slipped over his forehead. He looked up and he said to me, 'Oh Selina, yes you're very talented, you'll be absolutely fine, you've just got to do what I say and get that nose fixed' and the rest of the interview was spent telling me how to get a nose job!

What were the key events, productions, meetings, encounters or people, who influenced or helped form or articulate your artistic sensibilities?

John Dexter was key. John gave me a job in his company when I was very young, and I worked with him for three years. He had what appeared to be a very didactic way of dealing with the company; he would boss you about for the first three days, but that was just a beginning: he wanted to get the play on its feet as quickly as possible, because he didn't like people sitting around. What it taught me is that you have to have a structure. He taught me to wait, to trust that after a few days we would all have been through something quite frightening but then we'd all settle down and things would change constantly. He would demand that trust from you without actually mentioning it. I would have a problem with a part and say, 'John I was thinking about the part and would you mind if I...' and he would say, 'stop, don't tell me, if you tell me I'll know what to expect and you will not be able to do it as well. I want to see you do something 100% off your own bat, with your own creativity intact and I'll tell you whether it works.' That was fantastic. It would make you bold. He would say, 'never apologise, never explain,' and I've used that ever since. Instead of thinking will I be pleasing the director, what you're doing is working towards the play and yourself, using yourself to try to interpret the moment, after which the director can or may say, 'that really works'. If you're given permission, through discussion, in advance, you're so nervous about it you only give it 50%.

Is that because you intellectualise it by describing it?

Yes, but also, because you've mentioned it, you know they're looking for it, so it becomes self-conscious. John dealt with what was happening in the room.

So it was always a present tense transaction?

Always, even though the first few days' foundation work was military. He told us he used to have matchsticks and little triangles of cardboard in his attic, which he used to set a vague blocking for every scene so he could get the play on its feet by the end of the first week. It was an astonishing thing to do and anyone who worked with him more than once and let him do that, realised that he had to boss you about for the first week and then he would let you go.

And if you resisted that did you suffer?

You did and that was where he went wrong.

Or is it a waste of energy to resist a process?

It's how you resist a process. He would have been fine with questions, but he didn't want people to start saying 'I don't feel like moving there', he'd respond, 'it's not about that at the moment, I'm not doing the feelings, I want the shape, I want to see the play'.

Emotional journeys are linked to physical journeys and if that's imposed on you from the outset, it can inhibit creative discovery and development for an actor. It can limit your emotional horizons and, therefore, your character's horizons.

Yes, it can limit it but it depends entirely on how you respond to that moment of being bossed about. If you can let it be a technical practice, you can manage. I'm not advocating it but I have to say his results were often extraordinary. By giving it a skeletal structure, he freed the emotional underbelly of a production. I would far rather have someone boss me around for three days and then relax, than have endless table discussions, or, worse still, game-playing, just to find out whether someone should cross the stage or not. The thing that was extraordinary with Dexter was the text work: to me, the job is to deliver the text to the audience and the audience is the most important thing.

What actors helped you to shape your craft and your sensibilities?

Roy Kinnear was hugely influential at a formative time for me, when I was asked to be in the Actors Company at the National Theatre (an 18-month contract, to do *The Duchess of Malfi*, *The Cherry Orchard*, *The Real Inspector Hound*, and *The Critic*). One of the other important things about creativity is being in a company; it provides a liberating structure, based upon trust, gained through sheer familiarity. Because you know everyone so well, you can do anything, at any time. Roy Kinnear was my mentor: he taught me about comic timing, the art of invisible comedy, how not to anticipate a joke, he taught me how to be more brave, how to be slower, how to take an audience and use whatever they gave you.

What did he say about timing?

To set up a comic moment, internally, you must subliminally prepare the audience by letting them know you are about to do something, doing it and then letting them know it is over. At the same time, externally, they must not see you prepare yourself: so, for example, you establish the peril of the hole in the ground, but never look into it before you fall into it – it's got to be invisible. Everything you do comically requires 100% commitment, so it's often a contrast: if you really want the joke to work you have to not expect the follow up – whatever the gag is – you have to be absolutely certain that it's not going to happen, ever. Once he said to me, you know why you don't get a laugh on that line? I said no. He said, 'cross your legs when you're saying it'. I said 'why?' He said, 'to displace it, to take the pressure off it: they don't want to be asked for a laugh, they want to be given it'. It's so true, he taught me everything. That's why I love Shakespeare: he lets you decide whom you like, he gives the play to the audience. Some directors are all about waving at their mothers saying 'look at me, look what I did'. I don't want that, I want the audience to decide.

So whether you're a director or an actor, or any kind of artist, self-consciousness is not useful, that drawing attention to your own brilliance.

An ego is not useful. We all have an ego, but it mustn't dominate you. The most successful people know they have an ego but can give it away.

It is a delicate balance between confidence and arrogance.

Yes, theatre is not about the egos of actors or directors: it's about a greater thing – a process of play in front of an audience, about what happens then. The more you take your ego out of it, the more your real personality meets the author's, so you become a kind of conduit. By emptying yourself of ego you become much bigger, in a profoundly generous way.

There is a duality, in the sense of 'look at me', but then you get beyond that and you say, 'really look at me and I'll really give you something'.

That's right and it's the same generosity that tells you not to go for every laugh, when there's a fabulous one coming: you wait because you know the audience will have a better time, if you can just hold them until that comes. That's a perfect duality because you've got your ear open, your eye open – that's about you but it's also about them.

Are we always trying to trick ourselves about becoming our character, that you can lose yourself and sublimate yourself so much?

I don't believe you can become your character, nor should you try. You imagine how would it feel, if it were happening to you. You're not really a witch, but if you were, what would it be like? We do that in the playground: it's playing.

Any other formative people or events?

Ralph Richardson, my godfather, taught me technical tricks that I've never forgotten. When we did a production together, he asked me one day if I had a red pencil and I said no and he said, 'get yourself a red pencil'. He showed me his script – he was a great calligrapher, he drew beautiful, graphic designs all over his scripts – and before he'd even read the script, he would underline the last word of every sentence he had. He explained, when you're in the Olivier theatre, you had to lob the last word to the back of the theatre. It's what is called the upward inflection, but Ralph didn't like that term because he thought of himself as a technician. He thought of himself as an actor who had a responsibility to the man at the back. So if you underline it, it makes you aware that when you get to the end of the sentence, you've got to hit that word. It was an amazing trick and I still do it.

Does that apply to prose as well as verse?

Yes, it applies to absolutely everything. Our traditional theatre, from pre-Shakespeare to Ibsen and Shaw, is about the audience: the audience know the actors are on stage and the actors know they are on stage and that's the joy, the complicity at play between actor and audience: what do they know that I don't know and what do I know that they don't know? For instance, in *Hamlet* the audience are the only people who know everything, so the actor/character can talk to them and ask, 'what am I going to do?'. This sense of relationship with the audience is something that I find extremely lacking in most of the theatre that I see. People weirdly spend seven weeks searching for the truth in the rehearsal room, get on stage and pretend the audience don't exist: that's the biggest lie of all. To really use the audience is very exciting and you can only be present if you use it each night. To decide that they're not there, unless it's a play where that is the intention, is to do a disservice to the plays that were written with an audience under the canopy, in the daylight, because the audiences are not being allowed in.

How do you apply that to, for example, an Edward Bond, or an Arthur Miller?

It's always about holding the relationship with the audience and, even if you don't look directly at them, in the Arthur Miller play, you are certainly aware of the effect this moment is having on them and you could operate it flexibly each night. What I find difficult is when I see Mozart operas and Shakespeare plays and I see actors doing weird things, like thinking out loud: soliloquy is not thinking out loud, it's talking to an audience, an aria is not singing for no one, it is revealing to somebody your heart and soul. It's much easier to believe in the adrenaline produced by the people watching you, than to pretend that you're not going to get frightened as they come in. Audiences used to shout out. I long to shout out when I can't hear. I see productions at the National when I'm desperate to flip up my chair and say I've paid £38 and I can't hear a word. We should bring back eggs, it would be great; I'm tired of the audience pretending they don't have a say. It would be really exciting if we, as audiences, had some control.

Why do you think as audiences we don't feel comfortable about doing that?

Because we're so intelligent, we always know when we're being gulled and then we feel guilty: 'I don't want them to think I know how bad they are, so I'll clap louder at the end'.

Is there a curse of politeness?

There is now but there wasn't with Shakespeare, he used to change the ending if it wasn't going that well. Furthermore, if you've paid £50 you don't really want to acknowledge that you can't hear them. I was in *Pericles* at the National, which was a disaster on a huge scale. Now that process should have been examined: we were led blindfold into that process, we were slaves to the process of concept, borne out of the director's and designer's world tour, in which they'd seen many amazing funeral and wedding rites and processions. They thought, 'what play can we use those things on?' but that's not how you do a play. When we were on stage we could feel the audience leaving and moving. I used to think, yes, go, go but why don't you tell us why you're going.

In that instance were you invited to be party to the big idea?

Absolutely not. We were doing trust exercises every day, in the belief that we were participating in a collaborative production as joint stakeholders, but upstairs they were building things that we didn't know about. It was a terrible collaboration and a lot of people would acknowledge that it was a bad mistake. What I found depressing was that the National did that polite English thing of pretending it was marvellous. We had a meeting with the boss shortly after it opened in which we were told that the building was completely behind it, but we wanted to hear them say, 'look it's a bit tricky, things have gone wrong, this shouldn't happen again and we're going to examine what on earth went wrong, but in the meantime we support you as you get through these difficult shows until we take it off'. I asked if we could discuss it and I was told that we could at some point, but it never happened. Years later, one of the NT Board said to me I'd seen a number of people take the helm at the NT and was there anything I'd change and I said I would change what happens when things go wrong. Let's really talk about the failures and find out what went wrong – nothing ever happened.

Why is it difficult to have that conversation?

The nature of our business is that the workforce outweighs the work: we think we're on some course to success and might get thrown off it, if we speak our mind. The need to speak, without fear, is crucial. I led a workshop years ago at the NT Studio with Katie Mitchell, in which we each brought two groups of actors, designers and directors together, to discuss what happens when a production gets into trouble, when actors and directors are disagreeing. It was a discussion about how, why and what happened and how we could stop it happening. Of course it all went wrong, the directors took offence at the actors talking about getting a laugh, they preferred to focus on the 'mystery' of comedy, the 'mystery' of the process. A lot of directors felt threatened and a lot of actors thought if they said what they wanted to say, they might never work with that director again.

Is there anything you've read that's been influential?

The Craft of Comedy by Athene Seyler, a series of letters to a friend of hers who was running an amateur theatre group, is a little handbook of comedy and Michael Chekhov's *To The Actor* which I loved and ate up.

What was it about Athene Seyler's book?

The craft: like Roy Kinnear's advice, it was about the way in which you could help an audience enjoy something more and the structured notion of the craft of the comic world. I have met actors who don't want to discuss why they get a laugh and I think that's very odd, we all know it's a tenuous business and there is a craft. Peter Barkworth's book is good too, in that respect.

Why was the Michael Chekhov book so compelling for you?

Because it seemed to incorporate a world of physical theatre that I didn't understand. It was like coming across commedia dell'arte for the first time, the notion of secretly being a clown. I became more aware of my physicality.

What do you mean when you say it's not about the mystery it's about the craft?

You have to have talent, but how do you express that talent? That isn't a mysterious process. There are lots of directors who think they coax something out of you by doing weird exercises to release you, but, in my view, they inhibit you. If you have a good text, you have to understand what it means. The rigour of the text being clear to the audience is simply a matter of making sure you understand it. It's not a matter of 'does it feel right when you do that?' It's a matter of understanding what it means and then playing it – then it'll be there. There's nothing separate from you in that respect. There's nothing touchy feely about acting. It's a pretend game. I'm not suggesting there isn't art. The nature of the art is about lifting something, showing it to people and letting them judge it. You have to have the talent to express that in a theatrical way. There's so much guff about the nature of the process being mysterious: it's not mysterious at all, it's fun to work out how you're going to make it work.

I did a two-week workshop with Cicely Berry, the focus of which was the physical implications of language and the aurality of meaning. We did a sequence of fifteen exercises of displacement, which were designed to get your voice and body actively involved in the expression of the language. It wasn't a mysterious affair, but you were releasing vocal and physical energies which gave a different meaning to the words, beyond their sense-meaning. I think what I understand by the mystery is that there is an element that you just cannot explain, your instinctive response to something.

But isn't that your personality? I'm absolutely in accord with everything you've said; the physical and vocal response is what I mean by the craft. It is not an intellectual thing: it's about understanding how your body responds in your life, to use and choose moments physically and emotionally, and understanding how the physical and emotional worlds interact, so that you can begin to release the text. That little element you're talking about – isn't that about your personality, isn't that about the way that it happens to you? You've done the same physically and vocally as the person next to you, you've used the same word but it's different. Why is it different? Because it's yours. That's where there's a little difficulty in semantics: at the same time as wanting to get rid of your ego, it has to come from within you to be so truthful and when it's so truthful, as Peter Brook said, 'the coal is lit'. The coal can be inert for a long time but it's a treasure when it's alight, suddenly you're warm, it's glowing, you're on fire, everything works and that's when it's true to you. When you strip away enough by allowing yourself to trust your body, your voice and text, that little extra thing is just you, it's not mysterious, well maybe it is but that's not what I meant. What I meant by mystery was the directors who do the endless truth-telling exercises, there are a few trust exercises that I think are extraordinary. When I teach, I teach one exercise alone and the rest of the time I'm constantly using vocal, physical craft techniques.

I find those exercises useful only when they are specifically related to the text or, when there is no text, to a scenario we are hoping to create.

Yes, Sam Mendes is brilliant at that, he doesn't come in with a concept, he starts from the play and the company in the room and he creates things, almost on his feet, why don't we try this, and let's try that and what you try is always related to the text. When I resent that, it's because the director has a secret concept and somehow I know it has nothing to do with the text. You know when you're doing an exercise that is all about their ego and nothing to do with the text.

Can you consider your life as an actor as a career? Is it a collection of jobs you happened to have had, or can you think of it as a developing career?

For years I just accepted everything that came my way because I 'knew' each job was my last. I also had a family, we didn't have a lot of money in the early days and I don't think I made career choices. Now I do. There was a time when I played nothing but miserable spinsters. I got a bit bored because I thought, 'blimey I'm 40, playing these women who are 65'. I remember saying to my agent I'm going to grow my hair because I don't like the way I'm getting cast. She said, 'it won't change you, you'll always get cast like that.' She was wrong, because now I play glamorous women who are rather power-driven. So I've got a very interesting career now because I do a lot of different things. My attitude was, 'let's see what happens and I'll do everything for what it is'. I regret that I've never been employed by the RSC to play a leading part. I was brought up in the classical theatre world, so not to have done as much Shakespeare as I would have liked, is of great sadness to me. I'm hoping I'll do more, as I get older.

How important is luck in forging a career as an actor?

I'm a great believer in the maxim, 'if you want something done ask a busy person', and that luck is in the air around people who are open, optimistic and ready. I got a job not long ago that may have been regarded as luck, but I saw an opportunity and I used it. I was coaching an actress for a film. A new draft of the script came through the week before they started filming. Alan Rickman was in the film and he knew I was an actor and they wanted to have a reading of the new draft and hadn't cast it fully, so he asked if I would read with them and he asked my daughter, Lette if she would read the young girl. If Lette hadn't done that reading, I would probably have done a low-key reading – I didn't know that it hadn't been cast and I read three different women – but I was very keen that she should have a go, not do the mumbling thing, so I really performed, I decided to go hell for leather with the three parts; she did exactly what I did and went for it. It was a great day and we had a lot of fun. They rang me at the end of the day and offered me one of the parts. Now was that luck? It was lucky that Alan knew I was an actor but, on the other hand, I took the opportunity not because I thought I'd get the part, but because I wanted Lette to have a good day. There's a bit of luck in everything but I think there's much more choice than we imagine. When I felt frustrated that I was out of work and this angry sea that is the theatre was getting me down, I decided to do something about it. I rang the NT Studio and said, 'I'd really like to work on some texts, could I come and run some scenes on a Saturday morning, or a Friday night?' and they said yes – they might have said no and I'd have been in the same position I was before, I had nothing to lose. So that's always been my philosophy. Every time I've knocked on a door, it's opened. I've never had anyone slam the door in my face and say, 'no you can't do that'. A lot of actors wait for the door to open, but it's a profession in which you can't afford to wait for the door to open. Now I direct plays and do other things and people say yes to me, but there is still a glass ceiling.

Because you're known as an actor, even though you've directed a significant number of productions, are you still finding it difficult to get directorial work?

I don't get directorial work really unless I ask for it, just occasionally people offer me things, but I have to put myself out there and say, 'I want to do this directorial work, is that OK?' and they say yes.

Is that not true of all directors?

You asked if I get offered directorial work and I absolutely don't. I've done some very good productions and had good reviews and I'm not asked to do things. I think now that if I did take an idea to some of the mainstream places I would be taken seriously. However, I am also nervous of it because it has been my experience, as an actor, that when I've auditioned for a television or theatre job, if I've mentioned for instance, that I've just directed *The Way of the World* at Wilton's Music Hall, immediately they change their tone; they don't want me to be a director in the room where they are the director. Can I just add about the glass ceiling, that I also think it's because I'm a woman. I believe that as an actress I am not expected to be a director as well, because it's too threatening. I think that one of the reasons women don't run the theatre world is that they do often have families and find it impossible, unless you didn't give your family any time at all. How could you run the National Theatre as a woman, it would be very difficult, for a lot of us women, so we don't put ourselves out there. I also think that a woman in the rehearsal room is a very different experience from a man – they're much less threatened, they don't have to prove themselves so much. A lot of the men I know and have worked for, the ones who are successful, need to be right all the time and I think most women, the interesting women, are saying, 'let's discover it together, let's find out'. It's about being able to support the discomfort in the room, to support the flexibility of the moment, to say, 'it's not quite right yet, let's look at something else'. Women in a rehearsal room don't feel they have to win, the directors who don't have to win in a rehearsal room are always the winners.

Is the distinction between the creative team and the cast a useful demarcation?

I can't say, hand on heart, that it's useful; it represents a power thing.

Where do you think that comes from?

It comes from the strange idea that doing a play is about doing something *to* it: doing the play itself is the task I'm interested in. You don't need to be an intellectual to be a director and what happens is they go: 'what can I do to this play?' And the actors then are puppets. The people who don't do that, as I say, arrive in the room with the actors and together they untangle the play, make it clear and offer it to the audience and allow the audience to decide what they want to decide. The creative team also decides, sometimes on a message; they've decided they want to do this play because they want people to know that knifing is bad. As soon as you tell an audience why you're doing a play an audience goes away because they have to be free to judge things. If you think of Shakespeare, for example, you understand that *Hamlet* or *Macbeth* weren't even new stories: everybody knew the ending, so the only thing that's interesting is, could this actor make us forget the ending and take us on a journey where you felt, 'oh no, no it's not going to happen, oh god it's happened'. That seems to me to be fantastically interesting and that depends on personality and on releasing something in the moment, with the audience. No one ever talks about that, what they talk about is how shall we do this *Hamlet*, where shall we set it, which period should it be in, which costumes should we do it in, not which actor shall we have to play it and see how he plays it, his version of *Hamlet* should be the interesting thing. Adrian Noble, Richard Eyre and all those big people, in a seminar at the National Theatre on classic texts about seven years ago, all said that it's difficult because these big plays have been done before, you have to come up with new ideas. No you don't, the plays have stood the test of time for 400 years – the new thing is who's doing it.

Does the timeline of employment – the fact that you're employed last – affect actors' status within the creative hierarchy?

Yes, of course. I've never really thought of it like that. When I'm teaching young actors I always say to them you shouldn't just be actors, you should be directors, writers, do everything, just get out there and experience everything and in that way, I think you avoid that hierarchy you're talking about. That is part of the power game at the moment, that we are the last people; when we get the call from our agent, we immediately put ourselves on a lesser footing, we hope we get the job, we might not get the job, it's in their remit to like us or not like us.

At an audition, or at the early stage of rehearsal, a director will be more familiar with the text than the actors because he has had more time to access it, but that shouldn't necessarily affect the value, or status of the actor's input.

With the greatest directors it doesn't. We shouldn't be pawns in the chess game, we should be right up there with the kings and queens. The great directors do not make that divide between the creative team and the cast:

they elevate you, they hear you, they rely on you and they listen to you. A lot of it is about listening, together. What you're talking about is that so often we get into the rehearsal room and on day two we're thinking, 'I get the atmosphere: I'm not supposed to say what I think, I'm supposed to say "X" and no more because they've got this idea', and that's not right is it?

No. Do you find that you're encouraged to think of the big idea of the play? In my view, at drama schools and in the profession generally, actors are encouraged to think of their character, they're not required to think about the big idea.

One of the reasons I became a director was because I just couldn't understand why I wasn't being asked to think about the big idea of the play and about the function of the character in the scene at the time, which seems to me to shortcut an awful lot of business about what's your character and is much more useful. When I direct, all I demand is that we do the play in the style it was written, so if it's a Restoration comedy, for example, my job is to help the actors have the nerve to play it in the moment, talking to the audience, looking in their eyes as if they might answer, and using that. So I'm pretty tough on that but that's not a concept, that's how it was written. Gielgud said, 'Style is knowing what play you're in'. So people might say oh she's didactic about that; I'd say that was a way of making people think big about the play and that, to me, is essential. One of the first questions I ask my opera singers is, 'when was this written, do you know who this was written for and how it was written?' Even if you're going to go away from that, it seems vital to know.

How does that help you as a performer?

It helps me realise that I'm part of a team and I'm part of a picture – a dot in a surrealist painting – and, step back a certain amount, you'll see how I fit into that picture. That's one of the most interesting things about being in the theatre; what is the purpose of the evening? Shaw suggested that any fool can make an audience laugh or cry but it takes something else to shift their ideas. Knowing it's a play about hearing something different inside you, when you've been taught all your life to pretend something else, to know that it's a play about the human vulnerable condition, to know it's a play about the people who deny that, to know what the play is for, is sometimes the only thing you need to know; then you can really hold it and give it to the audience.

How could a director help an actor interpret a whole speech in a Shakespeare, for example?

You go through it line by line and you paraphrase it with everyone around the table, so, together, you begin to understand what the themes of the play are and how often they come up. That seems to me to be interpreting Shakespeare, you can't just vaguely interpret it, it's got to be completely exact and when it is, the audience understand it, because the acting is not generalized and they don't need a concept. Frankly, a lot of directors don't know how to do that and rather than go through that process, which might embarrass them, they will find a reason to do the play.

Theatre making is an act of generosity, of giving something over to an audience, your personal understanding of that text.

I've worked with five directors who I consider to be great, they're not frightened of saying I don't understand this and I'm going to find out but at the same time they've done a lot of work on the play and have an understanding of the history of the play, when and how it was written, but together we disentangle it and make it clear, and the journey begins on day one. They then take the role of the facilitator, they are the great directors and the people I've learnt from. It's very hard to direct yourself; you do need someone standing out there.

What is your responsibility, as an actress, in the making of theatre?

It's flexibility, it's listening, it's being open, but the purpose is to express the play to the audience, without the purpose it's just a series of self-indulgences. If you don't understand the nature of the actor within the profession and the nature of the profession itself – being so crowded with difficulties and deceits – if you don't understand that, it's very hard to have a balanced responsibility. You have to detach yourself from the notion that you're going to be a star – you're going to be picked out – and just decide that you're an actor not for those reasons. Otherwise you can't have responsibility that is genuine and generous and open and you're unlikely to ever have a career as a star.

The 'Why?' and the 'How?' questions are related: when you're asking why you are doing this, you're asking what is the point of theatre and what is the point of my involvement in theatre: does that relate to how do we make theatre-making better?

Yes, it is about the experience being one of equal creativity and the creative purpose being the play shared with the audience, by a team of people, at an agreed time, who have agreed on how best to make it clear.

All present tense transactions.

Without present tense transactions we're lost. One of the things that has governed the theatre with such destructive consequences is that set design has become something that has had to happen much earlier than when the actors arrive. The most successful productions I've been in are when the process hasn't happened yet.

How do you marry the pragmatic aspect of set design and construction and costume design and making/purchase, within a usually tight recruitment/ rehearsal timeframe, to the desired artistic environment where we all create together?

Well I've achieved that myself several times, working with designers who know the set is going to support the play but it's not going to be a separate, incredibly complicated, instituted art form. So it requires courage; I've worked with costume and set designers who are there at the beginning of rehearsals, I've given them a vague timeframe and a vague feeling but basically I suppose I'm talking about operating the simpler sets, at less money with simpler set changes, I'm talking about a theatre where I've often heard 'the audience expects more for their money' and I think that's rubbish. The audience want to be emotionally charged in some way, they don't need spectacle; there are films or musicals for that. I think you have to start from the premise that you're not going to engage in a massive set of spectacle theatre and that means being courageous. Sam Mendes does it. I've sat in rehearsals with him where we've had no design and then one day he says right we've got twelve chairs and we disastrously did the act on twelve chairs and that was an absolute fiasco. He said 'well that didn't work', then he said 'let's bring that props table over' and we did it with the props table and he then said 'yeah, that's great', and the designer came in and watched and talked and that was our design. Then the costumes and set evolved around that basic structure, because it was very, very simple. You have to have the courage that the play will work, if you support the play, simply. A lot of directors think, 'how will you do it?' but you have to start from, 'what is the play?' You can't start from how will I make this different, how will I get the award, how will I wave to my mother, it's much more collaborative. All of you have to agree the play is much more important than you. You have to start from the point of communicating to the audience something simple through the words. You can create incredibly sexy, creative things that will take them into a fantasy world, in fact the more they have to do, the less likely they'll want spectacle. *Pericles*, which takes you to God knows how many countries, was the most performed play when Shakespeare was alive. It's because it's a fairytale, it's because Gower leads the audience from nation to nation, from island to island, through god knows how many places and the audience presumably had to imagine that. Did he have huge sets? No of course he didn't, it's about the imagination.

How do you respond to the view that theatre in this country has, to its detriment, traditionally emphasised the text, or literary aspects of the theatre, at the expense of the visual dimension?

Theatre encapsulates both, of course, but you can be visual with very little money and huge imagination, you can also be more visually physical. You talked about the power of language within the body and I think we've been caught up in the head with our aural tradition. When I teach Shakespeare to black actors in South Africa I see Shakespeare that takes my breath away – I can't believe the things going through their body with the words, they just happen, because they refract it from themselves in a passionate way. I don't think an audience would be bored if they had nothing in the room but a football and a stepladder, because the visual thing is happening with the actor and because of the relationship they have with the audience. If somebody's saying 'look, look, she's coming down the Nile in the most

216

unbelievable boat', we all go where, where? When I was little I was taken to see *Peter Pan* an awful lot – my Dad loved *Peter Pan* – we never saw a crocodile, I thought I saw one, I heard him ticking but I was sure I saw him. Then I saw *Peter Pan* at the RSC or somewhere, I heard the ticking and then on came the crocodile and I thought, oh that's not really very frightening at all, I was better off imagining it. The power of the imagination is severely undermined. I see great performances and great plays, all over the country, but I seriously feel that we don't embrace the actor, the imagination, or the audience, in a way that the greatest channels offer us the opportunity to do. We have ourselves, our bodies, our imaginations at our fingertips but somehow we're so frightened of using them, frightened of saying let's not do the big set. Spectacle, ritual are great, but it doesn't have to be so expensive and not at the expense of the play.

In Italy, I saw two clowns on the street in a theatre festival and I watched them for hours. They didn't really have any props, so like the commedia artists, they had to keep the people in the market square – cover the ground, don't let the people get bored, if a space has been dead too long, move over, keep the people interested, literally cover the ground, but they had nothing else. I was never bored; I didn't know where they were going next. They come from a tradition of commedia where you have nothing and you give the audience everything. It's really about giving people the plays, on the night, in the room, the experience of it, just then. We don't trust our audience enough; we seriously don't think they'll understand a word. I think children understand Shakespeare; they understand the words and language, if you believe they do. In that square in Italy, we gave them our imagination because we were allowed to have one. The best director says we've got to make this line clear, because if you're not clear the audience won't be clear. If you don't trust the audience, you give them less, in giving them too much. I think we've got to recognise they love to supply the missing links, they don't want everything put on a plate for them, they absolutely love having to work it out. I think we've got to respect the audience, we've got to remember they're there. If we're talking about theatre, not television, we're storytellers and without them we wouldn't be there; presently, the show could go on without them.

As the people who are delivering the story aurally, how do you think actors might be better placed to make theatre better?

Their voices have simply got to be heard; it's not about directing by committee, the actor's voice and where he's coming from has got to be part of the creative team, if we have to have a creative team at all. In my view the whole thing is a creative team, it is a collaboration from the word go between the actors and the director; the designer and the rest of them come in to facilitate. Since the emergence of 'The Fourth Wall' theatre in 1912, the role of the actor has diminished. Prior to that, the actor was the most important person, now the actor is the least important person and I think part of that is the technological revolution that's happened. When Shakespeare was writing there were no iPhones or digital stuff, no cameras. The idea of going to the theatre and seeing a video screen up there is so weird to me. I want to say, 'that's a cinema, this is a theatre, don't mix your metaphors, or do a modern play about that'. What I'm saying is this technological impact is vast and I think most actors fundamentally feel they're being supplanted. It used to be that you felt, why are they putting music up in the middle of my speech? Isn't the speech enough? Now, why are they putting music, video, dry ice. What's happened to our believing that the audience will understand it? So the actor has got to be heard but the audience has to be given their intelligence back, we've got to demand more from the audience and we've got to be in a position where we can say, I don't want music under there. I want it to be hard for them. I don't know how we get there. We need conversations, we need a forum again, where actors will talk to all the people who run theatre, in a constructive, open way, to say this is what's happened to theatre and if you want that, that's OK but is there another way and can the people who are interested in that come over here and start that way, maybe it costs less to do what we want to do.

When you say a 'forum again', was there previously one?

It wasn't an actors forum; I was involved in a seminar, at the NT Studio, about classical verse speaking, but what happened was that actors got up and spoke – a lot of leading actors felt able to get up and say things in public, like I don't want to sign a two-year contract at the RSC, that doesn't mean I don't want to play Cleopatra, it just means I have a life. There was a voice and people were heard. It was great because it highlighted the need for a conversation. There's no conversation now, no space where we can have these debates.

How do you prepare for an audition?

For theatre I read the whole script, for television I don't necessarily; if it's a massive part I obviously do, so the script is absolutely everything to me really. I've got enough experience to skip a little bit of the story if it's television, but with theatre, I really look at the script in detail and I prepare a page that I want to prepare. If I've been told there's only one scene, I'll talk to my agent about doing another. I then underpin words with the thoughts. I don't consider what 'their' [the director's] input is, what I consider is, what is the text, what does it mean, how can I make people believe me when I speak, that's all I do.

Would you do any research beyond that?

I played Charlotte, in *The Madness of King George*, so I read a book about Charlotte and it was extremely interesting. I don't know what it did to me, Alan Bennett had already written an extremely interesting character, which seemed to convey most of what had been said about her. If it's a real person I do that type of research, but if it isn't a real person, to be honest, I don't. I look at the style of the play and at the time it was written. So, if it's an Oscar Wilde play, I'll think about Oscar Wilde, I'll think about when it was written, who it was written for, why it was written and who was watching it and that all helps me locate the version of me that will suit that play. That sense of what is the reflection of the society as it was written at the time is absolutely essential and that's how I teach Shakespeare or anything I teach, as if you've never seen it before, as if we were doing it for the first time, because then we can really broaden the horizon of the play and the relationship with the audience.

How do you reconcile that complete world vision of its period with a modern audience's sensibilities? What is the usefulness of finding out about all that stuff, in terms of a modern audience receiving the play today?

I'm not talking about doing a Shakespeare play in Elizabethan costume
necessarily. What I'm talking about is making you connect to the text in the
way that it was written. When you do the witches in *Macbeth*, you recognise
that witchcraft in 1598 was taken very seriously. That changes the way that
you operate the scene. If you think about divorce in any of the *Henrys* or
the History Plays, you recognise that those points were far more serious
then than they are now. It plumbs the depths of the play inside you; those
are the issues that you should be discussing and that research strengthens,
deepens, develops and explains the emotional world of the play as you are
doing it. It is easily accessible, via that life.

*So deepening the knowledge you hold within yourself of that world, will, in and
of itself, communicate itself to an audience?*

Simply put, it makes me more credible. If I absolutely play the whole play
as if I believe in God, when I'm St Joan, that is going to make me more
credible, because every time I speak, it's not going to be a light thing; it's
something that I live by. If, for instance, I'm a witch, the images I draw
are everyday to me, but have more weight in a society where witches are
hunted and found and believed in, so I have to do everything with more
intent and the intention itself, the depth of understanding and belief, will
convey itself. Modernity doesn't come into it; if the audience believe me,
then we've crossed the modern/old barrier. All we need to do is make them
believe us; bring them with us.

Do you do anything particular in advance of the start of rehearsals?

No, most of the time I don't do anything. If a director asks me to make a list
of what everybody says about the character in the play my heart sinks and I
do it really quickly and I'm not really interested in it to be honest.

Why is that?

I will be doing that anyway; that's what rehearsals are for. Making lists,
sitting for hours wasting time while I say to you what your character says
about me, when you know that and I know that because we've read the play,
seems to me to be a waste of rehearsal time. I think rehearsal time is about
getting up and doing it, stretching it, bending it, cancelling it, continuing

it and doing it again. I'm happy to sit round the table when we're doing Shakespeare and paraphrase the text; that would be maybe the only work I would do if I were doing a Shakespeare play, although, if that was with a good director, that would happen anyway. I make sure I know what I'm saying, otherwise I don't do anything.

So for you, the fundamental work only begins when you hit the rehearsal room?

Yes, but if I've got my wide, global view of when the play was written and I come up with a director who has decided to set this classic piece in Henley-on-Thames in 1992, then I will have had that discussion at the audition. I will have said, 'look, this is a great play and a wonderful part and can I ask you what you're going to do with it?' If you say you're going to set it in Henley-on-Thames, that might be quite interesting – but I want to know about it first and I want to decide whether I think that classic play, given the way it was written, will transfer and then I'll decide whether I want to be in it. So at the audition I ask who's designing it, what the design is going to be, is there a concept, can they talk about it and, if I don't like it, I don't do it.

How do people respond to that series of questions?

If you start being defensive, they respond defensively but if you openly say I need to know what your feelings are about this because my feelings are very strong and I'd love to do this in its context, but I wouldn't like to do this without that context, at some point, being available, they don't seem to mind.

Are there things you particularly like and try to do, with each rehearsal process?

I'm split in my answer, because I'm a director as well. I don't think there's anything I do in each rehearsal process. As a director, my aim is to release the play and to make the actors feel as generously creative as possible towards that. There's a thing about egos in rehearsals isn't there? Sometimes there are some egos bouncing around the room that get in the way of the play and there's an unspoken status tension between the cast and the director. That's not helpful and, as a director, you have to get everyone to feel that their input is valuable, because the play is more important than them. As an actor, I feel that very strongly. One of the ways I engage in a play is to work out what my function in the scene is, that's something I always do. I don't need to know what happened before I enter; I need to know, as I come in, I'm interrupting something very important and the author needs that interruption at this point – then I might get the dynamic right. So I look at the dynamics, very strongly, as an actor. I don't necessarily discuss that, unless someone gets in my way.

One thing I like to do is give the scene a little title. For example, in War Horse, one of the directors gave the first scene I do as a German Officer a title, 'The Good German Officer Saves the Horses from the Fighting': that's the purpose, the story of the scene and everything goes towards the telling of that story, primarily. Anything extra mustn't deflect from that storytelling. Is there anything like that, you do?

I've got a shortcut system, which is, 'front foot, back foot': how engaged is the character at this point? How disengaged is she at that point? Is she on her heels? Is she on her toes? Is she on her heels with one person and on her toes with someone else? What are the needs? How does the pace vary depending on the motivation of the entire play? So I work that out. A habit of mine is to start off slightly on the outside of it, trying to get somewhere quickly, too soon. I don't really like that, so in the middle of the journey, I stop, to ask myself, 'what if this was me?' and suddenly the whole thing starts to come from inside. I don't try showing off any more, I take it from, 'what if this was me?' and that somehow launches in me a centre from which I can operate more strongly. It has to come from me to be truthful. You can think, 'how do I play loneliness?' – you can't, but you can understand how it would feel, if it were you.

You can't play a state, so what do you do to create that effect?

I believe in the words I say. You can't play a mood or an emotion; if the words are good enough the emotion will happen. Too many people now play hysterics, moods. If you improvise, the main rules are you don't know what's going to happen; I notice that people get to hysterics really quickly now. I do that myself, suddenly you feel pressure to make someone laugh or cry or to shout at them. It's not very helpful; it's saying 'I'm pushing it this way'. So how is that relevant? People want to be seen acting well; consciously or not, they're saying, 'look at me, look at me'. This is what I mean by strengthening the relationship with the audience. The audience will pick up on the mood, if you play the lines and you believe in the words, the audience will do the rest, that's their job. It's incredibly important that the audience does the emotional work. Even if our characters fall apart, we're not indulging that, let that happen, play the action and let the audience do the rest.

What is the director's role, in relation to the actors?

Directors are essential, but the role of the director is as facilitator.

So is the director a super-audience member?

Yes, when I'm directing, that's what I am: I'm seeing it from an audience's point of view and saying, 'is this clear?'

They are more than that though; they lead the audience.

They do, because they have privileges the audience don't have – the time and the decision-making choices. Choices are made constantly for the audience, for the clarity of the evening.

What is the impact of the technical rehearsal on you as an actor?

It depends on how happy I am in my process. If I've had a terrible time with concepts and all that, I'm just going to be miserable when that time comes around, but I know I have to compensate for that and try to use it very technically, to get from A to B, to work out how the door handle does affect the way I come in. If I'm in a process that is gloriously fluid, open and creative, then I just shoot up in inches as soon as I get on stage and I absolutely love that. I love it when I think, I'd love a handkerchief and I ask the designer and he says, 'yes of course' and suddenly I've got one. It makes all the difference to a tiny moment because things are happening, really rolling. If the air is breathing between the actors and the director, things accelerate but if they're not, they stumble and fall.

What do you do if you have a costume you really don't like?

I risk everything and say I don't want to wear it. It's very difficult but if you do it, you have to be able to replace it with something and that's where I fell down early on because I'd say I don't want to do that and finally they'd say well what do you want and I hadn't supplied the answer – if you're going to make a fight you've got to have the answer. I memorably mucked up playing Cariola, the maid servant in *The Duchess of Malfi*, because I'd had a fight in the rehearsal room. I'd refused to wear a certain wig, the trouble was during the fight my confidence for the part had gone, so when I went on stage I looked at the floor the whole time. Ian McKellen came into my dressing room at the end and said, 'well you may have won your fight but you lost the battle because the fact is you've come on with nothing, you can't do that'. He gave me one thing to play and the next night I was fine. It taught me that it's all very well having the fight, but you've got to know how to work through it and that requires a lot of confidence, and also how do you play the fight? You have to be open and mature.

What strategies do you use to keep your performance live over a long run?

I try to make sure I never take for granted why my character is there. The other strategy is to listen, because I think listening can go downhill after a while. So as I'm standing in the wings, I tend to say, 'what do I want?' But if I'm in the midst of a long time, I go hang on a minute, listen and maybe don't know what will happen next, maybe do something new. If it's a comedy, that's difficult; but you can get a new laugh, just by listening again.

How do you feel about the curtain call?

Passionately. Curtain calls are fabulous. The audience deserves everything they can get. Curtain calls are a graceful ending to an evening in which the audience has participated as much as the actors have. If I'm directing I just say this is it, this is why you're performing, you need to come on and smile, it's over, it's fabulous, it's been great, now you're going home, you're just actors. So I think smiling is essential. I also think – and this may not be a popular belief – there should be an element of elitism about the curtain call: if you've played Hamlet, you deserve a curtain call, if you've just played Pericles you deserve a curtain call. I don't think you should stumble in from the side and that everyone supporting you through the extraordinary evening should get a position first. I think it should be organised, it's actually about structure.

Some actors experience a feeling of loneliness after the curtain call. Have you ever had that?

No.

How do you cope with rejection?

If I've done my very best in the audition then the rejection is fine; I don't feel it too much, because if they don't want me doing my best, then they don't want *me* and that is a very helpful process. If I think I could have done that better, I'd not listened enough or I was too nervous in the audition, I just didn't feel like I'd done my thing, I really mind. I also mind when I find that it's somebody where I think God, I could have done it better than them, of course I feel that, I can't stand it.

How do you cope with unemployment, how do you maintain your motivation, your skills base and your emotional sanity and stability?

I teach, but more than that, I've never thought that anyone owes me a living – I'm as good as my last job and no more. So for twenty-five years I've made sure I've had something else to butter my bread with – by teaching. I love teaching because I learn from it. I can develop my experience as an actor and my skills base by teaching. Most important of all, it gives me confidence that I can survive without it. When I go into an interview I think I don't have to have this job; if I'm offered it I might not want it; that keeps me sane. I teach businessmen, I teach actors, I teach opera singers to act; I have a huge teaching base. So sometimes I say to myself, 'I don't actually want to do that, I'd rather do my teaching'.

How does you're agent respond to that?

She's brilliant. We have an ongoing scenario where I say, 'RADA want to know if I'll do this, the National's Education Department want me to do this, can you pencil dates in?' As we get closer I say, 'OK we're going to confirm, is that alright?' She sometimes says, 'no, you don't want to do that because this might happen' and I spin all the plates. It's stressful but I would rather feel like a complete person than a pawn on a chessboard. When I teach at RADA, one of the things I constantly say to them is, it is your duty not to be small when you leave here, make work for yourself, go out and teach, go to schools, set up companies, find a way of doing something that will evolve your business.

What do you love about being an actor?

I love being on stage, in front of an audience and performing: when it's good, I love performing. What I love most about performing is the movement between the audience and the actor, the relationship that we've kind of risked together. I just love that sense of what we could have done and did, what we've achieved: a laugh, a moment and a sense of some shift. That quality of having engaged in peoples' emotional worlds is astonishing.

And what do you most hate about being an actor?

I hate the fact that we don't have a voice, we're not part of the creative team.

SIMON RUSSELL BEALE

Simon is an associate of the National and Almeida theatres, and an associate artist of the RSC. In 2003 he was awarded a CBE in the Queen's Birthday Honours List for his services to the Arts. He has garnered awards for a very wide range of work including Ben Jonson's anarchic comedy *Volpone, Hamlet, Uncle Vanya* and *Candide*. Extensive radio credits include *The Complete George Smiley* and *War and Peace*. He won Royal Television Society and BAFTA awards for Channel 4's *A Dance to the Music of Time* and presents BBC Four's *Sacred Music*.

POK   *How long have you been an actor?*

SRB   Twenty-six years.

What would you do if you weren't an actor?

I didn't go immediately into acting; I did try other things: I applied to a merchant bank and I also started a singing course, so I could have been a singer; I played with being an academic – I wanted a PhD in Literature – but there was only one choice really.

What experience made you want to be an actor?

I remember the first time the headmaster gave me a bit of Mark Anthony – the 'Dogs of War' speech – to read. It must have had some sort of impact because I remember where I was sitting; I remember what the sun was like. It was shining through the windows. I think I got the bug then.

What was it about that experience that thrilled you?

It was probably the attention being paid by the headmaster. Nobody had picked me out for anything particular by that stage. I was at a choir school and I was a very mediocre singer, so I wasn't a star in that musical world. So nobody really paid me any attention at all and then suddenly he latched on to me and said 'do you want to read this?' and it was a big speech. There must have been something visceral about this language because I don't come from a particularly literary family, it's a very musical family, but it became a bug from that point. In my senior school I had a wonderful English teacher, Brian Worthington, who, by the time I was 17 said 'do you want to play King

Lear in the school play?' I played Desdemona as a young boy and I did Lear for him at the end of my career at school.

Would that have been unusual for someone as young as you to play Desdemona?

No, especially in Shakespeare, the young boys always played the women's parts and the reason I was given Desdemona originally, was because I could sing and she has to sing 'The Willow Song'. But then he became such an influential part of my life. I'd never thought of reading English at university, I was going to be a doctor, like the rest of my family, but he took me by the scruff of the neck.

What did he do?

Well he was very strict and very puritanical, an intellectual, he was taught by the great Leavis at Cambridge. He had a rigorous, puritanical, unsentimental approach to literary analysis, combined with a passionate belief for the subject he was teaching. He was of the first generation of those pupils from Cambridge who established the subject as something fundamentally important rather than a sort of hobby. So he applied this vigour and there was something thrilling about that.

Has the rigour of his literary analysis influenced the way you work as an actor?

Completely: the idea of pursuing an argument and not allowing a loose thought in was his legacy to me. He was a keen amateur actor himself and he directed all the school plays and it was he who said to my parents when I was 15, 'has he thought about going into the theatre?' He used to come and see me; he hated everything, but I think he was proud of me.

How do you apply that philosophy to your work as an actor?

With the very great works of art, the great literary dramas, I try to get rid of any preconception I have; that's harder than you think because it's part of our culture. For example, I did Cassius for Deborah Warner: my preconception about Cassius was that he's a cold, political manipulator and then I realised he threatens to commit suicide in every single scene and then does commit suicide. So it was a question of saying OK that's a piece of information that's been given to me and now it's up to me to decide what to do with it. I decided to take the simplest option – which is probably what I always try to do rather than a more complex option – in other words that his threats are genuine, so it's not a piece of hysterical psychological playing, he will genuinely kill himself if Caesar becomes king. That opened up a whole other sequence of thoughts about him being passionate, disturbed and not very good at the political manoeuvring that he thinks he is good at. He spends a lot of the time panicking. I always have Brian at the back of my head saying that doesn't make logical sense, if you pursue that route.

So it's very much evidential?

Yes, absolutely, but trying to see the evidence as simply as I can.

What other great influences have there been on your career as an actor, in terms of how your artistic sensibilities have been formed or changed?

My family were musical, we didn't go to the theatre, so I can't say I went to see Derek Jacobi or Ian McKellen and think I want to be an actor, that didn't happen. I only started going to theatre when I came to London in the early 80s so I can't say there was a particular actor that made me want to do what he or she was doing. However, there was a person at university called Steve Unwin: he was the person everyone wanted to work with, he had fantastic charisma, a fantastic command of the undergraduate lot. I was at university when there was a huge group of very clever, funny people, like Stephen Fry, Emma Thompson, Hugh Laurie and on the serious side of the university's drama landscape were people like Tilda Swinton and Steve. Steve reinforced Brian's Puritanism. Until then, acting was showing off, and he taught me something, we were very, very serious, we were going to change the world and theatre was shit and we were going to revitalise it – the usual student thing – but the plus side of that was it was deeply important. He did a production of *All's Well The Ends Well* in the final term at university, it was the first time I'd worked with him, so for three years he'd ignored me, and I thought it was the most beautiful thing in the world, I thought it was perfect theatre. It was probably horrible to watch.

You said Steve reinforced the Puritanism, how did he do that?

I suppose he was hugely influenced by Brook, but it was about simplifying the picture and the idea of standing on stage and delivering something that has a purity in the stream of language.

Were there specific techniques or exercises that he applied, which you have retained, or have a bearing on the way you approach text?

Not exercises. You know when Trevor Nunn did his 1999 ensemble season at the National and he had those first workshop days, I remember he gave me a speech by Angelo where the verse is famously fractured, it's all out of kilter and we had a long, long debate where I insisted – and I still believe it – that I would prefer to ignore every single rule of verse speaking, if I can make sense, at first hearing, for the audience. If a line is split in an odd way, I know it's the sign of a fractured mind, but if it is a single thought, I would prefer to do that line as a single thought, regardless of the end stops. I might be misrepresenting Steve but that's what I remember taking away from him: the idea of clarity at first hearing – very, very important. You can be as breathtaking as you like, especially with fractured verse, but if the audience goes away thinking all I got was the impression of a disturbed mind, I really think that's a waste of time. Another legacy of Steve is to get the thoughts clear first: before you even think about emotional matters, fracturing, non-fractured, whatever, get the thoughts clear, really clear. Like the preconceptions, that's much harder than you think. A very simple example, this play I'm doing at the moment, one of the speeches starts 'Too hot, too hot…', I'm not saying you should say it like this but what he is, is *too* hot, it's *too* hot, that's different from saying it's hot. It sounds a minor detail but get that really clear in your head – that he's saying what they're doing is <u>too</u> hot.

So essentially that's an intellectual analysis.

Yes I think it probably is, yes. I like constructing an argument.

Can you tell me how you do that? Can you talk us through Hamlet?

To return to the idea of challenging one's preconceptions: with Hamlet I knew I didn't want to sexually assault my mother in the bedroom scene, only because that idea had been explored – that's vanity really – to the nth degree and there's nothing in the text that says he assaults her. I wanted to see what would happen if the last thing in the world he wants to do is touch her in any way and, using my own psychological make-up, I'm probably too middle class to think I could ever do that to my mother. The other thing I was puzzled about, was madness; admittedly I started with a preconception that I felt there was something supertextual about the way other people treated Hamlet's madness, so I looked at the moments he was mad and there was only one moment where we see him doing classic Shakespearian madness – with Polonius in Act 2 scene 2, about the cloud, words, words, words, words; the rest of the time he's perfectly sane. I thought that's interesting, it isn't page after page of this man going mad, it is one scene which he plays deliberately mad, to a man who we know doesn't have a particularly cute vision of human nature really and also to the man I suddenly discovered who is the first person to say he's mad. Polonius is the one who tells Gertrude he's out of his mind, therefore, to say Hamlet is mad is taking Polonius' argument at face value, it seemed to me. Now that's constructing an argument, which I could then support if someone challenged me about it: I could say look at the script. That led to further discoveries, so that he became a sweeter prince than I imagined him to be. If it had been a different director, it might not have gone that way. That's the interesting thing, because I was being directed by a man who is sweet, John Caird, that's the way it went, but it was supported by the argument about the madness. I was keen for it to be watertight.

That personality factor is crucial isn't it?

Yes and I also think it changes over your life too, don't you think? When I first started I played a lot of what they used to call high definition parts and high definition performances: so I'd be doing Richard III and Thersites and it culminated in Iago – hard-edged characters with an almost adolescent, bleakness of human nature, which was in tune with mine. Then my Mum died and that fundamentally shifted my perspective on life. That happened just before Hamlet. I think I've softened up a bit, I'm softer edged. Also doing Chekhov – he is the great writer of the fuzzy edge, isn't he? He is the great writer of people having diametrically opposed intentions, desires or thoughts, at the same time. With Uncle Vanya, you think he hates Yelena, he loves Yelena; he's embarrassed, he's not embarrassed; he's arrogant, he's not arrogant... You end up not being able to fix on anything except for your own personality.

How do you marry personality, or personal self-expression, with the disciplines of classical text?

Well that's a difficult question because, I'm perfectly well aware that I'll adapt parts to me, I'm perfectly well aware that that's a weakness.

Is that a weakness?

I don't know, it might not be a weakness, it might be a strength because you're building on firm ground aren't you, by building on yourself? However there is a certain relief in doing something like *Major Barbara*, playing Undershaft, a character way out of my usual personal and professional scope; I spent six years not doing alpha males and then I was asked to do an alpha male from a working-class background, so I couldn't rely on any of the old tricks or techniques. I think you probably get lazy, well not lazy, I'm never lazy, but you do naturally seem to use what you've got. I've also swayed in my career between sympathy and judgement as the natural position for an actor approaching a part. For example, I found it impossible to be sympathetic towards Iago and I felt at the time that was right, that the whole performance was a judgement of that man; I couldn't find any redeeming feature in him, any, but I'd been brought up to believe that you had to find such a feature in order to play a part and I thought I don't know if that's necessarily true. I hope I didn't distort him in any way but I was very conscious that it was a moral exercise. On the other hand, with Macbeth, I think I sympathised too much with him. So I should have judged him more I think.

You say you sympathised too much with him, how did that manifest itself?

It softened him, it softened him and Simon, middle-class boy from Wiltshire came out, it was a crack, so I felt terribly sorry for Macbeth at the end. I still do, I can't shake that off. I still have a feeling about that part, that he's the most miserable person I've ever played – genuinely, profoundly, existentially unhappy – having had the potential to be joyous and good; that was very important in the part, but I think you've got to come out thinking he's a mass murderer. I remember thinking there's too much Simon and not enough Macbeth.

When I played Macbeth, I tried to make him feel guilty which is not what he feels at all; he feels fear or regret at the possibility of not succeeding which is different from guilt or remorse.

I think you've hit the nail on the head. I presented a man as if he were guilty and it's different, it's within the same range, but it's not guilt. Mine was a man who did this to save a childless marriage, I'm sure a lot of Macbeths go down this route but it was for his wife and an obsession with children which is very Shakespearian of course. I should have been more precise about the accuracy of that range of emotion.

I'd like to talk more about the process and the detail of that. Do you do pre-rehearsal preparation or research?

It depends. If it's Shakespeare no, except for learning lines; I've now recently got into the habit of learning the whole part.

Why is that?

It's age, partly because it is more difficult at 47, it really is. I feel that it gives me a head start on the work, that I have done a lot of the boring stuff like stresses.

In the learning of it, you mark the stresses at the end of each line?

No at the top of the line. I obey the rules more than I implied earlier in the sense that I always try to obey the rules and if I can't then... The trouble with learning by yourself is that, obviously, you make mistakes and then it's difficult to unlearn. It's also almost impossible to learn disinterestedly and that has led to problems with making early decisions about how to say something that I've let go unchallenged. The first play I did for Sam Mendes was *Troilus and Cressida*, I was playing Thersites and there's one particular line which is 'The sun doth borrow of the moon when Diomed keeps his word'; it's a nice enough line but it's of no particular significance and after about a year – and this was the result of learning early – I got into the rhythm and Sam said 'could you stop saying that line as if it's the meaning of the play'. He was quite right, I was doing this as a rhythmic exercise without understanding the significance of what I was saying.

How do you guard against getting stuck in a thought pattern, from which you cannot escape, as a result of learning early?

I rely on the director really and the other actors. If you're worried about your own part, listen to the other person; that is the most useful piece of advice on acting I've ever had. It's an answer to boredom, to long runs, to getting stuck in a rut with saying something; it's so simple, but if you do that once, suddenly you're responding in a different way. That's where the learning early comes in useful because you have the lines so you can genuinely listen to people early and respond in a different way. But I suppose I do rely on an outside ear.

Do you do any form of research?

For Shakespeare no, but if it's a modern play, I may do. I did a play called *Humble Boy* about astrophysics, so I thought I'd better find out about String Theory and I did one about currency speculation and I did a bit of research about the City because it's something I know nothing about.

How did that help your performance?

I had a vague idea of what I was talking about. The research on Shakespeare is interesting because it's a hindrance a lot of the time.

Why is that?

Well if you're doing a history play it really is a hindrance because he wrote such bollocks historically. It's for my own interest that *A Winter's Tale* was written in 1610 but it doesn't contribute to the performance. It's fascinating sometimes to go back to the source of material: with Iago it was interesting to find in the source material that Iago and Emilia have a baby, so Shakespeare got rid of the baby because he was trying to say something about a childless couple – that's of use but those nuggets of information are kind of rare. And in modern plays it tends to be a specific project.

Do you think the fact that you've done that work helps the audience?

I hope so. At least I know that I know.

What bearing did reading about astrophysics have on your rehearsing of the part for Humble Boy?

The character, Felix Humble, had long speeches explaining String Theory, so John Caird asked me to explain it to the rest of the company. That is a very good exercise because you visualise it in your own particular way and then transfer it back to the speech. Directors sometimes ask you to do research for a specific purpose, like the masked ball in *Much Ado*. Now that was my job and was extremely useful because I've always been confused by how masked balls function: if you put on a mask and I put on a mask, you know exactly who I am. So you think well is it a game they're all playing, whereby they say we're pretending not to know each other, so you're allowed to say blah, blah, blah? But it just so happened that I had an Italian friend who comes from Southern Italy and of course *Much Ado* is set in Sicily, who explained how masks were used in his village: people would go from house to house, line up the chairs on the back wall, round the room, put all the chairs to the side, clear the chairs for dancing, and a masked group would come and knock on the door and be allowed in, they were completely masked, so you really didn't know who they were and you could dance with who you liked, you could dance with the 'wrong sex' if you wanted to without being pointed out for it and that was directly put into that production. That was a very tangible, useful bit of information. The chairs pushed back, the girls were waiting for the boys to arrive and that sense of excitement as the masked men appear at the door.

Would you say that research is best when it is specific?

Yes, I think it's interesting to know what Ben Johnson's world was like living in Blackfriars during *The Alchemist* but, it's of no significance to putting on the play.

What makes up a good rehearsal, what are the component parts?

I think the most illusive, difficult and magical thing a director can do – and I mean this seriously – is love you: love everything you do as a company, because it gives confidence, it makes people relax and risk things and the greatest directors all have that. I've worked with Sam [Mendes] eight times now and I'm absolutely sure he doesn't think this, but I can fool myself into thinking he wouldn't be anywhere else if he chose to be, other than in that rehearsal room watching me and I'm serious about that. I've just come back from NYC a few days ago, we were rehearsing on the 5th floor of a big building and he said at the end of the last run 'I just want you all to know that every time I get in the elevator at the bottom my spirits light up when I get to the 5th floor every day, thank you very much'. I don't care if it was a lie or not, it just makes us feel that when he walks into that room that's the only place he wants to be and I genuinely believe that's the most important thing you do as a director: it's just love, love, love, love – love what the actors are doing, find it absolutely and ceaselessly fascinating what they're doing and then they can risk anything. How you do that I don't know, how you create an atmosphere of complete relaxation I don't know, but it's a real skill.

And what about a bad rehearsal then?

I've been in a rehearsal room where I've walked in and there are people sitting totally silent, waiting for the rehearsal to start, with a sense of impending doom, like they don't want to get up on the stage.

They felt like they were about to be judged?

No, more than that, they were going to be judged and found wanting; there was absolute assumption that that would be the case. We've all seen directors destroy actors systematically, which I've never understood – well that's not true, I understand the psychological tick that makes someone want to do that – but I've never understood it as being a productive process. When I started out there were quite a few directors on the circuit who liked to do that sort of stuff.

Do they enlist your opinions ever in a bad rehearsal situation?

No I'd be left out.

Excluded?

Yes, from a process. It might be to do with playing bigger parts as you get older – I don't think it is – but in the 26 years that I've been working, I've noticed a culture of directors and designers especially, being much more inclusive of actors, which I think is very interesting. Funnily enough it's the same in the academic world. When I first went to Stratford in the mid 80s, lovely academics there, well we never really met them and now we have Arden editions with whole sections on the play in performance and a sense that actors have something to contribute to the debate about Shakespeare's plays, which I think is fascinating. I haven't worked with a designer now for ages who has said, this is what you're wearing: it just doesn't happen anymore and I think it applies to everyone, in most of the companies I work with now.

Why is that more useful? Is there not a danger of encroaching on designers' or directors' domains?

I don't think that's a problem, but I think there can be a problem – a bit like casting yourself – in that you do not see yourself as other people see you; that would be the danger – and vanity of course – in terms of working with some designers. I have that problem of how I look on stage all the time anyway because of my own weaknesses, I'm always disappointed with the way I look on stage but that's my own personal problem. So I don't think there's a problem with encroaching on a designer's territory so much as being aware that you're receptive to how other people see you.

What have been the most useful exercises for you or rehearsal techniques over your career, the things that have unlocked a character, or a scene that you can say, 'OK I can use that again or I'd like to use that again'?

Two diametrically opposed ones. When I worked with Katie Mitchell, in a production of *Ghosts*, she insisted on such hyper-realism that, before we got anywhere near even walking around the space, we knew where the bedroom was, what my sheets were like, where the harbour was, where the boats came in, how often they came in, even stuff that wasn't mentioned in the play: what my bedroom smelt like, where I'd lived in Paris, such an extraordinary wealth of naturalistic detail. I knew the ground plan of the house, what the upstairs was like. By the time we got on to the stage, I know it sounds silly, we had nothing to do.

Except to be?

Except to be. That's super-realism and I found that fantastic. That was linked in my head to a production of *The Seagull* which was a fascinating example again of giving people enough information that they didn't have to think about what they were doing: we rehearsed the first three acts of *The Seagull*, a four act play, which has a particular time set, there's a break of two years and there's a fourth act. We rehearsed the first three acts in a pretty conventional way for six weeks, didn't even look at the fourth act. One day we walked into rehearsal, he'd asked us all to learn it, he got what furniture he wanted, we did it and it never changed, that was it. It was pretty impressive, to get eight actors into such a situation that they didn't have to think. I'm a fan of pretty conventional working styles in the sense that I think you have to do the really boring work on the great texts together: in an ideal world, cut together, if you're going to cut it, but you do the really boring, plodding stuff and the meaning stuff, really thoroughly because you'll never get a chance to do it again.

That's the round the table work?

Yes, I think it's enjoyable but then I have a slightly academic approach, but if you don't do it at the beginning, you'll never do it again. I do remember Nick Hytner when we were doing *Much Ado*, we got to the last scene and he said 'Oh God I'm bored with this now' and I said to him we've got to do it because there are so many other things coming up. I like Sam's way of working: he creates a circle of chairs, immediately after the table work, you just do the scene and he'll do very simple exercises not frightening ones or silly ones, like pretend to be a reporter, reporting the event, but he'll suggest, 'what happens if Hermione's dead body is still there?' What he does, and it's genuine, is give the impression that he's finding out with you.

I enjoy all that table work too; Conall Morrison for example – this is really valuable doing a Shakespeare play – will insist that it's not even an approximation, every image is precise, so he'll ask you what it means and say, 'no, no it's not "it's <u>like</u>", what <u>is</u> it?' *It can be very painstaking and everyone is invited to participate.*

That's extremely important: as a leading man, you're in a very privileged position and your voice tends to be heard and allowed space, but it's absolutely imperative that everybody has an equal voice. I also think, and it's a delicate one this, up to a certain point in rehearsal – well the round the table bit – that other people's characters are not off limit; that's a very delicate thing to negotiate, but if someone wants to say something about Macbeth, they have a perfect right to do so as long as it's not done aggressively or offensively and as long as the person playing Macbeth has a moment to say, 'actually I don't agree with that' and has the confidence to be able to do that. Non-actors, stage managers, anyone who is sitting round the table should also be able to contribute. It's a delicate one but I think it's important.

There is a hierarchy in the rehearsal room and it does depend on what part you're playing, which isn't useful, in my view.

It's not useful for the leading actors either, that's the point, it's not as if it's protecting them particularly. At a certain point it has to stop and determining that is tricky. It's when you stand on the floor isn't it?

That transition from the table to the floor is always tricky: you sit round the table for a couple of weeks sometimes and as you do more readings of it, more excavations and conversations, you feel you're really getting into the heart of the matter and then when you stand up you think, 'Oh my god! How do I apply all that?'

We all do, that's the main reason why I learn early because I don't want to be standing up with a book and I'd rather get that agony out the way early. Sam has a very good way: he'll often say 'just get into the circle' (it's nerve-wracking for the first two minutes but it goes really quickly), he says 'just sit on the floor and do the scene to each other', so you're not thrown immediately into it, no staging and if you're both on your knees doing the scene to each other just running the lines, that's what it feels like and then he'll say 'Simon you get up and walk around while the other person stays kneeling.

Kind of arbitrary things, but in their arbitrariness, they allow you an access route?

Among other things, it allows you to not get self-conscious about your hands!

What strategies do you employ to overcome those moments of blockage when you think I don't know what I'm doing, I don't know who I am, I don't know what I'm saying, which we all get a lot in early stages of rehearsals but even in performances?

We've already mentioned the biggest one in performance, which is listening to other people, that's brilliant.

So why is that crucial?

If you listen without thinking of what you're going to say next, you will come out with something, I guarantee you, every single time, which is different to what you've been doing, not necessarily massively so, but there will be some slight inflection in your voice that will be different because you've just responded. Usually, when you're blocked, you've stopped listening. I don't know why the human mind works like that but it does. I have a blockage at the moment: I'm doing Lopakhin in *The Cherry Orchard* – slightly out of my comfort zone, a Russian merchant. Sam doesn't want me to do an accent, which would have been a way of hiding I think, so I'm speaking like this, a middle-class, middle-aged gay Englishman and there's a very particular way they speak; that's fine for 90% of the part, there's lots of sides to the part, it's very interesting not just about being a Russian merchant. However, there's one bit, which is his sense of humour, which I simply don't understand. There's one bizarre moment when he runs on stage and says 'mooo' like a cow; it's incomprehensible but it is a sign of his sense of humour that he does this. There are a couple of other moments: he misquotes Hamlet, makes the sound of a pig. I tried to ignore there was a problem and attempted to meld them into the rest of the part: it's rather difficult to explain but if he was a sensitive guy he'd do a sensitive mooo: it doesn't work. He runs on, says mooo and runs off and that's it: you have to do that mooo completely and you have to run on completely and don't complicate it, just try and do it 100%. I don't say I've got rid of the block yet but at least the last run we did I felt, well, that's just what he does. Edward Bond said don't look for consistency, the danger of an over reflective approach and the danger of constructing an argument is that you smooth out the inconsistency of the part. He might be a very sensitive guy, he might be barking, he might be acutely aware of what people around him think but he has one of those occasions when he comes on, does a great big mooo and runs off again.

It's what you were saying earlier; you're sort of doing it mechanically.

To try and release something, yes. Unless I commit to that moment completely, I will never know. If I hedge it around I will never know what Chekhov was trying to do with it. I get it all the time. It's like people being frightened of 'O' in Shakespeare, unless you go 'O'…

People will try and brush over it?

Yes they will and O is a proper word. It's not a warm-up word.

What do you think your responsibility as an actor is in the rehearsal room?

If you're playing a leading part, you have a responsibility to be generous, kind, to make it easy for others to work with you. If you're doing Hamlet you make sure that when you're on stage it's enjoyable to be on there with you, that's probably the most important thing. The leading men I've worked with, like Gambon, for example, didn't do anything specific but they had a generosity of spirit: I was never frightened of them. I was very young when I worked with Michael and he could have been really frightening but he absolutely acknowledged my function in the play and it's quite an unusual one with *Volpone* because Mosca does so much of the work, I can't remember what he said, he said something specific like it's your play to run, there you go, I have faith, go and run the play. We have a joke in the company I'm in at the moment about taking on problems that are not yours and we all have a tendency to do it. So you'll get someone come up to you and say 'do you like the set? Don't you think those trees are a bit unnecessary', well there are two options aren't there, you can either go up to the director and say 'we think those trees are a mistake' or you forget about it. The more difficult option, and more productive, is to forget about it – if you have faith in the director.

Is there always an element of a leap of faith?

Yes. The first show I did at the National was *Volpone*, with Matthew
Warchus: nowadays you have a revolve built into the rehearsal room, but
in those days you didn't, so we had different parts of the set spread around
the room, so when we did the final runs, people would have to move around
the room with you, it was frankly chaos. Michael Gambon and I, as Volpone
and Mosca, didn't really have any clue of what we were visually presenting.
In the back of your mind you're saying, 'this is a worry, I should be worrying
about this' and then there's a moment where you make a conscious decision,
'Matthew knows what he's doing' and indeed he did. Suddenly there the
set was, working beautifully and Matthew's vision came out. You have a
responsibility not to tread on other people's vision don't you? It's very rare
that you can safely say, 'I'm absolutely 100% sure this is a bad idea'.

*Was it Noël Coward who said, 'style is knowing what play you're in'? Often the
reason I sometimes feel I have a problem with an element of design or staging
is that I'm not sure what the function is. Do you think it's important to have a
sense of control over your creative process, or, if not control, ownership or even
a stake in the creative process?*

I think the reason why I don't do film is because of that. I want control I
have to admit. I think the great joy of stage acting is that we have the final
say.

Why is that important?

I just like being in charge: I like being in charge of telling the story to an
audience and I like the fact that, in the end, the director has to let go. I like
being in charge of pace, I love being in charge of trying to get laughs, timing;
that's always been the visceral thrill. I love trying to achieve that particular
silence we all know about in the theatre, the silence of concentration, that's
probably the most thrilling sound of all – when the audience are just thick
with silence. That's our skill, that's what we're trained to do, being able to
command a thousand people at the same time.

I think it's very difficult to tell the story unless you have a sense of ownership of the moment of 'to be or not to be', because, unless you have a personal stake in that, you're not going to be able to fully commit to the telling of that story.

I think you have to feel you have to have a 90% responsibility, it's as high as that, of course there are moments where there's a wonderful lighting effect or the design is sensational. I think it should be all on your shoulders really.

Do you think it's important to have a sense of control over your career?

No and I never have. I think I'm unusually passive about that.

Can you even talk about it in terms of a career?

No, I've never really manoeuvred myself in that way. I don't know how you do that in theatre, what can we do? Phone up casting directors and say will you see me for this? I'm a terrible caster of myself anyway, both because I think I can play roles that I can't and I'm also surprised when people offer me roles, which they think might push me in a different direction: Nick Hytner asked me to play Undershaft in *Major Barbara*, which I wouldn't have thought of, but if Nick thinks I can do it then I'll give it a whirl. That's by far the best way for me to go about it. I've been very lucky because I've worked in institutions that have looked after me and it is different if you choose a more freelance career structure.

How important is luck in forging a career?

It's timing I think, being in the right place at the right time.

Selina Cadell said that's all true but you also have to have an eye to identify the opportunity and then maximise it; luck identifies people who are open and receptive to it.

That's probably true. I'm quite well known for not being able to say no very easily, I think a lot of actors find it very difficult to say no and the couple of times I've had to say no, I think I've made the right decision, or my agent has. So that is luck in a sense, it could have gone either way.

Why do you find it difficult to say no?

Because I am genuinely greedy for a new experience. I want more.

So it's not a fear of unemployment?

I've never really been unemployed, which is extremely lucky. I find having a month off tricky; if I was unemployed for any length of time I think I would go mad.

What happens to you in that period of having a month off?

I'm fine for a holiday, a couple of weeks, but the truth of the matter is apart from family, friends, love and things like that, the most exciting part of my life is my work and I genuinely don't find anything as exciting as that. I've been exploring Leontes for the last eight weeks, I can't think of anything better. I think most actors would feel the same, that they're lucky enough to have a job: that is, genuinely, as exciting as it can get. When people ask you if they should be actors, I used to say all that stuff about, 'It's tough, you'll be badly disappointed': I've stopped saying that now. It's like people warning you about smoking and drinking – you know that. So I always say, 'Well if it works, for me, it is the most exciting work I can think of'.

How do you use tech time?

Techs are always thrilling for the first two hours, it's always so exciting and after a few hours you just want to go home and have a pint. I'm not particularly productive at techs to be honest.

So does your work on characterisation and all that go into suspense?

I go through a robotic repetition of moves and things but, to be perfectly honest, I take the time off.

So do you watch tech?

Yes, the only time I allow myself a drink is in the supper break of a tech day. Why do I do that? Well that goes right back to school. If sport was cancelled I would end up either in the main school because I had work to do or in the theatre, the actual building itself, watching the activity of the building is thrilling.

Do you use the time to check out the hot spots and weak spots of a given set in the auditorium?

Yes I do. If there's a scene that feels weak or under-rehearsed I'll ask someone to go through it, but most of the time we're on stage chatting. I'm terrible; by the evening session of a tech I'm hopeless, you get giggly, you feel the wall of silence in the auditorium: it's like laughing at a funeral isn't it? It's irresistible.

Is fear the enemy of creativity?

If fear restricts you, literally restricts you, if it makes you seize up physically then yes. If it's about saying I don't think I could ever do Hamlet, or I'd better not, I'm too frightened, no I will do it in spite of being frightened, then fear is good isn't it?

Because it can propel you forward?

That's why I did *Spamelot* really: because I needed a kick up the arse about something that would make me frightened.

What was it about Spamelot *that frightened you?*

Non-acting things, such as living in New York for a long time, experiencing the Broadway culture, which is different, and dancing! I mean, no, no, no, no, no not me – but I had to!

When I see you perform I'm always struck by your vocal and intellectual precision, but also your physical precision: you are a very physical actor. I remember, for example, in The Man of Mode *at the RSC, you were physically graceful and precise in the same way that you were vocally.*

I think I am a physical actor and I get angry with people saying you're either one thing or another: I don't think that's true of a lot of intellectual actors. I don't know about you but there is a moment with the physicality of a character when it suddenly clicks, in a way that the thought and vocal stuff never does: there's a moment where you realize, 'ah, that's what I look like in my head'. Whether that image is accurate, or true, is irrelevant, but in my head I know what I look like. A whole range of stuff opens up, if it works, that you're not even thinking about. With Richard III, I wanted him to look like a retired American football player – big muscles gone to seed. I know that idea had nothing to do with what I physically look like, but that's what I had in my head: suddenly the way you move becomes like an American footballer.

How did you arrive at that image?

Well that was a series of logical steps: he was a fighter who stopped fighting and I looked at my own body and thought, 'well, you know, big muscled legs' – you have to work on what sort of deformity you have! – he should be a sort of ex-athlete. There's a moment where you think, oh yes, it might only be a tiny physical moment, it just feeds back. Macbeth for me was, again, intellectually right; at the end he should be stuck on his chair, unable to move. Because I'd read something about Stalin not being be able to move in his final days that suddenly clicked.

Do you see things pictorially a lot?

I think I probably do more than I imagine I do, yes. I know I do. For example, I do learn lines now, before I start, but it used to be that I didn't have to learn them anyway because I would have a pictorial memory…

On the page?

Of the scene and yes of the page, some semi-photographic thing but I'd remember how it looked in the rehearsal room; so emotional journeys replicated physical journeys. Now that wasn't a conscious thing it was just something that happened to me, that I could see the picture, therefore, if I stood here that means something, so the physical picture… It was outside yourself, which is interesting.

Yes, I am aware of how a scene looks; however, with War Horse, *the scenes were too big to do that.*

Yes, I probably don't have an outside eye on this, as I said, that one moment, that one sort of clue that has a ripple effect through the whole part unless it's something completely cultivated like *Man of Mode*, absolutely precise, but that was sort of ballet-based. So it's different from you in that sense but I do have one or two moments when I think I know what I look like.

I know that you are a very accomplished pianist, do you ever have a musical image, or do you approach things musically as well?

No.

Do you find that your musical background has given you an advantage in the understanding of cadence?

I've been told it has but I don't know if I believe that. There are very practical things like when I decided to become an actor, after training as a singer, I knew what the diaphragm was meant to be doing but I'm not conscious of the music doing anything about the cadence or phrasing.

Even with a classical text?

No, I don't actually. It's a very separate part of my life really. I've been asked to do stuff with the BBC, presenting programmes about it, which I love, but I regard it as a completely separate existence. I pretend I'm a Radio 3 supremo!

That's interesting that you keep them separate.

I know. I've never been asked that directly and it's interesting I never think of music when I do Shakespeare.

Do you ever use music in the preparation for rehearsal?

Never.

I very rarely do but I do sometimes. For example, when I did Hamlet I sought out a piece of music that prompted, or epitomised, grief. I searched for music that didn't have words or if it had words, that was in a language I didn't understand. I went through a whole series of them, saying no, that's not right: it had to be specific to the level of grief that he started the play with and that's all it was for: as a starting point.

I understand people doing it. I did the opposite once with Owen Teale for *King Lear*: because it was four hours of complete misery, we decided to put on Barry White's *Can't Get Enough of Your Love* and we'd bop just before beginners just to cheer ourselves up and then go on stage and do a four hour descent into misery; that's the opposite, a prophylactic against Shakespearian misery. I never use music; I find it very disturbing. For the grief of Hamlet, my mother had died a month before and there was a particular image I had in my head of her, literally on her deathbed. Not being medical, I didn't realise she was in the act of dying. I was surrounded by doctors, she was a doctor – they all knew – she was dying, but I didn't. Dad asked if she was dehydrated and said 'stick out your tongue Judy' and she died, so that's the image, it still makes me go…so that was a very easy one.

I never successfully found one for that particular job. I chanced upon a newspaper article by Joan Didion, who wrote The Year of Magical Thinking. *It was an article about what happened to her husband and daughter: the level of loss, the shocking speed at which it all happened and the sheer, chance bad luck of it struck a chord for me that seemed to fit with the level and nature of Hamlet's grief.*

I think you've touched on something because I don't think I'd find music specific enough. If I listen to a beautiful Bach prelude, I think that's a beautiful Bach prelude, rather than thinking that's very sad.

It wouldn't draw you into a specific moment of the text?

No.

What do you do to achieve specificity or precision?

In the early part of the run I go though the whole part before the show – Hamlet takes about an hour – on stage usually, or, if not, in my dressing room.

Why do you do that?

It's probably superstition as much as anything. Later in the run I don't do it but for a substantial portion of the run, two months or so, I'll go through the whole part. I think saying the words is the answer to specificity. I'm trying to think of how you do the first lines.

Introductions and conclusions: first entrances, last exits are chief among my pet problems.

You're not alone there. I know with *Much Ado*, if the first scene went well, we were well on our way and if it went badly we really were struggling to keep up. It must have been a series of thoughts, I can't even remember now. But it is a physical thing as well, perhaps that's what I use, because I used to have a bunch of flowers for Beatrice, which I realised I couldn't give her: it would always be a very important moment when I put them down on the table and gave up trying to give them to her, so perhaps a physical thing. I remember the first soliloquy of *Hamlet*, looking at my flesh as if it was dripping off my bones; that wasn't exactly the first thing he says but I suppose if that speech went well I knew we were on our way.

How do you identify and quantify presence?

I don't know that I can answer that.

You know we all say Michael Gambon has great presence.

What does that mean? I don't know.

It means that the eye is drawn to him doesn't it and it means generally that it's drawn to him for the right reason, as opposed to upstaging, where our eye is drawn to someone for the wrong reason.

But could you define it?

Well, upstaging is drawing my eye somewhere away from the story, it's drawing my eye, quite often to a piece of brilliance, but it's about that actor being brilliant or clever, it's not about that actor being present in the telling of the story.

I saw Jeremy Irons in *Never So Good* and I remember thinking, 'my god you're a real star'; I don't know what that means but I know that his performance had an ease and an assumption that you wanted to listen to what he said; it had a grace and a beauty about it. He had the ability to make us want to listen to his every word and that's quite a specific quality. Michael's [Gambon] got star quality but he's also got ordinary actor's charisma, if you see what I mean. I've seen charisma on film, I've worked with Miranda Richardson who, a minute before a take, can switch it on. I think it's to do with the intention behind the eyes; well that's what it was with Miranda. On stage, I don't know what it is, I don't know what makes someone charismatic, that's the magic, that's the fairy dust isn't it.

Mystery? I'm not convinced that it's not a combination of being utterly present in every single moment and putting the audience at ease by being utterly relaxed. It makes it sound easy to achieve, which of course, it's not.

I think you also have to have some subliminal assumption that every single word you say is absolutely fascinating and, again, this might go back to the director loving you: if you've had a period in rehearsal where the director has found everything fascinating then presumably you can go to an audience and fool them.

Is acting a vocation or a job for you?

It's a vocation; I hate it when people say it's a job.

So what are the sacrifices and what are the rewards?

Being a theatre actor of course, the odd times of day we work takes its toll on a social life and I've sacrificed holidays because you're never free when all your friends are. The rewards? It's not the applause, it really isn't – of course I love being congratulated and being told you're good in whatever job you do – but it's not that actually: it's to do with the command of telling a story, I think there's nothing better.

It's the visceral experience of doing it?

Yes and saying to a thousand people listen, I'm going to tell you a story, being able to track their emotional response, or at least their interest. It's what I was talking about earlier, that thickness of silence. To get to the end of *Hamlet* on a good day and say the line 'there is special providence in the fall of a sparrow' to a completely silent house is, I suppose, a question of power, but it's one of the greatest feelings in the world really.

And is there an emotional cost?

When I was younger I never thought there was. I used to be very good at not taking my work home with me, but it is probably difficult to play Constantine, every evening, killing yourself, without some sort of damage to your wellbeing; on the other hand doing a great production by Nick Hytner, of *Much Ado*, you repair that damage by coming out and thinking two middle-aged people can fall in love and have a happy night together.

Yes, there are certain occasions when I feel like my battery is drained.

On very tough schedules when you're doing two *Hamlets* a day, for example, I remember feeling 'oh my god...' It was always after the ghost had gone and Hamlet has that heaven/hell speech, and I'd think, 'I can do this, I don't think I can go there today and I've got to do it again this evening'. There was always a moment in the evening when I'd think thank god I've done that now, that first bit is the hardest bit really, extremes of emotions. I've felt that a lot in performance.

But there are other occasions where, like a car, the battery is being recharged in the act of working.

In the act of doing, yes. And there are very rare occasions when you think that was fabulous, it might have been awful to watch, but it happens about once a year and you go, yes, every single thing was working then, just occasionally, for a speech, it's usually the Wednesday matinee when you're relaxed.

Isn't it funny how matinees are often the best shows. I'm convinced that it's entirely to do with the fact that everyone is completely relaxed.

Absolutely. And thinking from moment to moment – they have to because they haven't been thinking about it before! I remember one of the first shows I did: I came off from the matinee and I was so tired – usually at the RSC we were doing four shows – I don't remember a single thing about that performance, but I remember the director saying that was the best you've done it and I thought, 'oh fuck!'

That's the conundrum, you spend all your time meticulously preparing and then a director can say that's the best you've done it when you felt you were sleepwalking.

Well as you say it could be relaxation, you could be genuinely responding to what people are saying to you. It is a conundrum.

PATERSON JOSEPH

Paterson has played leading roles in major producing theatres throughout the UK, including the National Theatre, the Royal Shakespeare Company and the Royal Exchange Theatre and has won London Fringe and TMA Best Actor awards. His extensive TV credits include the award-winning *Green Wing, Peep Show* and *Sex Traffic* and films include *The Beach* and *In The Name of The Father.* He directed *Romeo and Juliet* for the Channel 4 documentary *My Shakespeare* and his play *Sancho – An Act of Remembrance* is published by Oberon Books.

POK   *How long have you been an actor?*

PJ   Including the youth theatre and the first drama school I went to, 26 years, but I left drama school when I was 24, so that was twenty years ago.

What would you do if you weren't an actor?

I'd still be involved in something creative. I was a chef and I might have continued to do that. If I had my way, I would also write plays and screenplays, but anything more academic or physical would have been out of the question!

What was your first contact with theatre?

It came out of the blue. I was 17, training to be a chef in a hospital; I knew that I didn't want to stay there but it was going to take a further year before they would send me to college to do my City and Guilds chef qualifications, so I started looking beyond catering. I went to The Cockpit Youth Theatre in Marylebone, which was then run by ILEA and they had a few really good teachers there. I remember walking into the building: there were 16-year-old kids there, who were so much more confident and articulate than I was. I was incredibly shy and didn't express myself in public. These kids amazed me and I wanted to be like them. We started to improvise and I didn't know what that even meant, but I saw kids doing stuff and I thought, 'oh yeah, maybe I can improvise something that I semi-know': my dad was a plasterer so I got together with this other kid and I said, 'let's pretend that we're building a wall and see how we go from there', so we did that and I was amazed at how quickly people recognized what we were doing. That was the first intimation that you could make stuff up that comes from within your own head and physicalize it. People laughed and they responded to it and that, for me, was it: I pretty much left the hospital overnight and started going to the youth theatre as much as I could through that summer. We did a couple of plays by Clive Barker, who's now a horror writer; they were really interesting, dangerous plays – about paedophilia and about the life of Francisco Goya – so they weren't little plays; they were really great and I loved it. I went to a drama school that year, which I picked, with my eyes closed, from *The Stage* – I didn't know where to seek advice. I went there for eighteen months, after which I knew I wanted to go to a proper drama school, because this one wasn't accredited and I went to LAMDA for three years.

Why did you apply to LAMDA?

I'd spent eighteen months with other students, so I'd gathered which were the good drama schools and which weren't. I had quite strong ideas about the kind of actor I wanted to be: I didn't want to be spoon-fed anything, I wanted to do it all by myself. So, I only applied to LAMDA and I got a grant, which you could get in those days – I wouldn't have been able to go otherwise.

What were your expectations of LAMDA?

I thought drama school would be all about learning how to hone your craft. I thought that I was going to learn skills; I thought that I would change as an actor and become increasingly confident. I wasn't very academic – I didn't get many qualifications and I bunked off school a lot – but I really applied myself to the learning, so I probably would have been considered a bit of a swot! I loved every minute of the training – apart from mask!

What was the focus, or ethos, of the training?

The focus of the training was, mainly, to get you to a place were you could be as neutral as possible, in your body, so that when you take on a character you're not simply bringing your own charms to it. The great thing about LAMDA is that it was not a methodological training. You can almost tell a

Drama Centre student from a Central student from a Guildhall student, by some of the methodology that they use, whereas LAMDA students, even in their manner, tend to be a little rougher round the edges, a little looser about their technique. At LAMDA they're not on at you to perform in a particular way, they're really interested in the whole being, the whole actor. I'm glad of that and I'm glad I went there, because I don't think that a lot of the drama schools would have suited my needs at that time. We did a little bit of Laban, a bit of improvisation, some clown work, a lot of Alexander Technique, which, of course is about honing your body and preparing it for performance. Later in the course we did the plays.

Was all that technical work successfully integrated into your work on the plays in production?

Because I was such an anorak about it, I really tried to use everything that I was given, so yes I really integrated a lot of what I learnt in classes.

What has been the impact of your LAMDA training on your career?

It's quite hard to define or to quantify, but I don't think I've ever gone into an audition on the back of having gone to LAMDA.

So there wasn't any strategic thinking about attending LAMDA? It was purely about honing your craft skills?

Completely – I wasn't sophisticated enough to think about the future.

Did you go straight from LAMDA into your first job; was there a long wait?

I left LAMDA a term and a half early, when I got a job at the Bush, *Raping the Gold* by Lucy Gannon. Jan Evans, at Evans and Reiss, had come to see a school show, just before Christmas, and she got me an audition for the role of a 19-year-old kid from Derby who was unemployed and very angry. So I left LAMDA – they were a bit funny about me leaving, but I did the show, which was very successful and I got great reviews.

I also left drama school a term and a half early, but at Central, they encouraged me to take the opportunity. It is interesting, given that part of the drama school remit is to prepare you for the profession, that LAMDA were less encouraging to you. Did they feel that you weren't ready, or that they hadn't completed their preparation, to their satisfaction?

No, I think, in my case, the strange response lay in a long-standing clash of personalities: When I went to LAMDA, the principal and vice principal, both had a kind of presumption that I knew more than I did; possibly because of the way I carried myself, and I did antagonise them, but not purposely, it was just my manner, who I was. In the middle of the second year, they ripped into me so vigorously, at one of our post-performance crits that I felt that I was in a semi-hostile environment. I think it was personality, I don't think it was anything more sinister. It will heal itself.

Is there anything about your training that you would change? For example, do you think that students are vulnerable to personal attacks, made by people who are not qualified to make them?

I had been warned about that before I went to drama school, about teachers who were not on your side, who were not fully qualified to give you their opinions – I have experienced a little bit of that – but not at LAMDA: all the teachers that I worked with at LAMDA were competent and generally very good at providing guidance. I was never given a bum steer, I was never told to do anything different with my acting, except particular, specific notes. I was always encouraged to express myself in the way I wanted to artistically and that is what I loved and admired about the LAMDA training I took what I needed from my training and I instinctively discarded what was not useful to me.

Do you have any recommendations that you would make about the training of actors?

It's been twenty years since I left, I haven't been privy to what really happens in the day to day running of a drama school, but I would say, the more they are bringing in professional directors on a regular basis – working directors, who are working at a very high level – and the more they are educating the students about what life is really like outside drama school, the better it will be. Drama school is a very particular environment, quite separate from the way the profession is run and so I'd like to see a lot of question and answer sessions with actors and other professionals, particularly casting directors, because we don't understand what they do and who they are – I didn't learn, until a few years after I'd left drama school that they were on our side – what agents can and can't do. All of that stuff is happening, but I would always push for more access to it, because the more you learn about it, the more prepared you can be for the shock of entering the profession.

In my memory of my experience of Central, they gave the impression that they really didn't want to have to deal with that aspect of an actor's life: there was very little outward looking preparation for the business of being an actor.

Yes that is problematic. There was an incident in the second year when we were in a class and somebody had said, 'I want to be playing parts in which I can show myself and my strengths, I don't want to be playing old people, because when agents come they won't be able to see who I am'. As a devil's advocate, I said, 'I think the training should be about the training, about improvement of our skills and agents shouldn't be allowed to see anything that we do until very late in the training. I think agents coming in the second year, or even early in the third year, to check us out is wrong: there should be a showcase at the end, I don't see why we should get picked off because that leads to a dissipation in the group's coherence'. In the end, it proved to be prophetic: some people were taken on even before the start of the final year and those who weren't chosen early were, inevitably, left to feel insecure and you don't need to feel insecure at drama school, before you have even crossed the start line. I still believe we shouldn't be placed in a position, while we are training, in which we are merely a commodity.

Did the job at the Bush catapult you into a new phase of your career?

In some ways it did, but at that age, you don't really know where you are in the profession, you don't know where to place yourself. It's difficult at the best of times, but in those early days you have no idea about the industry. I was very fortunate to leave drama school to do that job and, on the Monday after it finished, to start another job at the Young Vic, after which, I went directly into another job with Cheek by Jowl, for nine months – it couldn't have been an easier transition from drama student to professional actor. I remember going to work on my bike, for my first day, feeling like my dad, thinking, 'I'm a tradesman, I'm going out to ply my trade and I'm going to get paid for this, this is the most amazing moment of my life'. That feeling of plying a trade has not left me. However, the more work you do and the higher your profile becomes, the more you become aware of your place in the hierarchy of acting and the more difficult it is for you to keep your focus on what really matters – the work. I did a TV series about fifteen years ago and it was the first time I'd been among a group of actors who were so disgruntled: they'd been doing it for a while, the scripts would be late, there would be holes in them and they'd pick them apart, but I'd never been with a group of actors who did that. I'd been out of drama school for six years by then. However, for me, it also became about who was in the publicity shots, who was in the paper more than the others, how I'd be at the edge of the photo or the last in the interview line. All that stuff is entirely peripheral but it can get to you and make you feel, 'I'm not where I should be, or where I thought I was', and it was a real eye-opener to start looking at the profession in that way, rather than, 'How am I achieving what I'm trying to achieve as an actor?'

What are you trying to achieve, as an actor?

I just want to be one of those actors who keeps going on, who keeps learning, who is malleable, who avoids typecasting by doing a great variety of roles, who doesn't become mannered by doing things the same way. I want to keep un-learning what I think I know: I think that is really important. I want to achieve the longevity that people like Ian Holm and Morgan Freeman have achieved, people who keep plugging away, who never seem to lose their bite, never look like they're phoning it in, or doing the same thing again and again.

Can you view your work as a career, or is it simply a retrospective catalogue of jobs?

That depends on the actor: someone like Judi Dench has a career that has a clear pattern of development. She was a theatre actress, and then she became a TV actress and now she is a movie star and that's what she does. She's not what we would call 'jobbing'; she chooses what she wants to do. I can see that mine has spread from doing almost exclusively theatre work to now doing everything.

Has your work in TV informed your work in theatre and vice versa?

I think that my acting on screen and in the theatre are two different beasts and I suppose they shouldn't be. Some people say, 'Truth is truth', but it's a bit more subtle than that: you have to play your space and your audience on any given night and you don't do that on camera – on camera you have to truthfully do what you think is right for that character, you might make another choice if you did the same piece a year later, but that's what it is, on that day, in TV, so it's just very different.

Who have been the greatest influences on you as an actor?

Olivier's biography was the first actor's biography that I read. I loved the sense of fun and seriousness that he brought to his work; he was very focussed on the idea of acting as an art, although he was also irreverent. He wasn't sanctimonious about it, he was aware that there was a functional dimension to it as well. He was aware of the superficial aspects – the how you look and 'look at me' – but there was also a desire to bring the art of acting into the twentieth century and to make fundamental changes to British theatre practice. The biggest influence he has had on the way I act and the way I think about acting lies in the notion of transformation and in the bravery he displayed. He was aware of the daring nature of his acting choices and was prepared to take the risk of stepping beyond his own centre – he didn't want to play himself. While I'm not religious about that, I favour drawing myself towards different accents and different ways of being and of seeing the world, physically: I'm drawn towards habitual physical gestures or twitches that help to define the characterization; it may be as simple as where your jaw is set, or where your tongue lies in your mouth, how you hold your back. I'm not as aware of doing it as I used to be, it happens naturally for me now, but I have been influenced in this way of character building by Olivier's approach.

What are the advantages of that boldness of choice?

Quite simply, it's a matter of longevity: I am not fascinating, in myself, to watch – I wouldn't sit down to watch me, but I would watch someone who is a bit more extreme. The extremity is not always to do with the physicality; it can be in the mindset. Hotspur, for example, is so fixated by the principle of honour, he becomes a Vesuvius of rage because he encounters a world, which he perceives to be lacking in honour. Boldness of choice offers greater variety of minor choices within a characterization, it enriches the expanse and texture of my acting palette and I hope it will lengthen my career!

Who, or what, else has influenced your artistic sensibilities?

Reading Stanislavski's *My Life in Art* and *Building a Character* was a huge influence. There was a phrase of his that I would write in all my notebooks: 'From conscious technique to the unconscious creation of dramatic truth.' For me that was what it was all about.

How did you apply that?

I've learned to do this over the years, I haven't always been very good at this, but I apply it like this: you know who the character is, you've done all the research, you know his ticks and his twitches, how he walks and the kinds of things he would have had for breakfast, if you were asked. You know where he grew up, the kinds of friends that he has, and you've found his voice, through practice, you know his outlook on life and his spirituality, you know everything about him. However, when you get on stage, or in front of a camera, you chuck all of that away and you are as natural as you possibly can be. You are truthful to that moment, to what you are doing; you are not trying to push anything, you are not trying to make the audience think anything, you are just being that character, seemingly in an unconscious way and, actually, it is unconscious, because you've done all the work before you walk on stage. You are not on stage working it, you've done all the work already. So that philosophy led me to LAMDA and it leads me even now: looking at my script, learning my lines, I'm doing that all the time. I'm not doing it, consciously any more, because I haven't thought about it for years, but that is what I do. Daniel Day-Lewis has been another major influence, because, in his performances, you could see a fully rounded character, which could walk off that screen, at any time, and still be a believable person. He does that consistently and I admire him for that. I have had the privilege of working with him, briefly, on a film and he is a craftsman, in the truest sense of the word, he knows exactly what he is doing technically and yet there isn't any sign of that, it's just all there.

How do you try to bridge the gap between that aspiration of achieving the art, which conceals art, the act of being? What strategies do you employ?

The best strategy that I know is to not try hard, because when you do try hard to conceal, you are using energy that should be the character's for living the life that they are living, so you are using performance energy for things that the character would do naturally. This is the struggle and that is part of the game and it always will be. One of the best methods that I know is meditation. When you sit and meditate all sorts of weird and wonderful (and not so wonderful) thoughts will pop into your head: images, fantasies, fears and darkness will pass through your mind and the thing to do is never to try to push them away, because if you do you will end up being obsessed by them and use a lot of energy fighting them, instead of being in that state of peace. The meditational image of the mind is a vast sky and there are many clouds that will pass, but they are passing clouds, you don't shout and grump at them, you just let them pass. So when I realize I am out of my character's thoughts, I try not to worry about that and to keep being conscious of what you are doing, which is presenting another character who is not 'me' to the audience. You cannot fight your personality coming through, your fears – 'Oh my God, those people are really bored, that person is asleep, I've said that too quickly, no one is going to understand what I've said, Oh my God I'm shouting, I'm sweating' – all the things that distract you from just being, will always distract you, so you let them float past you. I do it unconsciously.

Are there any other strategies that you employ, either consciously or unconsciously?

Clenching my buttocks usually helps! Another major influence on my way of working has been Declan Donnellan, with whom I worked on my third job and he's just so good on acting, he is a mine of useful information about ways of stopping yourself getting bored. Declan suggests the reason why you drift off into these thoughts is because you are bored of what you are doing and you are bored because you are lying and you are lying because you are not using your imagination: this notion revolutionized the way I was on stage. He said you get your imagination from out there, in the auditorium, from the audience, you don't get it from looking at the ground, or your toes or inside – it is out there. That advice helped me enormously, to relax and let things come into me. He had a hundred tricks and they were all really good ones – you modify them and adapt them for yourself but he was genuinely the best director-teacher that I have ever worked with.

What is the ideal relationship between director and actor?

The ideal relationship is a collaborative one. It doesn't always happen; sometimes you find a director who won't allow you your voice as an artist. I know some film actors who won't do theatre because they think it infantilizes actors. It makes them children to the father/director and I can see why they think that, but I have been fortunate to work with a lot of directors who just don't do that. Most of the best work that I have done has been collaborative.

What do you understand by collaboration? It's a word we all use, often.

Simply, you listen to what I have to say, you assess it, use it if you can, you try it out and if it doesn't work we don't use it. You tell me what you think I should be doing, or what the character is doing or thinking, I try it out and if I don't like it or if it's not working we try something else. So we are literally creating something together, as opposed to you telling me what to do and me following orders.

Why do you think that is so difficult to achieve sometimes?

I think it is fear. Fear leads to all the strange manifestations of dysfunctional relationships between director and actor. If a director is afraid, and so many directors are afraid of actors, you know: they'll look at an actor and think, 'I don't know what the hell you are doing', not because you are doing something strange, but they don't know your methodology, they don't know how you achieve what you achieve. What you do is a complete mystery to them and they are fearful of it, so it leads some directors to be dictatorial, rather than allowing the actors to be creative, to create the magic in their own way. When a director is fearful of what an audience will think of the show it can lead him to attempt to control everything, and, in doing so, this leads him to dictate what the actor must do, what the sound designer must do…so fear is the root of all dysfunction.

What about fear within the actor? Is it always an enemy to creativity?

I really believe that fear is the biggest enemy. Any fear that causes you to stiffen, or restrict yourself, is bad fear. However, a fear that energizes you is great; it may be that you are fearful of not being able to reach an emotional high/low point and the tension such a fear creates can propel you into making the leap to reach it. As artists, you could argue – and this debate is eternal really – that we need to have our personal forms of darkness in order to shed light on the human experience. If we are endlessly and comfortably happy in everything we do, does that denude us of a creative power? Sometimes I need to feel fear to stop myself from becoming complacent, because complacency can sap the energy from a performance. Having said that, we also need to feel, at the core of ourselves, relaxed and confident because relaxation and confidence allow you to dare. Much of the energy, which feeds a desire for something to be good, comes from fear – of failure, of being judged to be not good enough. The part of you that says 'what the hell…' allows you to step beyond the parapets of your own comfort zones and know that there will be ground beneath you. Sometimes it will fail, but the more confidence you have, the more you are able to roll with it, if something 'goes wrong'. There is a mythic parable about the person who can walk through flames, without being burnt, because he is unaware of the danger, but the person who panics and thinks, 'I've got to get out of this,' and tries to zig-zag their way through is burned. The simple man makes it through the terrible gauntlet because he thinks simply. The innocence of attitude in, 'Hey, I'm going to make this work', can work for you; fear will always stop the attempt.

In the broader environment of our industry, do you think that we exist in a
culture of fear?

Yes, I'd say so. So the fear of career: 'What will this do to my career?' If I
try this new method, if I go with what this director wants, which is like
nothing that I've ever done before, what will happen to me as an actor, if
I allow myself to change what I do, will I ever be able to go back to how I
did things before? Fear of the audience: 'will they laugh at what I'm doing?
I've got to make them laugh, this is a comedy, after all'. Fear of not knowing
your lines, fear that there are other actors in the house... I think the higher
you progress up the professional ladder, the more fearful you become,
which is all about developing a reputation and, therefore, having a sense
of having something to lose. However, I think the nature of our job, which
is to make available, through you, all the different states of humanity, in all
of their extremities, lends itself to a risk-all personality. Many actors have
a daring-do; they will be brave about all sorts of life decisions, not merely
artistic decisions. The profession is a fearful one but it also generates a lot
of courage.

Have you ever experienced those fears, yourself? How have you dealt with
them?

I had a fearful experience when I was doing *The Recruiting Officer*, at the
National. I didn't believe the world that I was in, I didn't believe in the
relationships that we had created in rehearsal and I didn't, therefore,
believe in myself. It was like a slow-burn version of stage fright: I felt naked
because I didn't believe in any of it and I had to walk out on stage with that
lack of belief, in what I felt was a false wig, a false costume, a false voice, a
false accent and a false character, in front of an audience that knew that it
was just Paterson Joseph on stage, trying to pretend to be Mr Worthy and it
was terrifying. I thought that I might give up acting because I thought that I
didn't understand what I was doing any more. I just got through it for those
seven months and, thankfully, I have never experienced it since.

Did you force yourself, as an act of will, to go on stage and put it out of your mind?

Yes. I understand why actors can walk away and say, 'I'm never going to put myself through that again'. Thankfully, for me, it was remedied immediately in the next job – *Blues for Mr Charlie* by James Baldwin, in Manchester – which became, for me, about believing in who you were, believing in the world that you were in, which was the Deep South of America in the 1950s. It was all about believing in the cause of what you where doing, both as an actor in that play and as a black actor in Manchester, at that time, which was such a split community, in so many ways. The audience were almost literally caged together in an arena, where their own prejudices and fears were being played out: it was a significant, resonant piece of theatre, which rekindled my belief in and love of, the theatre. Meaning is very important for me; if I lose sense of the 'Why?' of what I am doing – its fundamental purpose – I can lose confidence. How you cope with that will depend on who is around you, who you can talk to, because you can't always work it out internally; an objective point of view helps clarify what, how and why you are doing something. For me, those moments when confidence has evaporated, have been crises of belief; they haven't been archetypal prima donna moments. Maybe that is my 'darkness'; maybe it is essential for me that I have moments when that sense of belief disappears, rather like someone who is struggling with their religious belief. Dark nights of the soul can be common for people of religious faith and I think they are familiar to artists as well; such experiences take time to unravel and you need good people around you to talk you through it.

How do you identify, or quantify presence?

When an actor is conscious, he is present and, therefore, has presence; if he is not present, he cannot have presence. He can still be lazy and get by on charm, but he will be using something that is alive, he will be using something that is active and it is that activity, intellectual, physical and spiritual activity that gives a sense of life, which has an impact on us because it means that the actor is in the room with us – they are not anywhere else – he is more alive in that moment than when you see him at the stage door. It is incredible how many actors have that quality and equally incredible when you witness a lack of it – when an actor cannot project himself beyond his own skin – which, I think, comes down to an inability to project a truth, held within, beyond oneself. It involves a sense of sharing; it is a communication of your humanity.

How do you prepare for an audition?

Essentially, auditions are just chats – and that is the most important part – and then you read from the script. To prepare, I read the script, I try to nail the character, as best I can, in the usually short time available to prepare. I will not deliver, in the audition, what I will deliver on the day, in front of the camera, or on stage. Come the performance I will have done more detailed preparation in the form of research and rehearsals. The audition is merely an impression of what it will be like; that allows me to take the pressure off myself to 'get it right'.

What about pre-rehearsal research?

That will depend on what the specific job is. If it is a play that I already know, or if it is not set in a specific period of history, desktop research will be minimal. For example, when I did *Elmina's Kitchen*, the play's dialogue was written in a North East London street-talk; although I understood what was being said, because I don't live in that environment I went to Hackney, Finsbury Park and also to Brixton, to study the way people were talking and how that affected, or was affected by, the way they moved and gestured.

Would you do research for an historical play?

Absolutely. If you are working for a large organization, like the National Theatre, they make so much information available to you that you could take a degree in that period of history! Sometimes that can reach levels of overkill, as you end up in discussions about what peripheral historical figures would really have done, as a matter of historical fact – but even that is useful, in order to see what the playwright has done and what he intends to express, in his treatment of an historical character. For example, with Shaw's *St Joan*, some historical characters were amalgamated in order to make a more compelling, compound fictional character. *St Joan*, of course is a play about history; it is not simply about the emotions and relationships of the characters – in a sense the history is another, crucial character, so research became invaluable for that project. I enjoy research; I know some actors loathe it and I appreciate the view that what we are doing is on the page and if it is not on the page the audience is not likely to understand that the historical figure never touched meat, or never drank alcohol, for example, and that it isn't important to the story because it hasn't been included in the play script. However I have done research, which has enabled 'eureka' moments to happen: at drama school, I played Bottom in *A Midsummer Night's Dream* and I discovered that a bottom was the name for a little, fat, spool of yarn, so I got a padded suit and played him as a very fat man. This, in turn, released so much comic potential in the performance because here was a very unlikely aspiring lover/warrior/lion. That single piece of academic research opened many opportunities for physical comedy, in performance.

Does a more generalized research ever help the rehearsal and performance?

When I did *Blues for Mr Charlie*, a knowledge of the American Civil Rights Movement and the social and political environment in the Deep South of America was essential for the playing of the scenes; it wasn't the done thing for black people to talk to white people, which seems so alien nowadays, but it directly affected the playing of the scenes and brought a particular focus to what was at stake when the young black musician confronts the town racist, on his return home from the North. Research of that kind generally informs you of the world you inhabit and, specifically, acts as an indicator of how your character would behave in the given circumstances of the written scenes. When I was playing Mr Worthy, a country gentleman, in *The Recruiting Officer* – and normally I never think of the race of a character, unless it is specifically pertinent to the play – I discovered, in my research, that there were 21,000 black people, in the mid-eighteenth century, living in England, the majority of whom were sailors or servants, but there were some in the gentry and this helped me defend myself against charges of lack of period authenticity, concerning a black man playing that part – it didn't help me directly in the playing of the part, but is was useful information in that respect. I am always staggered, however, when people raise such 'objections' about the casting of black people in 'white' parts. A prominent film director, known for the truthfulness and the verisimilitude of his work, said to me, 'why would you want to do *The Doll's House*, there would have been no black people in Oslo, in Ibsen's time?' Theatre isn't a documentary; people have not come to watch a documentary but a piece of drama played out by human beings, and as long as you can believe that you have and can communicate all the human qualities of that person, what does it matter what colour you are?

What is your view on colour-blind casting?

Casting should always be fair; you should simply cast the best person for the role. That may be idealistic; it may be more difficult for a white person, casting a play, to picture a black person playing some of the parts – it will be a lot easier for a black writer, or director, or producer to picture a black person in the scene, because, after all, people reflect who and what they are, in their art. It's not racist for a writer to write a play with fifteen characters, none of whom are black; however, at the point of casting, the onus is on the director, casting director and producer, to think outside the box. It is incumbent on them to consider all members of society, who need to be represented, and to be inclusive because it is important for us as human beings to see ourselves on stage, playing out our emotions and thoughts, extreme though they may be, for the good of all society. If you leave certain people out of the equation, they will feel disenfranchised and theatre has a place and a potential for both social reflection and communion. I know black people who won't go to the theatre because they say it is all about white people because that is whom they see on stage; when they go to the theatre they think, where am I? There are many black and Asian actors out there, so it is possible to achieve genuine social representation, although I think any form of positive discrimination would be counter-productive, as it would antagonise rather than ameliorate the situation.

What is a good rehearsal and what is a bad rehearsal?

A good rehearsal is one in which you get to burn the engine; you get to explore all the possibilities – however outlandish – of what you could do with a character and a scene. That is the great advantage of theatre rehearsals over film rehearsals; you get the opportunity to do just that, which you don't get in film because, in an environment in which time is money, there is no time to really push the limits of exploration in that way, or to collaborate with the other actors, the director, the movement person, the musical director and to throw ideas around and respond to each other's input, before getting down to the nitty-gritty of selecting/editing the choices available. The transition between the experimenting and the selection of material is often the trickiest period; that is usually when some of the collaboration breaks down, when the playfulness and openness gives way to dictums and edicts. The director Thea Sharrock is particularly good at negotiating that transition; the playfulness of creating in the rehearsal room becomes very focussed when we get into the theatre. Everyone raises their game by about 50%, and you feel that lift but it happens without a sense of external or top down pressure and is all the better for it. Non-collaborative rehearsals are the worst kind of rehearsals. Non-collaboration, when you have a group of collaborative artists gathered together, is idiocy to begin with, but is also disrespectful and professionally poor for a director to slam the door on creative ideas.

What rehearsal exercises or techniques have you found most useful?

Exercises need to be specific to the piece. For me, the most important exercise would be to be able to be your character beyond the script – speaking an inner monologue while performing an activity; interviewing yourself or being interviewed by others, in character; writing a letter to yourself, as the character – these types of exercises help to underpin the text by providing a rich seam of subtext. These are particularly useful for screen work, when you have little, if any, rehearsal time but they are also useful in theatre work because they can lead you into discoveries about the way you speak, the vocal cadence and the way you hold yourself physically – simply by walking around being and talking as the character.

What type of questions do you ask yourself?

The questions may be biographical such as, where did you grow up? What did you think of that area? Who or what you planned to be when you were a child. Other questions would be about the world you inhabit now. I usually only do that exercise once or twice, which may be because I don't want to get too obsessive about it and to return to the same biographical questions might create a rigidity, rather than a complexity, about who you are.

How do you bring the information gleaned from that exercise to bear on the speaking of the lines and the playing of the scene that is written?

I started doing it to help me get to grips with a particular Jamaican accent, so that I could speak in the accent without having to think about it. I would walk around the house answering questions to myself in the character's accent. It was useful to have this character's voice in my mouth and to connect the way he thought with the way he spoke, before I had to speak in front of other people.

What strategies do you employ to overcome blockages?

I get on the Eurostar! First impressions really do count – both for actor and audience alike – and it is worth keeping this in mind when you appear to run into difficulties. An audience will only have two hours or so to get to know your character, among many others, so the initial impression that you make on them is crucial – even if your journey is to confound that first impression later. By the time you finish the first reading, you have a strong impression of who the character is and what he does; rehearsal is a time for putting flesh on to that impression by adding the moment to moment detail and connecting it up (or sometimes showing the clear fault lines, where there is no connection). When in doubt, simplify things for yourself by returning to your first impression – your instinctive response. One of the best pieces of advice I was given at drama school was to trust your instinct because, much more often than not, it is usually right.

What is your responsibility in the rehearsal room, as an actor?

A teacher at school, when I was playing Bill Sykes in *Oliver*, said to me, 'you are the only Bill Sykes', which I thought was brilliantly insightful, because, for that production, I *was* the only Bill Sykes; I represented him. As the representative of the character, it is my responsibility to speak on his behalf and from his perspective, to express his needs, his feelings, what is working or not working for him. With a new play, that responsibility is usually even more crucial, because quite often there will be holes in the script, which will

269

sometimes be more readily apparent to the actor playing the role, because he will be aware of the difficulties of making connections and, therefore, of playing the scene, when a crucial piece of plot or character information is missing, or has been misplaced, or needs editing. It is important for the actor to express that, however small or large the role. A good director will allow and facilitate those contributions. Knowing who you are, where you are and what you are doing, gives you the confidence to perform your role and play together.

Do you think, as an actor, you need to have an awareness of the overview of the play, the mechanisms the playwright uses to tell the story and your function in relation to how those mechanisms work?

I have always thought that the actor – like a conductor – should know every part, how they function within the whole picture, so that you have a sense of why you are there; with this knowledge you will not feel lost, you will know why you are there, on stage, it will not simply be a matter of standing there, in a nice costume (or not), saying lines. It is horrific to have to stand on stage and not know what the play is about, why you are doing it, what the world you are in is meant to represent to the audience and who you are; that, for me, must be what stage fright is – the stripping away of the reason for being where you are.

Why is it important to have a sense of control or ownership over your creative process, or your characterisation?

It is important because you are an artist delivering a piece of work, which is, by its nature, communicative; if you don't know what you are saying and why you are saying it, how can you possibly articulate it, how can you commit to it? I don't see the point in that; without that knowledge it becomes an empty noise. You need a love of the audience and a love of the thing that you are communicating to them, in order to communicate it with any sense of joy, élan or creativity, and you cannot have that if you have no comprehension of what you are doing. I can't imagine members of an orchestra would not know what the overall piece of music is, however abstract it might be. However small your part may be, you should know what it is that you are communicating. I will always try to get to the essence of that in a rehearsal; I will talk about it and ask 'why?'

What strategies do you employ to keep your performance alive, over the course of a long run?

One thing I do is to blank my mind before I go on stage – every time, not just for my first scene. I reassure myself that I have been doing this play for quite some time and I do know the lines, I do know what I am doing, so what I need to do is to blank my mind, so that I can surprise myself and this helps you return to the moment by moment progress of a scene. Most of the time that works for me; when it doesn't work I revert to technique, which is just to tell the story, very simply, to an audience who have never seen it before. If it is possible to do so, within the lighting for any given scene, I will move to a different position on the stage, which, again, surprises me, gives me a new energy and puts me slightly off kilter and brings a freshness to how I say the lines. As long as it doesn't adversely affect your fellow actors, that is a legitimate way of keeping yourself alive.

How can you gauge whether it will have an adverse impact on the other actors?

Other actors will soon let you know, directly or indirectly, if they think such improvisatory interventions are helpful! You discover in rehearsals who you can play around with and to be sensitive to those people who are uncomfortable with it. The restrictions placed upon you by another actor's needs can also be a useful and exciting challenge to you, to keep it alive without upsetting them.

It seems vital to have at least one sequence of moments in which you really do not know how you will say the lines each night, which will not materially detract from the storytelling or interfere with another actor's work.

Really, it is only impossible to do that when there are technical restraints on the scene, such as a fight or a dance, or a physical set piece, which you can't change because it may endanger someone or cause a breakdown in the scene because you are not in the required physical space for a stunt to take place.

Is acting a vocation or a job, for you?

It depends on the job! At heart, it is still a vocation but the pragmatic demands of familial needs and the geographical location of where we live, in France, mean that it is more of a job than it used to be. When I was young, free and single I was monk-like about it: I ate, slept and drank acting, it was all I was consumed by, sadly! Now I lead a fuller life, which means I am richer, I hope, for when I do give myself to it. I don't think it can be a vocation, or, if it is, unless you are very blessed to be working all the time, that can be very damaging. It requires a mixture; you have to be both wise and crazy about the job. As an actor, you depend on other people – to act with, to write for you, to cast, direct and promote you – if it is simply a vocation, you risk making it all about you and it really isn't, you are so subject to the wheels of fortune, in this profession; you have to understand that it is a job within a business and you need to make money out of it, you need to make a living out of it because I don't believe that financial anxiety is either necessary or good for making art.

After the birth of my first child, I noticed a quantum improvement in the quality of my work – I'm not sure anyone else did! Like you, when I was younger I was consumed by acting; after his birth, my awareness of time was heightened and I became a more effective time manager; there was less seepage of work into my domestic life, so time and the work itself became more specific.

Yes, because I have a family, it stops me feeling desperate about work and notions of career, because I have to care for my son – that is my main job.

What are the sacrifices and what are the rewards of being an actor, for you?

You sacrifice economic stability and you constantly question your status and abilities. You miss out on a renewal or development of a career because you never know what is coming so you sacrifice a sense of absolute peace with the future. The rewards are that you don't know what is coming, you are constantly having to renew yourself, you are never sure whether you are standing on stable ground or not! The curse and the blessing are one and the same. The self-consciousness that plagues you as an actor is also useful for knowing how you present yourself; it is a double-edged sword, but both edges are equally sharp.

What do you think theatre offers that other media or art forms can't?

Theatre is an arena, which provides a direct communication with an audience that is often beyond your control; you are a conduit for the writer and, although you are in control of the performance of your own character, there is always an element of uncertainty because it is live, which is in no small part due to the composition and the individual and collective mindset of the audience on any given night: that is magical in its way. It is rare, when you work on camera, to get the time to really live your character in the way you do when you work in theatre. In theatre the audience has control over where they direct the camera of their minds; you can watch an actor who is 'not doing anything', who is merely listening, and get so much from him. On stage you can be completely within the character, all the time in a three-dimensional way, that is always available to an audience.

What is the greatest threat to theatre?

I don't think that it will ever disappear; in a recession, theatre may come to be regarded as a luxury that people are less prepared to pay for – although they may still be prepared to go to the cinema because it is cheaper. I can't think of a time when people will not need to hear and see stories about themselves; we are much too interested in ourselves to let that go. The greatest threat to theatre could really only come from within, by disappearing up its own backside, by not understanding the plays that we are doing, by not speaking to the audience and by not enabling the audience to understand what we are doing; that would be a threat to its relevance.

Is there a creative hierarchy in the making of theatre?

In some ways there has to be because there is so little time; if you were to have six months to put on every single play and everyone was paid accordingly, so that you could afford to have people working only on that particular play – in The Moscow Arts Theatre model – you could aspire to a completely collaborative venture in which everyone could contribute to the conversations about what costumes they could/would wear, the setting, what the play is about, its writing mechanisms. Inevitably there is a hierarchy within the way we currently make theatre in the UK, because of time limitations, so that you arrive on the first day of rehearsal and the set and costume have been designed.

Is that 'timetable' hierarchy useful?

I understand that the timeframe is in place to best enable the theatre to make money, or, at least, avoid losing money; if they can't make money there will be no jobs, so I understand why that has to happen. As long as people are prepared to listen when you say this costume or this piece of stage design will not work for me and are prepared to compromise, in the way that actors constantly compromise, in rehearsal and performance, I see no need or reason to affect the fundamental design discussions. When I did *The Emperor Jones*, I was able to suggest that the material for the surface of the floor might be reconsidered, as I spent a lot of time on the floor, but there were no fundamental changes to the look of the design.

If the head of the National, or the RSC, or The Arts Council, were to invite you to contribute to a review of how we make theatre, what would you suggest?

A lot of fine actors are reluctant to work in theatre because of what they perceive to be a lack of collaboration; they feel infantilized because they believe they are made to feel that they are lesser creative artists than when they work on camera, although that may be more to do with an individual director than a culture of working practice.

What do you most love about being an actor?

I love doing it, getting to grips with great words, great thoughts, great stories. I also love the experience of sitting down to learn the lines; it's as if you never say them as well again as when you are first learning them because they are coming out naturally and new-minted, because you are never quite sure what is coming next. It is the doing of it; it is like chipping away at a big block of wood or stone and beginning to see the face taking shape and being realized.

JIM NORTON

Jim has won Olivier, Tony and Obie awards in the course of a long and distinguished career working in the major theatres of Ireland, the UK and America, including the Abbey Theatre, the National Theatre, West End and Broadway. In addition to working on the major classics, he has appeared in premieres of the work of writers as diverse as David Storey, Alan Ayckbourn, Trevor Griffiths and Conor McPherson. He played the role of Bishop Brennan in the seminal sitcom *Father Ted* and has featured in many films, including Peckinpah's *Straw Dogs,* Ken Loach's *Hidden Agenda, Harry Potter and the Chamber of Secrets* and, most recently, *Water For Elephants.*

POK   *How long have you been an actor?*

JN   Fifty-one years, as a professional. I've always been an actor. I was a child actor. I started acting as far back as I can remember and it never occurred to me to do anything else. Many years ago I realised that this is what I would do with my life. It goes beyond being a profession: it becomes a vocation. It's how I make sense of who I am, I don't know what I would do if I wasn't able to act.

What was your first contact with theatre? What made you think you needed or wanted to be an actor?

I went to the cinema a lot as a kid, there was a cinema at the end of my road and I loved the movies. I used to go with my mates every Saturday to see *Hop Along Cassidy* and all the Westerns and, of course, Laurel and Hardy. Strangely, I recently did a movie for the BBC in which I played Stan Laurel; it was extraordinary playing him as Stan, not his movie persona, but I did a lot of research on what kind of person he was and I found that fascinating. So my interest in the possibility of being other people started off there: acting is the great imaginative leap you have to make in order to become someone else and I was always interested in being other people; I've always been happier when I'm playing characters far removed from me. I love playing that other person I have to create: how they walk, talk, what they wear. I had a very inventive, interesting grandmother, a great storyteller – I suppose the Irish tradition is the Shanakee. My sister and I used to go to see her and she would tell us a story and my sister and I would act them out. I remember she'd turn orange peel the other way round and make funny teeth and I invented this character, this man who came from the country and used to visit Dublin; we didn't realise that what we were doing was improvising. She was a country woman from Clones, County Monaghan, with a great interest in music and storytelling and theatre and she told me the first time my grandfather took her out, probably one of their first dates, he took her to the old Abbey Theatre in Dublin; she'd never been to a theatre where the curtain went up before, and when it did she screamed because she thought her seat was descending into Hades and I thought I'd love to see theatre. The first thing I saw in the theatre would have been pantomime; every year we went to see Jimmy O'Dea, a famous Irish comedian, playing the dame. I had a very good singing voice, so I sang quite a bit. I had singing lessons, entered various festivals, won various things and one day I was coming home from school with all my mates and there was this woman quite close behind, paying a great deal of interest in us and when I got back to the street where I lived, she was at my mother's front door talking to her. When I got into the house my mother said Mrs O'Brien just called in to say 'I was walking behind your son and his friends and that boy's got a terrible Dublin accent.' At the same time my singing teacher was saying my diction wasn't so good, I sang in a competition and they said we can't hear the words, which is very important, so my mother sent me to elocution lessons. There was a famous drama teacher in Dublin at that time called Ena Mary Burke, a very formidable lady and my sister was already going there for classes. I didn't want to go – the idea of going down there and learning poems was an anathema to me – but I did go and I did do my poems and I realised that I was actually quite shy, standing up in front of a room of other kids saying a poem. Basically what she said was, 'I don't want you to lose your accent, I just want when you're speaking to people, that they understand what you're saying, it's very important'. 'Articulation!' was the word she would constantly shout at me. Then she started doing drama classes and suddenly I was in heaven. She had a little studio in Dublin, and a little theatre with curtains, sound and lighting, so I got stuck into that. I was the stage manager; I chose the music for the plays and helped with the lighting. The whole backstage world fascinated me and I did a bit of acting as well; that was really the beginning. Around that time I was asked to audition for a radio show, they wanted a kid of about 13 who could sing and act and I did a children's radio series, which led to *The Foley Family*, a well-known show in those days. I played the kid for *The Foley Family* for about four or five years until my voice eventually broke. I was working with a radio repertory company there, we didn't have any television in those days; there was either radio or the theatre. So when I left school at 18, I joined the radio repertory company full-time. And that was it; I was a fully fledged actor of Irish Equity and that was fifty-one years ago.

So you went straight into the profession without formal training?

There wasn't any form of training available, so I went as far as I could with Mary Burke's classes, I stayed there until I was about 17 and then I was a professional actor. The rest of my learning was within the profession, working with truly wonderful people and I think that's where my education began because my school days were very unhappy. I went to Christian Brothers, a really rough, tough place and I didn't fit in there very well but when I began to consort with actors, who were a lot older than me, they were all very caring; it was like being part of a family and I was the young kid. I started to read: I read all of Steinbeck, I read Brendan Behan – I was in the first two plays he ever wrote, as he wrote for radio originally and I wasn't aware that these people were truly masters at what they did. The other actors in the company advised me, I started to go to the theatre a lot, maybe twice a week, there was a lot of theatre in Dublin in those days and my aspirations then were to work in the theatre rather than radio. So my first professional job was at the Gate Theatre, in the early 60s, in a production of *A Moon for the Misbegotten*; I had a small part at the beginning, a young boy who runs away, and I was also hired as the assistant stage manager. My job was to go to the Gate Theatre every evening at 5.30pm, put all the props on stage, about 120 props in that show, and turn the lights on. I suddenly felt, for the first time ever, somebody had given me responsibility. I went to that theatre, unlocked the door, went up that dark stairway, in total darkness, turned the working lights on and there I was on my own for maybe an hour and a half before the company came in and that's when I really thought that's what I want to do, this is absolutely wonderful.

Who or what were the key influences on your developing artistic sensibilities?

I was always fascinated by what was happening in London; it seemed that's where the exciting things were happening. I was a huge fan of Alec Guinness; he was just the kind of actor I wanted to be, having seen him on film and heard his recordings on radio – fascinating voice. Olivier was in the ascendance then as well. Every Sunday I'd rush to get the English Sunday papers and I'd read Harold Hobson's reviews and Kenneth Tynan's reviews and I realised there was a world elsewhere, where they seemed to take acting a bit more seriously than what I was seeing around me in Dublin. By now I'd done a few plays. *A Moon for the Misbegotten* was my beginning of moving out of this very kind of structured world of being a radio actor. Then I thought to myself one day, who is the best radio actor in the world? No one knows. It's not a world in which you can develop as an actor even though I learnt a huge amount without realising I was learning a technique from these marvellous people I was working with. I then did a number of plays in Dublin and eventually ended up working at the Abbey Theatre. I did *Red Roses For Me*, the O'Casey play. That was really my big breakthrough role at the cradle of genius at the National Theatre of Ireland, the Abbey, with these famous actors all around me. I couldn't understand why they only rehearsed in the morning because I had so much energy and I was so motivated I wanted to work all day. In that play there was a dance sequence with some songs that we had to do and I felt we were under rehearsed, and so I asked some of the other actors to get together and do some work in the afternoon, for which I was seriously taken down a peg by the then artistic director who accused me of calling rehearsals, and I said well, I just want to be better. Maybe I was a bit insensitive in the way that I said it to him but he seemed to take it as a criticism of him. So as time went by I did more and more theatre and then I worked with Peter O'Toole and Jack MacGowran and Siobhán McKenna in *Juno and the Paycock* at the Gaiety and that was it. I really thought this is the kind of work I want to do all the time, this kind of sense of heightened excitement which those actors brought to it and it seemed to me the only way to achieve that would be to go to London. I had been to London a few times to see productions and realised that the standards were very high, the level of acting was terrific and eventually in 1969 I moved to London. I'd gone over to London to do television but I just decided I needed to go there and see if I had what it takes. I was in London I suppose about a month and the first audition I did was at the Royal Court with Lindsay Anderson directing a play by David Storey called *The Contractor*. I got the part; it was a wonderful part and T.P. McKenna and I played the two leads. That was like the turning point in my life, in the sense that this was how I always felt it was going to be like, if I was ever a professional actor.

How was it different from the work you'd been doing at the Gate and the Abbey?

First of all, the whole auditioning process was fascinating. Lindsay was a genius and a great director. I learnt a huge amount from him. His auditions consisted of several actors getting together and playing the scene, whatever the scene was from the play, and the presumption was that you'd got the job and you were now rehearsing and that went on for three days. He would direct us for three days, all of us in our designated parts. Then the next week if you were lucky enough to get a call back, you arrived and maybe not the same six people were there, other people were there, so basically he was fitting in different actors to different parts until eventually he got the balance that he wanted. I just enjoyed the whole process so much, it wasn't like an actor standing alone on stage with a script, we were being directed by a really fine director, our opinions were asked for, our input was demanded, we were expected to go away and do homework and come back and show how our performance had improved over the few days that we had to study the part, and I thought this was wonderful. I think there were about eight or nine actors in that play and eventually he put the team together.

What was it you learned from Lindsay Anderson?

He was just so articulate. He made it seem very simple: well he would ask for very difficult things but you knew what he wanted. He gave wonderful copious, detailed notes on the performance. He was very good at giving the actor confidence. He used to say 'they've all come in, wearing their best furs, the air is redolent with perfume, they're all there waiting for the play to begin'. I opened the play and he said 'you're the most important person in their life, I want you to come on with arrogance, not the arrogance of you as a person but with the proper arrogance of an actor who is taking the stage because he has a story to tell and these people are eager to hear the story because we are all eager to tell the story of our lives and hence we need help to actually construct the story of our lives and that's what going to the theatre is about: it helps people make sense of their emotional lives because there are people up there articulating it. So take that time, come on and just be there.' He always used to say to me, 'do less, you're doing too much, it's too ornate, you're exhibiting too much'. He talked about organic acting, I asked, what do you mean by that, and he said 'acting with roots; we have to believe this person has come from somewhere, that he has a life, that he had breakfast, that he had lunch'. So I guess these were basically Stanislavskian principles but I hadn't had much of that while I was in Ireland because we had two weeks' rehearsal, you learnt the lines, learnt the moves and got on and did it. Whatever creativity you brought to it was up to you. First of all we had the time because it was the Royal Court Theatre, dedicated to good writing. We had maybe four or five weeks' rehearsal and I just found this wonderful. During that time at the Court I did a second play called *The Changing Room* about rugby football and we trained: there was a guy called Bev Risman, a Welsh international, who was our coach. We played seven a side, we went to the gym, we got fit. I was in heaven because acting was now a 24-hour job. The Royal Court also chose about twenty actors to go to classes for about six months, where we did mime, mask work, comedy, text, movement, improvization with Keith Johnstone and we had these amazing people that the Royal Court provided.

Why did they do that?

To create a company of actors; even though the Royal Court is really devoted to writers – this was Lindsay's idea.

So were they investing in an ethos of theatre-making?

Yes.

Even specifically of acting?

They were basically investing in the actors that they liked or who had worked at the Royal Court. Penelope Wilton was there and Ken Cranham and lots of others. Some people fell by the wayside because it was very tough. Bill Gaskill was a particularly tough teacher and took no prisoners and some people couldn't deal with the astringent way he dealt with actors, it wasn't very pleasant, but I remember thinking I'm not going to leave, I want to stay, I don't care what they do, what embarrassments I have to go through, I'm going to stay because I'm going to learn something from this. Some of the exercises were very difficult to do because you were revealing more and more of yourself and as I said earlier I was all about hiding myself behind the character, behind a voice or a funny walk or whatever; suddenly I was having to be open and vulnerable and I realised the way to become strong was to acknowledge your vulnerability first.

And you think that's an essential ingredient?

I think it is. All actors reach a point in their careers where they are afraid; it is quite frightening and actors have suffered terribly from stage fright. These classes gave us a chance to experience that in a slightly safe environment and I found that very good and I suppose what I learnt from that was the way to deal with the fear is to embrace it: acknowledge it and move on because if you push it away and pretend, you're never going to get over it.

About Bill Gaskill's astringency; is it useful for actors to have both the carrot and the rod or is it ultimately damaging because it affects confidence?

It can be very damaging and some people in those classes were damaged to the point where they left: they couldn't take what seemed to be a form of abuse. I found it very upsetting and it made me very angry but I rationalised that by saying this man is a proven man of the theatre, a great intellect. He's not very good with people but I'm here to learn. I'm sure I can learn from his classes. He was wonderful on text and Restoration plays, but he was tough and uncompromising and didn't have any people skills and didn't have a great deal of charisma in the way that great directors have: they persuade and cajole you and get you to give a good performance, better than one you thought you could give. He didn't have those skills but he did know a lot. Some of his classes I found fascinating and frightening but I stayed in there.

A determination not to be beaten?

That's it, yes. I did end up being very angry a lot of the time but I tried to use that in the classes. It seemed his way of working was to get you to breaking point to see what you had to offer.

Do you think that kind of approach is necessary on occasion?

I don't think bullying is ever necessary and having been to a school where I was bullied, not by my fellow pupils but by the teachers, I had a really bad reaction to this – I don't suffer bullies well. I think apart from him and years before, when I was doing *Juno and the Paycock*, a director called Denis Carey was a bit of a tyrant; it was only afterwards that I discovered he had one whipping boy in every production and on that occasion it turned out to be me and I found that very tough. I remember Peter O'Toole being so kind, taking me aside to explain that sometimes directors do this for whatever crazy reasons they have; it can be all kinds of things. He said, you're a young actor with a career ahead of you, this is an older man coming to the end of his career, maybe there's an element of envy, maybe you upset him with your enthusiasm, your youth, and he's using that opportunity not to help you but to hurt you. Carey would justify himself by saying you have to learn the tough way. But after that experience I never would allow myself to be bullied again by a director and I realised you can be assertive without raising your voice: it doesn't have to be those big shouting matches that used to be quite prevalent in those days, where actors would walk out and slam the door: it seemed to be part of being an actor but I decided I don't want to be like that, I want to be able to deal with these difficult situations you sometimes find in rehearsals without it coming to a head, so I devised my own way of dealing with it by putting all my energy into the work. I found the best way was to approach the director and say 'don't do that, I don't respond very well to what you're doing, it might work for other people but it doesn't work for me and it's not helping me'.

Any other key people or events that formed your artistic sensibilities?

When I came to London I realised I'd never had any real schooling in movement. I was aware that I was very angular in my acting; I wanted to be more fluid, malleable, so I went to classes with Litz Pisk, a great movement teacher, put on the ballet tights and danced around. I felt embarrassed but I had to break through this, I guess, Celtic inhibition about movement. Then I thought about it: all our Irish dancing is very rigid. I wasn't able to physicalize what I intuitively felt, there was a block and, even though I was interested in athletics, I wasn't fit: my body wasn't responding to what I wanted it to do, so I found these classes very helpful. I went to various people and classes over the years in order to align my body with my intuitive acting process.

That's crucial isn't it? Acting is a physical, experiential job.

It is and *The Contractor* was a huge physical play. In the course of that play we have to build a tent on stage. We had a movement teacher every morning. I just got great joy from doing physical roles and after that I began to look for parts where I could actually do this. When we did *The Playboy of the Western World*, I played a very physical Shawn Keogh; I threw myself around a lot – it was like I suddenly broke out of this box I was in and I found there was another me there that had been locked away.

So we articulate ourselves physically, more than intellectually?

I think so, but having worked so long in radio, I'd worked a huge amount on the vocal element of acting, to the detriment of my physicality. When I did Conor McPherson's *The Seafarer*, on Broadway, because I played a man who was blind and who was drunk a lot of the time, it required a lot of physical dexterity, to get ready to play the part; a lot of people who came backstage said they loved the way I moved, obviously you trained as a dancer! I'd had two left feet for the first ten or fifteen years of my acting career and that meant to me that I had broken through, it worked – but it took a lot of hard work because I had to overcome all my conditioning that I had as a kid, to be seen and not heard.

What books have you read that affected the way you thought about acting?

I've read most that's been written about acting over the years; I've always been fascinated by how other people do it, approach it. I read Kenneth Tynan's reviews over and again because he wrote so wonderfully about actors. He obviously loved the theatre and actors and he was able to put down on paper what he saw on stage. He wrote about Olivier brilliantly, he wrote about Alec Guinness wonderfully and I found this fascinating.

What was he identifying?

He was celebrating something that was nearly impossible to articulate: the process of acting, the alchemy that happens. Sometimes the more you talk about it, the more ephemeral it becomes; like a piece of mercury, it keeps slipping out of your hands. When Olivier was playing Richard III, his director said, 'you were absolutely amazing this afternoon' and Olivier said, 'yes I know but what did I do?' So sometimes there's something about acting that is inexplicable: you do all the preparation, the work on the text, the physical work necessary, you rehearse and then hopefully something magical happens that is hard to describe. I sometimes don't know what I'm doing and when someone says 'I love the moment when you…', I say don't tell me, because if you tell me, I'll become self-conscious about it. I don't know what I did and I'm sure I'll do it again tomorrow night but if you draw attention to it, it loses its magic.

Self-consciousness is clearly an enemy to good acting.

Absolutely, yet there are some actors who are very self-conscious, who are very competent and successful and can tell you at any given moment exactly what they were doing and what they wanted you to feel. I don't understand that because I don't act that way.

But the preparation is crucial?

I remember hearing an interview with Alec Guinness, in which he was asked what's the main thing about acting? He said the main thing to remember is that preparation is all and I know he wasn't the first person to say that. I was interested in athletics and I was quite a good runner. I was trying to run a fast 400 metres. I did all the winter training, the stamina work, then the speed work and the work in the gym. Before the race, my coach said to me, 'when you step out on that track, forget everything that you've done, forget everything about any training, any technique, just get out there and run and all that work will pay off', and that's how I try to think about acting: you do all the preparation and when you walk onto a stage you're just that character.

And therefore everything becomes a present-tense transaction.

Yes, exactly because what's really important in acting is living in the present and the best definition I've heard of the present is what you're doing – you and I talking, there's nothing else. We can't change the past, we don't know what's going to happen in five minutes' time. So as an actor that's the thing that's really important.

How did you go about preparing for an audition? Or did you prepare?

Yes I did. It's terribly arrogant to walk into an audition assuming you're going to wing it. I remember years ago an actor saying to me, if you're going to go for an audition you have to think, first of all, do you really want to play this part and if you do, do everything in your power to prepare; find out everything you can about the character. Sometimes in auditions you just get a page, but if it's a play, read other plays by that playwright, find out what you can about the playwright, find out what the intention is because your job as an actor is to carry out the intention of the author. I read any information about the writer because sometimes at an audition the director may well want to talk about this writer and getting or not getting the part could depend on you saying, well I also read his earlier plays, I know this and that about him, which shows interest on your part: I don't think you can know enough. So yes, I used to do a lot of preparation, otherwise I wouldn't go.

How do you prepare for the beginning of rehearsals?

A funny thing happens: you do the audition and you pretend to forget about it, if you really want it – it's foremost in your mind – and if you don't get it you just have to move on; the green-eyed monster is a very destructive element in our profession and you can linger too long thinking I should have got that part – you just have to accept it and move on. But when the phone call comes and you're offered the part, I often think that's the highest moment of achievement for the actor because you have been chosen out of all the people who were available. Then they do the deal, the money's fine, it's exciting, it's a wonderful director and you try to find out who else is going to be in the play and then there's a moment I always have: 'well now I've got to do it, it was wonderful getting the part but now I have to do it' and the fear enters the soul. But after that moment, yes I go on working: I read the play over and over again. There was a time when I would write down everything the other characters said about my character. Then I read a book, I forget who the actor was who said don't do this because that's only their opinion; truth is a point of view, that's how they see your character but you are the only person who knows who your character is, so I stopped doing that and just began to work on who I was playing. I read the play over and over and try to forget which part I'm playing; I try to get an overall picture of the story and then slowly, maybe after a week or two of this, if I have the time, with my marker, I will mark my character and then I will read the play looking at what importance my character has in the story.

So why is it crucial to have an overview?

I think it's important to know what the intention of the author is and to know the story: to know the intention of the evening. As an actor, you're part of this jigsaw puzzle, you're part of this picture we're going to present to the audience. I love working with and being part of a company, I'm not so happy when I'm the central character, when it's just me with maybe actors around playing supporting roles. I love being part of an ensemble, that's really what I think I learned working with Lindsay Anderson.

Why do you feel more comfortable in that situation rather than as the leading man?

I just enjoy being on stage with other actors. I remember Lindsay saying, 'the stage is an inter-related world', and I love being part of that inter-related world. He used to stop rehearsals mid-run and say, 'so what are you thinking about that person to your right? What's your feeling towards this person who's just come in?' He was just fascinated by the interaction that we all had with each other and I find that fascinating. It's good: it keeps you mentally very alert, whereas if it's just you, droning on in a monologue, I don't find that so exciting.

What is a good rehearsal for you?

A good rehearsal is where you can trust yourself, the other actors and the director. You can come in to rehearsals genuinely not knowing what's going to happen, being open: it's about not coming in with any preconceived ideas. Actors often come to rehearsals with their emotional cloak around them, they don't want input from anybody else because they've worked it all out; they know what's going to happen. I like to be open to what anybody says – a fellow actor, a director, whoever – that's when you discover new things, that you, on your own wouldn't discover; it can only happen when you get in the room with other people and that's why it's important to work with people you respect, who you know are there for the good of the play. I don't like competitive rehearsals or acting. There's a lot of that about, you have to have your own bullshit detector to see where that's coming from.

How does competitive acting manifest itself?

In all kinds of different ways: people are needy for all kinds of reasons and you have to be mature enough to separate their artistic needs from their personal needs, so a little knowledge of psychology helps.

So in that situation the event becomes about them.

Yes the event becomes about them because they need the attention for whatever reason. That can be difficult because a lot of time is wasted in dealing with a selfish actor: that's where the good director steps in and is able to give everyone what he thinks they need.

To go back to the movement classes you did with Litz Pisk: did you seek those classes out because you were aware that in order to be receptive to ideas and other people's input in rehearsal, you had to be physically open as well?

Yes I felt there was a kind of barrier between what I wanted to do and what I could do physically. I could see the other actors I was an admirer of could do it with gesture, and I thought, 'how can you do that easily?' I wanted to break through this physical inhibition I felt I had.

Did you find as a result of doing those classes that you were able to interact more freely with other actors on stage?

Yes.

So it opened you up physically and emotionally?

Yes, I acted from the centre, I imagined I had an eye in the centre of my chest.

So what techniques do you find most useful?

I like to warm up. I like rehearsals where there's a warm-up, a lot of directors don't do that.

What does that entail and why is it useful?

I've always thought of acting as an athletic event; you have to get to the theatre, get ready, you're on stage for two and a half hours; if you're going to run a race or play football you wouldn't go on without stretching, so I do a lot of vocal work before a rehearsal. Usually now a lot of actors will do that and I like rehearsals where different actors suggest different exercises; we all have different physical stuff that we can do, so you share that around the company – one person says this is a good back exercise, this is a good exercise for getting your shoulders loose, this is good for opening up your chest. That's what I mean about being a part of a company: I like it when everyone is contributing. I don't like those rigid rehearsals when you walk in and start. In a perfect world – and happily I've worked in that perfect world at the National Theatre where you do have vocal coaches – a person who will come in and listen and say your voice sounds a bit tired let's do some work on that, or they do have the physical person who either does movement or someone who does Pilates or something like that, who helps the actors to be fitter, more mobile, more flexible vocally and physically. I think that's terribly important and in the perfect rehearsal situation I think a warm-up is great.

In rehearsal, what are the most useful directions you respond to?

I suppose being left alone: the really wise directors will. I love to be able to offer up stuff: can I try this? It doesn't mean I have to *do* it, but can I try? Can I make a fool of myself, go too far? The director's job is to step in and say I like A, B and C: the rest, while fascinating and entertaining, isn't required in this play. I've worked a lot with Conor McPherson and I love the way he conducts his rehearsals: he gives the actors tremendous freedom but when it comes to the actual choice of what he wants, he is shot through with steel; suddenly this affable, easy-going person becomes really tough and decisive in what elements of what you're doing he wants. Sometimes it's sad because you're losing stuff that was good, organic and truthful, but he is the final arbiter. I like a director to ask me to do things that I don't think I can do, to go beyond what I think I can do. I like a director to make reasonable demands but in order to do that, the director has to create an atmosphere in which it's safe.

Does Conor work like that because it's a new play and subject to change?

There is that. It's also because, rather like Alan Ayckbourn (who's a delightful director to work with), when he's written the play, he knows what he wants. I remember saying to Alan Ayckbourn once, because there were a lot of '…' at the end of the speech and I said if I'd gone on speaking what would I have said and he said, 'nothing, if there was more to be said, I'd have written it.' But of course, as an actor, you go home and have your own take on it. I think when most writers write a play they envisage it, they know how it is and when they're getting what they want, when they are able to say that's exactly what I meant, then it's wonderful for the actor.

How do you manage that situation, when he says there's nothing more to be said? Is that useful for you to know?

It is useful for me to know but there are always elements in a part and performance that you never talk to anybody about, that you never tell anybody, least of all the director or your fellow actors.

Why is that?

By nature that's how we are: we are who we are and it's virtually impossible to articulate every thought or feeling that we have. There are always things, always notes about a character I'm playing that's my secret, and I think most actors have that. There's always an element that nobody knows about but us, as people: it may be too painful, an area of high sensitivity that you just don't share. As an actor you share it but you don't talk about it, you just do, you manifest it through the acting.

I remember Conall Morrison directing me in a Tom Murphy play and he said, 'I need to know what you are thinking at every moment in this sequence'; I thought about and I said, 'no, all you need to know is that I am thinking. If you know exactly what I'm thinking then there's no work left for an audience to do'. Do you think that's part of the need to retain secrets?

I think it is. Again back to the alchemy of acting, for the audience, different people will get different things from a performance based on how their emotional life is, or how their life's journey has been up to that moment. Some people will come up to you afterwards and say that speech was so much about...it wasn't about that at all but that's what it meant to them. That's the joy of theatre: it's a live act and it will mean different things to different people. That's the magic of theatre, when those two things meet, when the umbilical chord is held at both ends, one by the audience and one by the actor. There's a lot of mystery about it; good theatre is a very spiritual experience.

Can you explain a bit more about that?

A lot of it can't be explained, I think something happens. I remember seeing a play at the Royal Court years ago called *This Story of Yours* with Michael Bryant, about a detective chasing down a child murderer. He finally gets the man into a cell, beats him up and loses his job as a result, but he is so overwhelmed with rage at what this man has done. He has spent his life as a detective dealing with dreadful murder cases and he is sitting with his wife – the relationship is in a really bad way – and she says you never talk to me or tell me about your work, you never discuss it. I'm here, I love you, I'm here to help you, why don't you? And he says OK and he enumerates all these different crimes that have been committed, these terrible crime scenes that he's come upon, the state of the body, the terrible things that he's seen that people are capable of doing to each other, in the course of a page-long speech. It was the most extraordinary thing: he did it like a shopping list, it was as if he was saying I'm going to get half a pound of sausages, buy some flour, some bread, it was an absolutely unemotional reading of these horrendous crimes. I remember getting on the train to go home and getting off the train and going back to the theatre, going to stage door and asking to see Mr Bryant and he came down in his dressing gown. I said I just had to come and tell him that I'd never seen anything like it before, I'd never been so moved and horrified and I just don't know how you did it and he said it's called resistance, so I wrote that down and that was the end of that conversation. Years later we worked together at the National Theatre and I said tell me more about resistance and he said let the audience feel, give them the chance to feel. He said if I'd played the emotion of that, there would have been nothing left for them; everybody in the audience is able to relate to that speech from some point in their life, they may not have seen a dead body, they may have seen a dead dog on the side of the road, the shock, and to have that as your job every day, let them feel the emotion, give it to them as a gift, that was a huge lesson I learnt: less is more.

It's a great pitfall I know, that I've certainly fallen into on occasions.

We all do, because there's a huge emotional comfort in playing a big emotional scene; it's very therapeutic, you can get rid of a lot of your own emotions, your own hurts and pains. It's very good being an actor; it's a very good way to get rid of the detritus of your emotional life because we get a chance to play, if we're lucky, saints and sinners. In the course of a year you play a killer, a psychopath, someone who is very cruel or someone who is very kind and these are all emotions that have to be truthful in order to present them on stage. So it's a good emotional journey through life, being an actor.

And yet it is crucial that it isn't therapy?

Yes, there's a huge difference. You have to know what you're doing.

Is that to do with always having in mind that you're handing something over?

Yes, the storytelling; it's the great emotional leap you have to make to become somebody else but you have to leave that somebody else behind you. There are actors, and I've worked with some, who have had breakdowns on stage or in rehearsal, who have been unable to play the part because they allowed it to get into their own psyche so much and that's very frightening. You always have to be at one removed.

How do you manage to guard against that situation happening to you?

The thing is to take the work seriously but not yourself because in the end we're just storytellers, strolling players, we're coming along for an hour or two of an evening to tell a story and to be as real as possible in that situation, and then you go off stage and check the football results.

We all accept that being as truthful as you can be is crucial for the playing of any given moment on stage. How do you try to get to that point of truthfulness?

At some point in the rehearsal – it could be the very first time you read the play, or weeks into rehearsals, or when you're going for a walk or a run – there comes a point, and I can only speak for myself, when I truly really feel the emotions of that character; they may be of exaltation, happiness, of dreadful unhappiness, of hopelessness, whatever it is the character feels. There is a moment in the preparation – I don't have any control over when it happens but it does happen – when I feel I know this person, I know exactly what that feeling means and that can be quite frightening because if you go on feeling like that you end up having a nervous breakdown. My job then is to recreate that moment of intense, heightened feeling on stage every night for eight shows a week for maybe six months and that's when technique comes in – all the training, the vocal and physical expression – because you have to reproduce that every night as truthfully as is humanly possible without actually experiencing the intense emotion because it would kill you if you did. That's what acting is, in as much as I can explain it and there are actors who genuinely have to feel it every night and they don't survive. The stress on their whole physical, vocal, emotional make-up would be too much.

There is a duality there isn't there? On the one hand you have to be utterly present within the construct of the scene you're playing and, at the same time, you have to be aware of the audience and how they're receiving that. It seems to me, if you get too wound up in the emotion of it, if you have to feel that intense emotion every night that you're neglecting the audience.

Yes you are and you're also neglecting your fellow actors if you are so involved. You can appear to be completely involved but you'll still notice somebody in the second row getting up to go to the bathroom, and make the adjustment that you still give the performance while being aware this is happening. You have to find a way to overcome the person coughing every six lines: you get to the point where you become so perceptive that you can hear when someone is about to cough, you hear them breathe in before they cough and you hold the next word but you're still giving the performance, you're still being truthful, you're still, hopefully, moving the audience or entertaining them and that's the skill, the technique but in order to be able to do that, you have had to, at some point, felt the emotion and sometimes that can be very frightening. I find it very frightening when I finally nail the essence of the character, of the black hole that you have to go into and I really experience it. It's very frightening but it's also a feeling of great power, you feel very powerful but then your job is to bring that on stage every night, it's like carrying something very precious in your hands on to the stage and saying here it is.

Over a long run, how do you guard against staleness? How do you reproduce it without losing truth or immediacy? Is there something you say to yourself?

Yes, I usually write myself a little letter, at the beginning, about how much I want to play this part, what it means to me, the reason I'm doing it and that sometimes things will have happened in my life that make it hard to go on and do it. I always have that note in my dressing room and I look at it most nights before I go on. Then I warm up on stage, which I always do – I'm always reluctant to leave the stage, I'm always the last to get off before the audience come in. I go to my dressing room to get ready and I usually say to myself, these people have never seen this play before and I give myself a little lecture that there might be someone who has never been to the theatre before so it's important they see something that will justify their journey and that kind of does it for me. Then, before it begins, I'm always, I hesitate to use the word nervous; I have never gone on stage bored or feeling, 'Oh God I've got to do this': I've always gone on with that little thing in my stomach, which I've come to recognise as an adrenalin rush – it's not fear, it's excitement. I remember somebody telling me, I don't know how true it is, when they were doing the film of *Glengarry Glen Ross*, Jack

Lemmon would go into a corner and have a little mantra to himself before each take and somebody asked him, 'what do you say when you go into the corner?' Jack Lemmon is alleged to have said, 'this is what you always wanted, now you have it'. And it is true, it gets us back to acting being a vocation: it's the most wonderful gift to be given, to earn a living doing something you love. There are times, of course, when you're tired, or maybe the show isn't a success, or the audience isn't full, tensions within the cast, or you're dreading the scene coming up with someone who is doing something which isn't germane to the issue, but that kind of thing gets you through the preparation; you have to prepare before each performance otherwise why do it? You can always say no, we always have choice in our lives. People say how can you do eight or twelve months in a show, eight shows a week? It does require huge discipline; it requires great selfishness in your personal life – getting up, going to the gym, having a swim, whatever, having your lunch at a certain time, having a little nap in the afternoon – your whole day is about doing that show. It is hard work but you don't have to do it, you can always say no. But if you're going to do it, do it as well as you possibly can.

Do you think fear is always the enemy to creativity?

Yes, because to be creative necessarily means being self-doubting, questioning and vulnerable. Overcoming it is of course the great test and great experience: there are many ways of doing that, people take different routes, different paths in order to overcome the fear but in the end it's only a play.

Have you had the fear? Had stage fright?

As a young actor I didn't have stage fright, I was fearless. I might have been twenty or thirty years an actor when that little voice that you have to keep dealing with, says, you're not really very good, how do you think you're possibly going to stand on the stage, in the Olivier theatre, where I was doing *Tamburlaine* and I had this huge speech at the beginning, in one of the most wonderful theatres in the world, the place is full, it's the beginning of the National Theatre, you're going to go out there as Calyphas, what is it – two minutes that you're going to do that speech? – in iambics and have to make sense of it, you're going to have to hit the back wall, you're going to have to really woo them, do all those things that Peter Hall said you could do, yeah! I began to get frightened. It came and went but luckily in that production I was working with Albert Finney, who appears to me to be one of the most fearless people in the world; he has such hoots-pah, he just didn't seem to be afraid. I remember walking forward and suddenly you're hitting this invisible wall that moves and it's pushing you back. And you want to hide: I went through a period of not wanting my face to be seen, of turning away from the audience, wanting to play parts where I was wearing masks and wigs; I wanted to cover up. I don't know why that happened. During that time I had a very good friend, Ari Badaines, who is a psychologist and great lover of the theatre. One of his areas of expertise is psycho-drama – he uses theatrical exercises to deal with his groups and he used to come to the theatre a lot. We just met at a bus stop and got chatting. He was fascinated by the whole process of acting. Why actors didn't go insane. I can't understand, he said, the demands you make on yourself every night. We were friends for a long time and when this began to happen I asked him if we could talk and we talked about fear, in your daily life and, in particular, on stage and this resulted in me going into therapy with him. That was enormously helpful because it gave me the opportunity to deal with a lot of things in my life that weren't to do with acting but were to do with acting, because the two things are inseparable. We dealt with the fear and dealt with the embracing of it and dealt with the reality that if something does goes wrong, when it's over you're still the same person you were before it happened – it was just a little glitch in time. Because it's so important to you, the possibility of an actor dropping a line or making a mistake – actors are so unforgiving of themselves if they make a mistake or if they dry or if their forgetting a line upsets another actor, or some of the play or the audience notice – it's like it's a public humiliation. Yet I know from talking to audiences and being in audiences when things happen, the audience in many ways enjoy seeing it. So this was very helpful to me in dealing with my fear but the extraordinary thing was, having been in therapy for a while, a huge change happened in my work: I suddenly began to get lots of work, I suddenly became quite able to do interviews, I became fearless and much more myself, much more who I was when I did meetings about future work and my career shot up, my earnings shot up because I had learnt how to deal with this terrible thing of walking into a room and meeting a director. Somehow, I'd found a way to do it and that way was actually to be who I was.

Is that because you didn't subjugate yourself, consciously or subconsciously?

I was always guarded and I was always presenting what I thought they wanted rather than what I was and I learnt to tell the truth but pick my words carefully. I learnt to say what I felt as soon as I felt it. I learnt to be more in touch with my feelings and not deny them and to acknowledge and deal with my fear and my feelings of insecurity. The work that we did was very helpful; I learnt a lot of techniques to compartmentalise things. If you were really worried about an acting problem or the fear of going on stage, take a moment in the day where you go into a quiet room for maybe half an hour and deal with all the permutations of forgetting my lines, or what would happen if I went on stage and said I can't go on and at the end of the half an hour it's done, you put it away: you are dealing with it in a way that it's in a compartment so it's not polluting our day. So it's one of many techniques I use. That went away but it comes back. When you're in a long run, when you know it and you know it works, you have more time, your brain has more excess space for these kind of defeatist thoughts; sometimes you're on stage battling for your own sanity and confidence, it never ends but it's a fascinating journey.

Can we talk about how important confidence is? Or is it?

Ideally it would be great to feel confident all the time. The nature of the work means you don't. Every time I start a new part or a new play, I try to – although I can't – sweep aside all that I know. I try to start from scratch, I try to be pure and as unknowing as I can and just approach this part, this text, and see what happens. Inevitably you will use all the techniques and things that you've learnt, the things that you know will work for you but you try not to. Laurence Olivier said, 'mannerisms are easements between the actor's insecurity and the audience': you go on stage and cross your arms because that's comforting, it's also a way of pushing people away, or you rub the back of your neck to relax the muscles and as time goes by and, if you're not careful, those things become mannerisms and the actor will be recognised for that gesture. But what it comes from is fear, so the thing is to try to remake yourself. I think W.B. Yeats said 'You do not know what is at stake, it is myself that I remake'. Every time I come to a new script I try to approach it as truthfully as I can and with as little guile or knowingness as possible.

Have you ever felt blocked – I don't know where I am, I don't know what I'm doing – in rehearsals or a performance?

I nearly always have that. Usually when I read a play or a part I've been offered, I pretty well know what I'm going to be like on opening night – how to play the part – and unless something happens in the course of rehearsals I will end up on the opening night playing exactly what I envisaged. Of course, to reach that point, I have to do a huge amount in rehearsal. In the course of that journey, I invariably hit the wall and think I can't act anymore and I have to deal with this creature again, who's waiting for me every time. The best way I find to deal with it is to leave it alone, to back off; walk through it for a few days, or say to the director, 'give me space here, I'll say the lines today but I'm having some difficulty getting into this'. It's like a knot in your shoelaces: you can't open the knot but if you leave it and come back to it the next day and start picking at it, you find that you can undo it. So yes it does happen – a lot; it's frightening and real and people who aren't in our profession don't understand that it's so real, you could say, 'I'm going to stop doing this because I can't act anymore' and there are no words to express what you're feeling; it's like going into a dark tunnel but just keep going and it will be OK. I use mask a lot when I'm rehearsing at home, I can play it as a different person, play this as a telephone call, I can lie on the floor and if all those techniques don't work then you just have to leave it alone.

How does mask work help you?

I'd never done mask work until I was at the Royal Court, when we had those classes. In fact we didn't have masks, we just had newspapers and we cut out faces and I remember cutting out a clown's face and putting it on. We had to come in a door, first of all as ourselves and be physically funny, which of course no one could do because we were so infused with self-consciousness. However, put the mask on, look at yourself in the mirror and you see this wonderful face and those people who said they couldn't move very well put a mask on and moved like a ballet dancer and people who thought they weren't funny put a funny mask on were able to actually play comedy. The masks freed us up: it works because if you can't see your face then your body is free to be the character. So when I'm really blocked I will use a mask. If actors did a whole day's rehearsal with masks they would free up a lot of the tensions they may feel in the character.

What do you do to work towards specificity?

It's a really good question because I pride myself on being specific, in fact on being meticulous. I hate general acting; there's no real truth in that broad sweep of emotion. Every time there's a full stop, there's an electrical charge for the next speech, the next sentence. I try to look at big speeches. I did a play once with Michael Blakemore, a wonderful director I think, a great actor's director. We did *The Wild Duck* in which I played Gregers Werle. I had this long convoluted speech, and I was having a real problem. He took me aside and he said I can see you're having a lot of trouble with this, Gregers doesn't intend to make a speech, he intends to say the first sentence and then there's an electrical impulse at the end, at the full stop, and then he has to say another sentence which reminds him of something else, so eventually it's a series of sentences. He said if you can, think of it as beads that you're putting on a string: eventually at the end of the process of putting these different coloured beads on the string you have this beautifully coloured necklace and that's the speech. That was a technique I learnt and I try to apply that to everything I do; I make lots of notes in my script, different colours for the different thoughts that are there. You have to work on it, like a draughtsman, break it down into its component parts and reassemble it. All this of course should appear to the audience as seamless. Sometimes you have to present them as difficult ideas or arguments to an audience but make them crystal clear and that's what I mean about specific.

And in terms of the storytelling, the detail is the story; it's how it happens, it's the specificity of each moment.

That's the art of great storytelling; it's 'Once upon a time…' and the audience leans forward, you hope and you have to keep their interest.

What do you think theatre offers that other art forms don't or can't?

It's a question of getting back to the present: when you're in the present, in that auditorium with all those other people, it's a unique experience because the only people who can experience it are the people in the room at that time. You can watch a film over and over again and break it down into its component parts but in the theatre it's gone. I think of it as being written on the water. I remember when I left the National, the last time, I don't know why but I wrote on the mirror all the plays that I'd been in and at the end of it I simply wrote, it's all written on the water; it's gone into the ether. It's a spiritual experience that everybody there that night had and they remember it and, as the memory wanes and changes, they remember it in different ways. It's just a unique experience that brings together everybody's emotions; we're all involved in this inter-related world: it's very special, it's almost like a religious ceremony. If you see a really good play that moves you and the audience around you, you experience something that hopefully changes you.

Like an act of social communion?

Yes, I think so.

And what do you think is the greatest threat to theatre and to theatre-making?

A lack of awareness of its importance to the psychological wellbeing of the community, may, in the current financial climate, lead to a reduction in funding in the subsidised sector, while in the commercial sector there's a danger of it being dumbed down because the financial difficulties we're in at the moment can be used as an excuse to make it a cheaper thing to do: it is a business after all and producers are there to make money. If we lose subsidised theatre, we lose the heart of theatre. Hopefully that won't happen; it's been going on a long time.

How important is it to you to have a sense of control over your career?

I gave that up years ago. It's pretty impossible. We're swept along on a tide of other people's decisions. I'd like to think it was possible to manage it but I don't think you can. The only way you can have any control over your career is what you choose to do or not to do; sometimes you have to have the courage of your lack of convictions to turn a job down for whatever reasons, either aesthetically or financially. You have to be brave to be an actor.

In terms of accepting financial poverty?

Well exactly, yes; we're always on the cusp. People get a false sense of actors because they see them on television or in a movie and they assume that they're doing that all the time, which, as we know, we're not. Sometimes to do the work that we really love, we don't get paid for it or we don't get paid very much; either it's in the theatre or an independent movie where they don't have much money. In the end I've always gone for the part, I've always tried not to think about the money. As time goes by, when you have the opportunity, you get a little bit more selective.

What do you most love about being an actor?

I love the excitement and challenge of a new part and in recent times I've been fortunate enough to do a lot of new plays; that journey is really exciting. I suppose I'm getting to an age now (70) where it's important that my name is on that; I'm the first person to have played that part. When I was a young actor, when I got a copy of a play I used to go straight to the front to see who played it first and then I would imagine what they would have been like and now my name is on the front of lots of plays and that kind of means that I exist, that I survived.

What do you most hate about being an actor?

My instinct is to say I don't hate anything because I love it, it's what I've done all my life; I've never actually done anything else and I've been fortunate that I've never done any other job other than being an actor. I believe there's always a job, always something going. There have been times when I haven't earned a lot. I suppose I hate the fact that it's always someone else's opinion as to whether you're right for the part or not and I hate the fact that their decision is often based on very little knowledge of you as an actor. I also hate the fact that sometimes you don't get the chance to ever meet for a part you want to play with a director you want to work with, and, as has happened to me now on numerous occasions, I meet the director later on and he says I can't wait to work with you, I'd love to work with you. We're not given the opportunity to meet that person because of the process of going through the agent, through the casting director, being barred from the room; not being allowed to be a contender sometimes can be very hurtful.

Do you ever try to by-pass that business mechanism?

No, I'm too bloody proud! I'm naïve enough to believe they're going to discover me but I know in the real world it isn't like that. I always want to be asked to do it because they really want me and not for any other reason.

So what does it mean to you to be an actor?

It means everything, it's my life, it's my vocation, it is how I earn a living, it's what I'm here to do, I really do believe that. I've been involved in some plays that moved people to maybe a heightened awareness of issues, of their relationship to other people. I think it's wonderful being an actor. Looking back on my career there are things that I could have done differently. When I was young, I didn't realise how successful I was and that I couldn't have asked for anything more but I was still striving to become better, to get better parts, I wasn't living in the present then, which I am now; now I'm much more centred about it and when I'm doing a play or a part that's all I want, that's enough.

The apparatus of the industry is very future-stressed though isn't it?

That's exactly it. I was conditioned to believe, 'do this now and it will get you a good film or a nice television series, do the TV series and it'll get you a nice play'; it was always about the next thing and a lot of my energy was dissipated: we're saying I'm in this but I'd rather be in that. There's no guarantee that I will ever work again. It's always someone else's decision that can stop your career in its tracks – that's the bit that's not good about being an actor – you are not in control; it is always someone else who decides whether to hire you or not and that's the big problem, that's insurmountable unless you set up your own company. I don't know about that though: are you the best person to decide what you should be doing? I like to be given difficult parts to play, I like to be given challenges from other people, so I'm an actor for hire, that's what I am, I'm a strolling player.